SUNDAY
MORNING
IN
FASCIST
SPAIN

A EUROPEAN MEMOIR,

1948–1953

Willis Barnstone

SOUTHERN ILLINOIS UNIVERSITY PRESS
CARBONDALE AND EDWARDSVILLE

Copyright © 1995 by the Board of Trustees,
Southern Illinois University
All rights reserved
Printed in the United States of America
Designed by Chiquita Babb
Production supervised by Natalia Nadraga

98   97   96   95   4   3   2   1

"Salonica," copyright © 1993 by Maria Kodama, Executrix of the Estate
of Jorge Luis Borges, from *The Collected Works of Jorge Luis Borges* by
Jorge Luis Borges. Translation copyright. Used by permission of Viking
Penguin, a division of Penguin Books USA Inc.

Library of Congress Cataloging-in-Publication Data

Barnstone, Willis, 1927–
     Sunday morning in fascist Spain : a European memoir, 1948–1953 /
Willis Barnstone.
          p.   cm.
     "The first four chapters . . . were published as a 'literary memoir'
entitled 'From Hawthorne's gloom to a whitewashed island' in
Contemporary authors, autobiography series, vol. 15 . . . (Detroit :
Gale Research, Inc., 1992)"—p. xi.
     Includes index.
     1. Barnstone, Willis, 1927–   —Homes and haunts—Europe.
2. Poets, American—20th century—Biography. 3. Americans—
Europe— History—20th century. 4. Translators—United States—
Biography. 5. Europe—Social life and customs—1945–   .   I. Title.
     PS3503.A6223Z477   1995
     811'.54—dc20
     [B]   93-15493
     ISBN 0-8093-1883-0   CIP
     ISBN 0-8093-1884-9 pbk.

Frontispiece: Willis Barnstone at the Acropolis, 1949

The paper used in this publication meets the minimum requirements of
American National Standard for Information Sciences—Permanence of
Paper for Printed Library Materials, ANSI Z39.48-1984. ∞

CONTENTS

Contents

ILLUSTRATIONS

ACKNOWLEDGMENTS

The first four sections of this book were published as a "literary memoir" entitled "From Hawthorne's Gloom to a Whitewashed Island," in *Contemporary Authors: Autobiography Series,* vol. 15, Joyce Nakamura, ed. (Detroit: Gale Research Inc., 1992). I thank Gale Research for initiating this process.

Grateful acknowledgment is extended for permission to reprint the following:

"Salonica," by Jorge Luis Borges, copyright © 1993 by Maria Kodama, by permission of Viking Penguin, a division of Penguin Books USA Inc.

Poems of Federico García Lorca, by permission of Manuel Fernández-Montesinos, for the Fundación Federico García Lorca. Copyright © 1993 by the Heirs of Federico García Lorca.

Poem number 3 of *Mythistórema,* by George Seferis, from Edmund Keeley and Sherrard Philip, trans., eds., *George Seferis: Collected Poems,* copyright © 1967, renewed 1981, by Princeton University Press. Reprinted by permission of Princeton University Press.

for Robert Barnstone, my son and boss
in Cambridge, Vermont & Serifos

and Tony Barnstone & Sarah Handler,
companions in China

Hurrah for oxygen, especially in southern Europe where sun makes the air look blue. Or even in the north where mists of Paris and London comfort our aloneness following birth. Our genesis is the air. Genesis is narrated at the rim of Asia in the major book of the West. And that telling began with the word and light. But oxygen came soon after, giving us rust and fire, gusto and death. Life is a slow burn.

—*Pierre Grange, "Origins"*

I

BEGINNING

IN

MAINE

One's origin is never experienced. It is learned. Then one spends a life experiencing that learning, which is half information, half speculation, and a third half favored myth. I was born in Maine and so have always felt smugly like a Maineiac, not a New Yorker, although my mother went home to Maine only for my birth and returned to New York after a week or a year. I have no memory of those first days in Maine but have the information, which is enough to engender nostalgic roots.

As I look back into the ignorance of my background, I think of orange wingseeds on brick sidewalks and huge chestnut trees on a lawn around a four-story Victorian mansion dominating Laurel Avenue in Auburn. There my grandparents Lempert lived, and I visited them in summers in the early mid-thirties, whose memory is a few images floating in and out of darknesses. After boisterous New York, in Maine I was careful to be almost silent since my grandmother was nervous with Parkinson's disease. Her hands and face shook pitifully and any loud voice upset her.

She stayed mainly in the kitchen, cooking hot dumpling soups, stewing meats and potatoes in chicken fat, making apple-cake desserts, or sat for hours on a chair by the potbelly cast-iron stove, opening its doors and dropping wood into it. At times she would walk trembling into the den where I hung out, never too quiet on my own.

"Don't upset Bubbie with all your noise," my mother or older sister inevitably warned me.

Bubbie had nice black-and-white-speckled dresses and she'd come to kiss me, brushing my face with her lips and her cheek lightly gowned in a flower bed of soft long white hair. She had been stunningly attractive, everyone said, a twin, like my mother, though their doubles had not survived. I'd feel all her years quiver as she pressed me against her freshly pressed cottons.

Before Maine there was the European Pale and a Jewish shtetl in what is today Poland or Lithuania (then Russia), near Vilna, from which my grandfather emigrated in 1881 to come to America. Hyman Lempert, who had attended the Yeshiva high school in Europe my mother proudly said, had led a horse and wagon around New England to sell his junk metal. The peddler was an early recycling ecologist. Eventually, he seems to have dabbled in real estate, at least enough to leave an inheritance for some of his descendants' living and schooling. Hyman was a short, good-looking man with silver hair, adored by my mother, perhaps stingy, who was given to long feuds with two of his four children over religion and money, which resulted in years of silences and resentments.

I have few clear memories of the grandparents—they died in the mid-thirties. I do remember Hyman, whom I called Zeda, davening in the early morning by the beautiful stair banisters, with small black phylactery boxes on his forehead and a leather strap wrapped around his left forearm. He was chanting and rocking as later I would see the pale Orthodox Jews chanting and rocking in Jerusalem. To me he was good and tolerant, since I was an unpredictable scamp, climbing, running, not offensive but in a constant fervor of shy eagerness.

My brother, Howard, who was to become an architect, was almost five years older than my six years. One day Howard carefully erected a small clubhouse out of old scraps of wood. As I watched him measure, cut, and nail, the operation amazed me. Next morning I discovered a pile of fresh lumber in the garage, delivered a few hours earlier. I wished to emulate my brother. No one was around and I took a saw, hammer, and nails and sawed and hammered for hours, trying to make an upright room. Nothing stood up and what I created was mangled deconstruction. When the family came back around noon, I waited nervously for their approval. Zeda stared at the mess and laughed. All he said was "Billy!" No one rebuked me but the drama of my folly must have been strong, since in the haze of unfocused memories I still have a clear picture of the chaotic house I built which even a small cat couldn't enter.

My father's family is more obscure, since I never met any of the early main figures. How many were there? Their names? The closest to a real-life encounter occurred one Sunday morning in Manhattan, in our apartment facing the Drive. I overheard a racket coming out of my parents' bedroom. My unknown grandfather was on the phone. "I need some money."

"You never gave me anything but your belt!" my father was screaming into the phone.

My father's father and mother's father were first cousins, making my parents second cousins and me a third cousin to myself. The unseen old man—my paternal grandfather—had been a tailor in Boston. He had come to America in the nineteenth century as Bornstein, meaning (like Bernstein) "amberstone," which is also the meaning the unabridged *Webster's* gives for "barnstone." His son William Anglicized the name so that by the time I took it up, my name, which in Europe would have been Velvel Bornstein, had fully altered its ethnic glow to become a spanking, odd, New Englandish "Willis Barnstone." It was a name, together with my face, made for "passing."

Peddler and Tailor

My grandfathers come to me in an old film:
peddler and tailor gone to the New World.
In the Old World the image blurs, unknown.
My bones, nose? I must be a bit like them.
Old photos say, look, here you were with a
black hat, white beard, dark faith in the one God.
But they stood dully in the light that day
in Lutz. They were despised. It wasn't odd
a century ago to flee. They wandered here
in steerage, climbing seven flights, and sat
in safety in their tenements. I hear
a plane, a wasp groaning under the sun.
Below I'm undespised and free: the son
peddling a soul and wearing no black hat.

But if there is any saturated color in the myths I have lived by, it is from the Boston tailor, his wife, and his black mistress. It began with my father's birth, an event that would determine his early life. My recounting of the birth happened soon after my fiftieth birthday, the evening I began a pentalogy of sonnets under the general title *The Secret Reader*. The first book, *Gas Lamp, 1893*, begins with a poem carrying the title "Gas Lamp" when it appeared in the *Times Literary Supplement*:

Gas Lamp, 1893

In brownstone Boston down on old Milk Street,
up two dark flights, near the gas lamp, the tailor
waits glumly for the midwife. August heat
has worn the woman out. Amid the squalor
she looks around the bed, clutching a cape
she brought from London as a child. It's dawn
and dirty. The dark tailor wants to escape
to his cramped shop. The woman's sheets are drawn

below her waist. She isn't hollering now.
Her eyes are dark and still; blood on her thumbs.
Her name is Sarah. No. I'm guessing. How,
untold, am I to know? Hot day has worn
into the room. The midwife finally comes.
Grandmother bleeds to death. My father's born.

That life in Boston led my father as a boy to go into the world
on his own, living by his wits in the tradition of Spanish picaro
scamps from Europe's first realistic, episodic novels. Who knows
why the algebra of chance led him, when he was over fifty, to
marry a very young Mexican who at the age of seven was already
selling ties on the avenues of Mexico City? Although Matilde
Franco worked as a child in the streets, she did so for her family
and did not leave home at an early age. In fact she shared her
bed with her mother until her marriage and only then left it to
share sheets with my father from the North. But Mexico was
near the end of Father's life. The turn–of–the–century Boston was
another scene, one of his turbulent childhood:

Grandfather

Born over there in mist, not even God
or Germans have a record of the house
or village outside Vilna. Here, the old
poor tyrant snips a cloth, stitches a blouse
or shirt, and finds a black woman to live
with when his wife is dead. His smart son sells
papers in Boston subways, won't forgive
the tyrant fool for whipping him. The smells
of steam and cooking mix with yellow cheeses
when suddenly the wrathful tailor seizes
a belt and flogs his son for rotten grades!
Last drama. Twelve years old, my father leaves
his home and school for good. The tailor fades
from all of us forever, stitching sleeves.

After my father left home, he worked in the subways selling newspapers; he sold papers himself and also distributed them to other boys working for him. There were no laws in those days against minors entering saloons and so his way of finding a good lunch was to go into a bar, sit down by the workers, and order a nickel beer. The beer came with all the cold cuts, sandwich bread, and fruit you could eat. Dad ignored the beer but ate enough side dishes to carry him through the afternoon and sometimes the evening. At some point in his late adolescence he moved to Maine where he had relatives.

"I was a wild one in Maine," he told me proudly. "The French and Irish kids attacked me but I never ran away from a street fight. I stood there as they rushed me and threw them to either side." With the same French kids (most of Lewiston was French-Canadian) he liked to walk across the railroad bridge over the Androscoggin River, especially if a train was passing by. Then they would hang from the wooden track ties and, if it was a good place, drop into the roaring river between the boulders. In Auburn he met and married his second cousin Dora Lempert. There is a romantic picture of the young couple, lying on the grass, a high rich grass before a forest, both looking up toward the camera. Although they are on the ground, they are handsomely dressed and groomed, confident of their success to take on the world. They are holding up their radiant faces with very strong fists. Dora and her sister Jane were two beauties in those twin cities of Auburn and Lewiston. I was once told that they could not appear at a public dance because they were Jews. My sister, however, threw cold water on that story, saying it was probably our grandfather's ploy for keeping his daughters away from Christian suitors.

Before settling permanently in Auburn (separated from Lewiston by the Androscoggin River), my father, Robert, worked for an older brother in Boston—I think his name was William. William Vincent Barnstone had a jewelry store, and apparently the collaboration did not go well. All these assumptions derive from vaguely overheard remarks. In this instance my own name was a clue to their bad relationship. When I was born my mother wished to name me after her father's brother, whose name was Velvel ("little wolf"), usually translated from Yiddish into English as William. But since the older William V. was still alive, I could not be given that name, for Jews, like American stamps, cannot bear the name of a living soul. I suspect that the Orthodox law was obeyed by my unorthodox mother because she didn't care for William anyway and so had a good reason to come upon the unusual name of Willis. I've always been grateful for that uncommon name. Among other things it is a fine Buddhist description of an egoless thing on the earth: a "will-less barn stone."

In the early twenties Father opened an elegant jewelry store on Lisbon Street in Lewiston in an art deco building. His eye was like a magnifying glass. He saw into the interior of precious stones and knew their inner colors and qualities. He always had good taste and an instinct for design. Later, in New York he imported a Swiss watch that he named Pierre Grange (Stone Barn). The designs he chose turned the cases and movements into miniature Bauhaus buildings, with some imaginative Corbusier lines to give measured curves and angles. When he and the family moved to New York in the late twenties, he established a firm for importing Swiss watches, but the '29 stock market crash wiped him out. He was three-quarters of a million dollars in debt. When facing bankruptcy, he transferred ownership to Dora and Dora's brother Joe Lempert. The store was saved for the next fifty years but its ownership remained a source of controversy and anger.

When I was born, youngest of the three children, Mother and Father were having domestic problems. So they brought Lucy Thibodeau, a beautiful brunette, slim and bosomy, in a black kerchief, down from Auburn to be my nurse and live with us. My sister, Beatrice, once observed to me, "Lucy took possession of you like a tigress. It was unnatural, but Mother had her hands full and accepted it." As for my feelings, Lucy was my first great love, we were engaged, and we stayed that way even after the first five years of my life when Lucy left to work for another family, the Lanes. We were living in the seventies on Riverside Drive, and I scarcely remember the apartment. My sister, twelve years older, was still with us and Lucy had her own room. But I remember Lucy clearly, even without pictures to conjure up and create realities. In fact my first distinct recollection in life is being held in her arms outside the hospital—perhaps I was two—on the landing just outside the hospital door, at the top of a stairway leading to the street. I'm looking up at the cement gray sky, and she is comforting me after the removal of my tonsils, promising lots of ice cream. More darkly I recall entering the corridors of that hospital and being taken to a room where they gave me gas and put me under.

After Lucy left, I was down. "He's almost six, too old to have a nurse," Mother said. But Lucy was employed at the Belnord on 86th and Broadway, only a few blocks from our new apartment facing the park and the Hudson River on 90th and Riverside. I visited her, even though I was an outsider in that bright, modern apartment. When I got too excited, she calmed me down, and warned, "Billy, you've got to be good now. I'm not *your* nurse anymore."

"Yes, you are."

I knew I was lying but what she said hurt my feelings. Worst was when she married Jimmy the doorman and had her own child—who was palsied and never learned to walk. I lost her for a while, because Lucy kept moving around the city. Then things changed as did our friendship. A few years ago I wrote a novel, *A Swan Over Manhattan*, drawn in part from childhood, and Lucy enters it, undisguised, and the details are not invented: "But you move again, and I lose track as I start grammar school. All I know for sure is how good it is when Jimmy dumps you (I'm over nine) and we fix it for me to come daily to your place for lunch between classes. You're back in the city, a block from school. When I get to your building, I shout up at the third-floor window, 'Lucy!' I run up the tenement stairs to the smell of potato soup. I kiss a French beauty and we talk like old times."

Eventually, I did grow up and Lucy did disappear. She was

My mother, Dora Lempert (*left*), and her younger sister, Jane Lempert

My mother and father, Dora and Robert Barnstone, in Maine, about
1920

Billy Barnstone (*left*) and
Mitchell Rosenheim with
Babe Ruth as Professor of
Swat, preparing to hand out
Academy of Sport diplomas
at the World's Fair, 1939

Digging privies in Mexico
with the American Friends
Service Committee, 1946

Our wedding picture in front of the Mayor's Office, Sixth District,
Paris: (*front row from left*) Robert Payne, Katherine Harper, Norman
Rudich, Helle Tzalopoulou Barnstone (bride), me, Jack Sanders,
James Emmons, 1949

Visiting the Acropolis in the company of classical scholar and poet Louis MacNeice, newly arrived in Greece to direct the British Institute, 1949

With Helle Barnstone at the Temple of Poseidon, 1949

the first nonfamily woman I loved. In those first five years in the same house and the next five of rendezvous visits, I can't say how Lucy formed and changed me, but I suspect the effect was profound. "You have a smile, a sexy film star's look, with white teeth and warm full lips. But the look, with all that northern light in it, is all your own. And what's more, you're built like a sexbomb. Most of all, no one talks as we do together. And even when I was a real shrimp and a slimy brat, you never spanked me. No matter what my folks say about how you managed in your own things, I don't see a pin of sadness in you. I assume it will always be like this—after all we made a pact—but you move out of the city, and I never see you again. My lover fades, but only the way a photograph yellows in a drawer, someplace under other important papers."

New York City has neighborhoods and kids stick to them and act out their after-school activities. Twice, I got held up by toughs: once with ice picks at twilight on 93rd and West End, the second time with knives at night on my way home from my scoutmaster's house down in the 70s where I had passed a test in semaphore. Up on 93rd I had just said goodbye to my chum Eliot and was daydreaming about women's legs, between their legs, when suddenly three ice picks were against my ribs. The Price gang. Brothers. They'd been in a reformatory.

"Empty your pockets or we'll stick you," one guy said.

I jammed a nickel into the lining of my knickers and they got nothing, but I was like stone, unbreathing, so scared I felt like a pickle with their spikes inside. Just a few months later, down in the 70s, in the shadow near the brick building some toughs were waiting. As I came near—no one else around—they moved away from the wall and blocked my way. This time three high-school kids pushed knives against my stomach.

"Gimme your change or we'll cut you up," the biggest fellow snarled. Then he stuck me.

I didn't say anything but did the same thing as in the last stickup—jammed a quarter into my lining. I'd felt a glow after leaving the scoutmaster's place but it hadn't helped. Yet they got nothing and didn't even slug me. They left empty-handed. All they did was draw a little blood and tear my clothing with their knives. But I felt punched somewhere inside my chest. Let's put it this way: I wasn't shaking but was shrunken and pretty stiff. My shirttail was soggy with the muck from that first blade that cut me when the gang first pressed against my body.

Just to feel safer I changed plans for getting back. Instead of sticking to quiet West End Avenue, I went one block out of my way to walk home by Broadway where there was a lot of light, where plenty of people went in and out of delicatessens, buying the next morning's papers outside the subway. I bought a bag of hot chestnuts with part of my salvaged quarter. The chestnut seller, a Greek, was standing next to a woman with a metal cigar box, asking for money to fight the fascists in the Spanish Civil War. On her high-breasted black sweater she wore a white sign showing a photograph of the bombed city of Guernica, with dead people in the street. I looked close at the sign between her breasts. A beautiful woman. And noble ideas. Maybe it was the gang and their knives, but that woman was fire to me.

Each season had its games and every kid was into them. In the fall we set our marble boxes out in the gutter and shot at the square holes to pick up some winnings; in the park we played football (I broke my front tooth when I got nailed catching a pass and fell right on a stone in the grass); when snow filled the big gully we greased our sleds with butter and dragged them to the park and froze on the slope until it got dark; in the fall and spring we played stoopball and stickball on 89th or 88th streets. Stickball was our street baseball, the sport for little bambinos.

Babe Ruth, the great Bambino, lived in the same wide building as I did, a gray-orange whale lying slightly curved along the Drive that goes up west-side Manhattan to the George Washington Bridge. Poor Babe. All we tenants heard about him (as if he were a charity case) was that he was a Catholic orphan boy who grew up to pitch, hit sixty homers in a season, and once, when he felt like it, pointed to a place high in the stands and boomed one up there. The Babe also made it his off-hours practice to visit sick children in hospitals. For one sick boy, Johnny Sylvester, who the papers said was near death (the boy recovered and actually lived another sixty years), he even promised to hit a special home run, and the next afternoon in the Series he smacked three goners. Yet despite all the charity work and mastery behind the plate, he had, they say with a grin, a softness for women and drink. Even when you're famous—and have a national candy bar named after you—you can't win.

Babe Ruth lived on the other side of the court inside the whale. His brother-in-law jumped from the eighteenth story into the same handball area where we played, after school, unless we made too much noise and tenants got angry and threw us out. I heard the thump of the body at night when I was in bed. Like a steamer trunk had fallen out of the window. I wondered who had to clean up the bloody splash. One day the same doorman, Joe, who slapped me for not being nice to retarded Jerry (it wasn't true), took me to the Babe's for the photo that came out on the front page of the *Daily News*. That's when the Babe gave me a baseball diploma, saying on it, ACADEMY OF SPORT, World's Fair, 1939.

Sunday afternoons at home we heard Father Coughlin and Hitler live, shrieking on the radio. They were both ranting against Roosevelt and Jews. Hitler was screaming in German all the way from Berlin. Why did we listen? "We have to know them," Dad said, "even if it makes us vomit." Everyone in the building hated Hitler, including the Babe, who said so over the slow thundering speakers at Yankee Stadium.

When the men who worked in our building, elevatormen and doormen, went out on strike, the new fellows kept billy clubs behind the entrance doors. The scabs were very friendly—big, reasonable men, with out-of-town accents. I liked the scabs as much as Ruddy and Joe outside on the sidewalk in the wind, picketing, the guys we brought corn-beef sandwiches to and hot coffee. I heard Ruddy got hit trying to bust in. They almost broke his head.

It was funny for men to ride me up the elevator. I was just a kid and they were doing it for me as if I were a grown-up with my own money to pay rent and give Christmas tips. I always ran downstairs, leaping as many steps as I could, my hand on the railing, trying to float. They slowed me down as I raced across the marble lobby floor to the front entry and outside into the North Pole wind and gully in Riverside Park.

But often I spent the afternoon sitting in a corner of the elevator, going up and down in the tired coffin. When no one else was riding, they let me close the accordion brass gate. I did it like a grown elevatorman. One afternoon I was sitting in the corner on the floor when the Babe walked in. The Professor of Swat was a little drunk. He wasn't too young, but this big bulk had a kindly iron smile. Ruddy, who was back on the job, looked at me, winked, and said, "Go to it, buddy." I jumped up and grabbed the brass controller stick that made the cage slide up and down, and we descended safely toward the lobby. George Herman Ruth stood staring at the floor numbers slipping by. Lucky, I leveled the car on the first try and snappily pulled open the folding gate. As the Babe wobbled out, he mumbled, "Clean hit, kid."

At home, it was Mother, Father, and Howard. Beatrice was away and had her own life. Mother was always gentle with me. Beautiful but far on her own mountain. We were trusting and she was sometimes affectionate, but we conversed like strangers from two generations. She worried about me—that I might turn out like Father. I adored her, almost as much as I did Father who told me secrets and was a fellow conspirator. He was a man of enthusiasm, really a dreamer, sometimes about me, and I got caught up in it. He gave me belief that nothing was impossible. Only he wasn't there much for us to talk. My brother and I had an early wrestling relationship. I got up in the morning and we'd wrestle. I came home, and we went at it. It was sport, fun, and real conflict. Howard and Dad had a strange conflict, fighting over Mother, which increased over the years. After my father's death, he became her surrogate husband.

One morning I heard my father and mother arguing. I think it was the sore point of ownership of the store in Lewiston. Father was screaming, "You Goddamn bitch you, you Goddamn bitch you." He went for the door and I tried to keep him from leaving. "Don't go." But he left. About a year later, he was in bad shape and came in occasionally to see Mother through a special entrance facing the Drive that went down along the boiler room. None of the tenants could know he had come. He'd stay until dawn and I would accompany him down the metal stairs and up to the Drive and the few cars outside coming and disappearing in half light.

Father had lost everything, and when I was thirteen I spent some wonderful months with him—I didn't go to the expensive camp in Maine that summer. We had a room at the Greystone Hotel on upper Broadway, and I accompanied him downtown as he went from jewelry store to jewelry store, selling what watches and straps he had left in his satchel.

Clockman

My father was a jeweler and in late
Depression days I went from store to store
with him, selling our last supply of fate:
Swiss kidskin leather straps. Once in the door,
I opened up the case and spread our brand
of luxuries. When someone made a slur,
enraging him, I didn't understand.
When things looked good he laid out gems and myrrh,
the balms of Bible nights, pulled a gold watch
out of his pocket, Corbusier in shape,
whose name, *Pierre Grange*, was ours! Such was his past
till bankruptcy and deep depression botch
his life. I loved this man of time, but vast
with pain he leapt through time to false escape.

We made just enough money to pay for meals and the hotel, but he was feeling optimistic—I was too. When his business

13

would collapse he went through a manic phase to hide it all and then a depression. He was coming out of depression and it was one of the happiest periods of my life. By the next summer, he sold diamonds and pearls rather than watches as he moved from city to city from coast to coast, and with his good eye and charm he was driving a white Buick convertible.

Meanwhile, I finished a year at Stuyvesant High School, a school for students "gifted" in science. I had been disappointed when the School of Music and Arts turned me down. I drew a railroad engine with a pencil, which was the main component of the entry examination, and it didn't make it. So I took the science test for Stuyvesant and passed. The standards were very high in this New York public school, but Howard thought I should get out of the city and he wisely selected the George School, a coed Quaker boarding school in Pennsylvania, which I entered when I was fourteen. The divorce and need for a change was the main reason for sending me out of the city. It would help me when applying for college. Not least was the thought that my Maine speech was being overcome by a New York accent and that was unacceptable to Howard and Mother, who were concerned with social proprieties.

I loved every aspect of the George School, where I learned about women, dirty jokes, pranks, peace, civil rights, and meditation, and also studied Latin and the regular curriculum. It was January 1943 when I went to the Quaker school, and unfortunately I rushed through. The word used then was I was "accelerating." Everyone was telling me, "You better have some college behind you, before the Army grabs you." I expected to be drafted at the end of 1945 when I would turn eighteen. So I enrolled in extra courses and took advanced Latin. After the first year with the Quakers, Dad suggested I meet him in Boise, Idaho, and spend the summer together.

I took the train from Philadelphia to Boise—three days on a train crammed with soldiers and sailors—many of them sleeping overhead on the luggage racks. We set off from Boise, going through Reno down to San Francisco where we spent a few weeks at the Saint Regis and ate codfish at Bernstein's; then we drove up the redwood coast to Seattle, and down through desert America to Colorado, Texas, and Mexico. Sometimes we drove through the night. Once at midnight a deer leapt into a headlight, struck us, and disappeared just as quickly. In Colorado he taught me to drive. At dawn in Amarillo, Texas, we saw Air Force cadets marching in ranks through the street, singing "Off we go into the wild blue yonder."

When we reached the border, Dad was called into the custom man's booth by a very stern-looking gentleman. I was worried. A few minutes later Dad came out smiling.

"What happened?"

"That fellow said almost nothing. Just sat mum till I threw a few dollars on the table. Then he was happy and said 'Welcome to Mexico.' You must understand that these officials make next to nothing. So they hit us when they can. It's a mess, awful, don't you think?"

"It's scary."

We took our white car through the harsh desert that smelled of cactus and millennia, climbed up through the rain forests of the Pan American highway where we often picked up entire Indian families to take them to the next village, then sloped down through the astonishing colonial stone cities of Querétaro and Guanajuato near Mexico City. After reaching the capital, we kept going south to Taxco, the silver city, and dropped a hundred miles into Zapata country. In that Nahuatl-speaking region, each house had a portrait of their revolutionary hero Emiliano Zapata, who, like Madero, was gunned down. In the southernmost village we were given a room in a small inn. It was late afternoon and the *patrón* closed the door behind us without putting on the light or opening the shutters.

"Duck!" I screamed.

The room was swarming with bats. We rushed for the windows, tore open the shutters, and the circling creatures darted out into the darkness. Within minutes, the full moon kindly came up over a mountain and walked in through the window used by the departing bats. In all that lunar luminosity, I slept safely, with no desire to pull the sheet over my head.

In Mexico City, Dad showed me this great ancient city of the Americas. My favorite street was Avenida Francisco I. Madero, a street with jewels and precious silver shops, brightly lighted behind steel window cages. Madero Street led to the Zócalo, the huge sixteenth-century plaza, with its cathedral (built on the foundation of a major Aztec temple), the grand palace of the parliament, and other old administrative buildings. On the Zócalo was also the Monte de Piedad (Mount of Piety or National Pawn Shop) where Father bought jewels and silver pieces he was later to reproduce and manufacture in Colorado. He also introduced me to two sisters, Matilde (Marti) and Adela Batista. The four of us went out on a double date, which was also the very first date of my life. As the evening came to a close and we were taking the women home, I sat in the back seat, necking with Marti. She was about two or three years older than me. She gave me a red handkerchief with a guitar painted on it that I lost on the Pullman going north. A year later when I went to visit Dad in his new home in Colorado Springs, Marti was his wife and she was expecting.

After three terms with the Quakers, I went to Phillips Academy at Exeter for the summer term to finish high school at the "accelerated" rate. So at sixteen I found myself a freshman, back in Maine, at Bowdoin College. That fall I began to smoke a pipe and wear tweedy jackets, which made me feel older and more dignified, yet it hardly made me less eager and immature. I came to Bowdoin with many lessons from George School, not the least being an awareness of the American Friends Service Committee. As a result of the Friends' connection, I went twice to Mexico to dig privies in Indian villages in their work camps. That was the beginning of my Spanish-language world and the beginning of a life of wandering.

Bowdoin was a disappointment after George School. I was sorry I was there. College meant fraternity bigotry, a silly, big-man-on-campus anti-intellectual atmosphere, and, above all, the lack of idealism that had dominated the Quaker school. For all the pranks, George School had an ethos of idealism, whereas Bowdoin was a microcosm of urbane prejudices and the frailties of a rich small college. Everyone was in fraternities with the exception of twenty-two students who lived in one wing of Longfellow dormitory. Of these, twenty were Jewish, one black, one a nonconformist tumbler. I did continue with sports, diving for the swimming team and winning my Bowdoin letter. In a year of minimum competition, with most potential students in military uniform, at sixteen I came in fifth at MIT in the competitions for the New England College Championships.

Slowly I saw more. After all, there were professors, with their own dignity, knowledge, and wisdom, and so the George School faded. My calculus teacher, Professor Holmes, relished the eighteenth-century English novel, the courses I took in philosophy altered everything for me, and I had a few crucial friends who made Bowdoin the eventual place of despair and illumination. When I took my first step as a writer, two older students, a Dane and a Czech, were there to help me make the step permanent. While I was busy fencing with Bowdoin, I heard from Dad. It had been a while.

Father had fallen low again. His silver empire was in trouble. He made it grow too quickly and couldn't control it and did extravagant things to prove to himself that he was invulnerable. When he called, he asked me to come to New York, and I went down to the city immediately. I was finishing my sophomore year. We talked the night away, from bed to bed, long after we put the lights out. I tried to raise his spirits. I had almost become his father. Then I returned to Maine to take my finals. A few days later, Dad called again. "Come down to New York. I need you."

"Give me a few days till I finish my exams. Just a few days and I'll be with you."

I was almost annoyed, but I promised to come. We talked a while, and then click. Then I didn't hear from him. He left New York. He went to Mexico City and saw Marti. Then flew to

Colorado Springs. I got through exam week and the next afternoon there was a message to call Colorado. I called and spoke to one of Dad's assistants. He told me that my father had climbed to the eighth floor of the building, went onto the roof, folded his light topcoat and put his hat on top of the coat. Then he leapt into the May air. The funeral would be in three days.

I saw Mother in New York. She was weeping and saying, "Why did he do it?" Indignantly, as if he had pulled another terrible stunt. But that was a facade. She was heartbroken. I took the plane and met Marti. She was three months pregnant. My younger half brother, Ronald, a little more than a year old, was in Mexico City. When we passed by the open coffin, I did not let Marti look at it. I didn't want to remember, or have Marti remember, Father dead. Years later I felt the same about my mother. It was too unfair to them to have their whole lives recalled and reduced to a few moments at the end. Father had given me voyage. I would never stop dreaming of him—in China, in Tibet, wherever he would show up to talk and give me half information about where he was. He is with me even now.

Father on Glass Wings

Death calls from Colorado spring. The phone
tells me you jumped: angel with dizzy stone
arms, floating on glass wings. But you don't land.
Childhood. We're selling watch straps, store to store,
sharing a shabby Greystone room. The floor
is spread with schoolbooks. As you take my hand
we ride downstairs for papers: SNEAK JAP PLANES
SMASH PEARL HARBOR! I've got Latin to do
but we walk Broadway. Plunging through the blue
air (I'm in Brunswick in the tedious rains),
you shatter in the gutter. You'd be gray
by now, I guess, and coming up the stairs
is my young son I love the same old way.
He can't see you. I won't know his gray hairs.

2

FISHING

FOR LIGHT

IN VERACRUZ

After two years at Bowdoin and the suicide, I decided to go to Mexico for a year. I was a junior in college, only eighteen, in need of a change. George School had been coed and I had begun to be less shy and perhaps more natural with women. Bowdoin was all male and socially in the Dark Ages. In compensation there were blind dates from other colleges (I had one dreary blind date in two years) and the famous Bowdoin fraternity house parties, where drunken, masturbating Bowdoin men were supposed to turn into happy, drunken copulators. As for the wild house parties, I was not in that favored company. Hawthorne, Longfellow, Admiral Peary were asleep. Mexico was calling. I had been there once with my father and then between semesters at George School when I went to Miacatlán, an Indian village near the volcanoes, where the American Friends Service Committee had a small work camp.

Now I went to Yautepec, a bigger village with a plump red jukebox in the main square, pastel-colored houses, and many privies to be dug. On Saturday evenings there was a dance in the small city of Cuautla, and the women at the Friends' camp a few miles away came to join us. A male singer sang standard songs in Spanish, but his speciality was "Kees me wonce and kees me twice, and kees me wonce again, it's been a loong, loong time." I liked best the tropical rhythms of the huapango from coastal Veracruz and danced through the night. By mid-September, my five companions in the camp were in their cots, recovering from yellow jaundice. Somehow it spared me. And I went into backyards of the poorest campesinos and dug their privies.

A few days after I got to Yautepec our numbers were increased by the arrival of two Spanish students who, like myself, were to be there for two months. Paco and Tomás were orphans from the Spanish Civil War, living in an orphanage in Mexico City. In 1939, right after the Spanish Civil War, Mexico, which never recognized the Franco regime, took in some five hundred Spanish refugee orphans, sending them first to the city of Morelia, west of the capital. Now, seven years later, they were living in scattered buildings in Mexico City. I spent all my time with Tomás, the scientist, and Paco, the writer, and when our brief but glorious experience in the ditches and cantinas was over, I went with my Spanish friends to the capital, where they managed to get me into one of the orphanages. I slept on the floor of a soccer-playing chemistry student. Hugo and I made up a funny Spanglish. When we woke in the mornings, before putting on his silver-rimmed glasses Hugo would say to me, "*Bueno, Guillermo, vamos a get-earnos up.*" (Okay, Willis, let's get up.) Each day we left the house very early, since my stay as a guest was still a secret to the bespectacled director. A week later, however, Hugo found me an official place on the roof of the other male orphanage in the city, sharing a small white room with Tomás García Borrás, my pal from Yautepec. Tomás, a Catalan, was also in chemistry, and smart, lusty, and obscene. He always wanted to *gatear*, meaning "to look for cats," slang for "maids."

"*En la cama todas son iguales*" (In bed they're all alike), he'd say.

By agreement we spoke English one day, Spanish the next,

and he taught me Catalan popular songs. I was never hungry at the orphanage, but neither was I deliriously well fed. One afternoon Paco took me to the elegant apartment of a French lady who was his friend. An attractive woman in her late thirties, who had had polio as a child, Thérèse waddled boldly around the living room in her steel braces. I thought I was in love with her after five minutes. She put on Offenbach's *Gaieté Parisienne* and served us dish after dish of the main course and then plate after plate of pastries. Both Paco and I ate with no embarrassment, yielding to Thérèse's insistence that we keep eating, and I think my love increased with each bite.

I got my cot on the roof and my share of cold beans and potato tortillas in exchange for teaching English to the fellows. Soon I also taught five outside people of different ages and backgrounds: a fifteen-year-old girl from a wealthy family on the Lomas de Chapultepec, an energetic lawyer, a serious bureaucrat in his forties, an elderly secretary who was cultivated and always gave me wonderful desserts, and a young Swiss, Peter Bach, who had been admitted to George School and needed tutoring in English. At his house Peter's father, an economist, talked to me at length about Leon Trotsky. When Trotsky was in exile in Zurich, Bach had been Trotsky's friend and advisor. When the Russian leader settled in Mexico in 1936, Bach joined him there. Ramón Mercader, a Catalan, worked his way into Trotsky's entourage and one afternoon, while Trotsky was looking at his library, Mercader buried his alpenstock in his skull. Later, a list of other dangerous Trotskyites marked for assassination was found in the Stalin agent's room, and among them was Mr. Bach.

With these students I enjoyed each lesson and felt part of Mexican life. It gave me enough money to enroll in two literature courses at the Autonomous National University of Mexico and take an outstanding course in Spanish phonetics at Mexico City College. The latter was offered by a Spanish refugee intellectual. It was my first acquaintance with a body of writers and intellectuals who were to shape my life. One very lonely Sunday morning, Juan, a tall, extremely morose Spaniard at the orphanage, said,

"*Guillermo vamos a la corrida. Lucha Manolete.*" (Willis, let's go to the bullfight. Manolete's fighting.) Manolete, the grave, gentleman matador, who looked like Picasso's drawing of Quixote, was on the posters for that afternoon. I don't know why—because of some passivity in a year of venture—I declined. It was not the slaughter itself, which in later years would alone have dissuaded me. In a few years Manolete, the most acclaimed figure in tauromachy, was gored in a provincial Spanish bullring near Jaén. Under very primitive medical conditions, he died a few hours later. He and Federico García Lorca's friend, Ignacio Sánchez Mejías, the literary matador to whom Lorca wrote his extraordinary elegy *Llanto por Ignacio Sánchez Mejías*, were the two failed bullfighters in the twentieth century. Manolete was the essential Spanish tragic figure, sacrificed to the ritual of an anachronistic, savage game. Sánchez Mejías died as a result of a series of miscalculations when the older man returned foolishly to the ring. The bullfighter-scholar had lectured at the 1927 tricentennial conference on Luis de Góngora, the baroque Spanish poet whose work inspired a generation of modern poets. Lorca's elegy on Sánchez Mejías is often taken as a mirror reflecting and presaging the poet's own violent death in 1936.

That Sunday while Manolete was awing Mexico, I hung around the orphanage, restless, and finally reached Margaret, an older Canadian woman with whom I went to restaurants and on dates, and took the bus to her apartment. Margaret was a good, romantic friend. Although she was only thirty-two, she had the languid beauty of an expatriate who had seen perhaps too much. We were moments of innocence. She thought me too young for her to have sex with—which she conveyed to me as we lay near each other on her bed, giving me blue balls—but she introduced the notion of lovemaking, urging me to know that world and that light with someone else, and I was hotly in agreement. Margaret was a passage. We had a secret, candid understanding of affection, and never lost it during the year in Mexico.

The orphanage locked its gate at 10:00 P.M. and unless I could climb over the iron fence and get someone to unlock the door, after ten I had to spend the night elsewhere. My private classes kept me beyond that hour, so several evenings a week I went to crummy restaurants on San Juan Deletrán street and read Thomas Wolfe, John Dos Passos, and D. H. Lawrence novels through the night. Prostitutes argued with their companions in neighboring booths, mainly women cursing out men. One evening a tall woman in a flimsy flowery dress was sitting opposite a well-dressed gentleman who made no reply at all as she insistently told him, using the formal mode of address, "*Yo le digo a usted que vaya a chingar a su madre, yo le digo a usted que vaya a chingar a su madre.*" (I am telling you, sir, to go and fuck your mother, I am telling you, sir, to go and fuck your mother.)

At daybreak, when I headed back to the orphanage through the damp-smelling city streets, there were inevitably mounds of twelve- and thirteen-year-old boys sleeping on the sidewalks, in piles like vegetables, to keep warm in the winter, "the forgotten ones" (*los olvidados*), as Buñuel called them in his documentary film.

> The moon dogs of midnight,
> night half mad with cold:
> white cement of the street,
> white children of nothing.
>
> Who are these children
> that sleep in the street?
>
> All the doors were soiled,
> all the walls were mute;
> windows were tongueless,
> the night without ears.
>
> Indifference was pure
> without future or past.
> The brats of the moon
> were asleep in the street.

Sunday Morning in Fascist Spain

Who are these children
that sleep in the street?

Sometimes I went to the place of George Ballou, a friend who had a room in a typical downtown residential building that had three or four stories of rooms around a patio, with stairways going up each side to the interior tile walkway around the patio on each floor, giving the rooms an extra place outdoors and animated a social life among the occupants. George's desk was filled with "manuscripts of sunlight" (as he described them) about his trips to Jalisco, and his extra bed held cages with the small animals he had picked up. His talent was as a naturalist and he handled animals with savvy, traveling from country to country, through customs, carrying small snakes and rats in his pockets. His first publications were in naturalist journals. A year earlier he had convinced the Smithsonian to send him to Central America and he lived in the jungle for some months, sleeping in a hammock, catching, taming, and writing about small beasts. He glorified these adventures by wearing a Spanish beret over his shaven head, which he said he had shaved to be more comfortable and keep away jungle diseases and pests.

"George, can you put me up again tonight?"

"Sure."

"Where you going to stick me?"

"Over the stairway."

"You son-of-a-bitch, why don't you move your rodent zoo and let me sleep on the other bed?" It was useless. The little beasts were tranquil in their home on the cot. So I hung up the jungle hammock and went to sleep, but took it down very early, soon after dawn, so that the tenants wouldn't have to walk under me. I was following George's orders.

George had interesting connections in the art world, usually made through his mother, Jenny. He showed me pictures of an American black dancer, Jimba, a tall, plump, sensual woman, whom he later introduced me to. In the publicity photographs the dancer was sitting or standing naked, except for an African cloth around her waist. Jimba didn't have a girlie-shot look but rather a glare of artistic meditation with religious overtones. George said she also posed for the painter Diego Rivera, who was much in the news because of his mural in the dining room of the Reforma Hotel, which contained a declaration in large letters—DIOS NO EXISTE (God does not exist)—that incited a series of angry blotchings out of the word NO. When Margaret and I ate supper and danced at the Reforma dining room, the letters were again restored to read DIOS NO EXISTE.

If I didn't go to a restaurant or George's, I spent the night at Marti's. After Father died, Marti left Colorado and moved back to Mexico City. She had little money and lived with her mother Rebeca, a Sephardic Jew from Istanbul, and my infant brother, Ronald, in a very old barrio behind the cathedral. Soon she would buy a stunning white suit and become an interior decorator, the first step on her way to great wealth and several marriages. Now she was pregnant with my second half brother, who would be born six months after our father's death. In January she flew to Nuevo Laredo, crossed the border into Texas to give birth to Robert Barnstone, and flew back to Mexico City. She was only twenty or twenty-one. Dad had left her some debts, nothing else. But she said he had lifted her forever from her past and given her a knowledge of business that liberated her. In reality she had a genius and a constancy for business, which Dad never had, and within a few years she was a millionaire, with diverse properties, theaters, a furniture factory, and department store. She also was given to philosophy and religion, flew to Spain to study the works of José Ortega y Gasset with his disciple Julián Marías, and spent time in Asia in pursuit of Tibetan Buddhism.

Now she was poor, young, and filled with plans. Even then Marti was a candid mixture of self-educated, dreamy student of religions and implacable businesswoman.

Since I had little money, I often sold my blood to a clinic near the orphanage and once, when I was very broke, I managed to sell it to two clinics in the same day. I got about ten dollars out of that bloodletting, which could easily carry me through the week. I had come to return some pesos Marti had lent me. "Here's the money I owe you." "Thanks, Billy." I reached into my side pocket, but found that someone on the jammed bus had got there first. He stole my blood. I don't know whether Marti believed me. Though her face changed with disappointment, she said nothing. (I sold more blood and soon got her the money.)

Marti and her mother slept in the bedroom. I regularly slept on a mat on the floor between her brother Sam, who was a captain in the Mexican army, and the Indian maid. A captain in Mexico in those days made a miserable salary, and so the officer chose Marti's floor when he was on leave; but the army was his career. Sam wore dark sunglasses, even at night, which gave him a certain allure, though once, years later at a party, his older sister, Luisa, screamed at him to take off his Mafia shades.

At Mexico City College I met a young American woman in the phonetics class. We became good friends. By this time I had moved from the orphanage to a Mexican boarding house where the food was much better and where we even had a cook who liked to hide hot chilies in my mashed potatoes to see me holler. I will call my new friend Katherine, although her name has eluded me for years. Katherine was twenty-four—I had just turned nineteen—and, she told me, a virgin, a condition she would be happy to change. I went to her apartment after class and we had a fine supper on the balcony. The night was good and at one moment we must have looked so happy there that some good-willed men got out of their car below and shouted up to us, "*A la cama, a la cama!*" (To bed, to bed!) We did lie down on the bed and made plans about mutually changing our innocence. We would take a bus to Veracruz, the seaport on the coast to the east of Mexico City and spend some days there.

The bus descended from the high capital and crossed the great plain of Puebla, which Cortés marched over on his way to his conquest of Tenochtitlán and the Aztec empire. Those plains were filled with ancient building stones and the three hundred sixty-five chapels at Cholula that Spaniards built on the ruins of destroyed Indian temples. We descended through lush mountains of flowers to fast plains of sugar cane to reach the tropical coast. In the afternoon the sun over the coastal area didn't seem to move. It hung in the sky like a grapefruit of fire, and everything under it was touched by its still energy until it finally relented and descended into the ocean.

In Veracruz we found a room in a private house. White pajama costumes were still normal dress. A perfect fabric for the climate. That evening there was a dance in the city square. We bought masks, a green and a silver one, and behind our masks we were lost in dance. The *huapango* guitar and the horn and drums casually lifted the street and it floated for a few hours on incandescent light and tequila. We came down to walk back through the streets to our rented room:

Tropical White Pajamas

In Mexico in a poor village near
the live volcano with its summer snow
and smoking heart, the Quakers settled here
and I dug privies in the mornings. Oh!
one evening in the streets of Veracruz
I danced, wore a green mask, we heard the wild
huapango song, big stars cooked us. Those loose
tropical white pajamas and the mild
faces of Indian friends soothed us. We went
back to our room, our bed, took off our clothes,
both innocent as Eve. The *patrón* laughed
at us, smirking. Dawn found our bodies bent
for the surprise and birth of light! Who knows
your name? We fished through white night on our raft.

When summer came I left the rich year in Mexico to attend Middlebury College where I enrolled in the French School. One course was in the Spanish School where I was also allowed to take my lunch. I learned to speak French very quickly in their saturation program. The heart of the summer, however, was my own immersion into everything Spanish. I attended lectures by Pedro Salinas, one of the major poets from that extraordinary Generation of '27. Years later I translated his book *La voz a ti debida* (*My Voice Because of You*), a sequence of seventy love poems. As with all books of poems I translated, the activity became my instructor for knowing the poet and for absorbing lessons into my own work. Like all writers, I have learned and stolen constantly from reading—but never as much as I learn and steal from translating.

I spent time with Salinas's daughter Solita and her husband Juan Marichal. But my closest friend was Jaime Salinas, Pedro's son, who became a friend for life. And then there was Edouette Quillivic, an instructor in French from the Midi, who the next year in France invited me to her house for some good days in Carpentras. That summer I spent with Jaime and Edouette.

It was a summer of poets. One evening Jorge Guillén and Luis Cernuda came to visit Pedro Salinas. I was to see Guillén often in later years and spend a week at Salinas's house. But this was my one glimpse of Luis Cernuda, who had been a year at Mount Holyoke and was about to return to Mexico, where he passed the later years of his exile. When I shook the hand of this shy, arrogant poet, whose work has only grown in importance since his relatively early death, he was wearing a white sport jacket. I see him now shining elegantly among his fellow poets.

In the evenings we tended to walk for hours in the Vermont hills. Sometimes we would walk almost to dawn. I spoke Spanish to Jaime, French to Edouette. Our common language was French, which Jaime, born in Algeria, knew natively. One night about four in the morning the moon, like a yellow buffoon, suddenly rose over the hills, dimming the stars. I stared at it so long Edouette asked me whether I was having a mystical fit. Jaime, given to dramatic statements, was complaining about the role of being the son of a famous poet. He claimed not to have read his father's books, yet at the same time said his father read him each new poem as he wrote it. I countered with something to cheer him up when he came out with, "*Willis, en tu caso es distinto, porque tú eres poeta.*" (Willis, in your case it's different, because you're a poet.)

"What are you saying! I've never written a poem in my life—or even thought of writing anything."

But Jaime was almost right. Poetry was less than a year away.

After Middlebury I was back in New York before returning to Bowdoin. My friend from Mexico, George Ballou, called to invite me to supper at the Santa Lucía Hotel to meet two Greek women, one of whom had arrived that afternoon by liner from Europe.

"Yes, of course." I knew the place, a small Spanish hotel in the village. Aliki Tzalopoulou was on her way from Athens to Mount Holyoke, her sister Helle was beginning her senior year at Wellesley College.

Aliki had had an intercontinental affair with George's father, Harold Ballou, while he was in Greece, working with the United Nations Relief Organization. Now to complete the web, George was there at the hotel with his mother, Jenny Ballou, a novelist, usually estranged from Harold, to meet Aliki, Helle, and me. Two Greek women. What to make of it? If he had said two Slovenians or Bulgarians, I wouldn't have known more. Jenny played the part of a 1920s expatriate Bohemian. She had lived in Paris, was in Spain during the Civil War (George was born in Madrid); her novel *Spanish Olives* was the second winner in the annual Houghton Mifflin novel awards—the initial prize having gone to Robert Penn Warren. Extravagant, whimsical, Jenny froze George into a loose image of herself, and he was to spend his life arduously and agonizingly trying to write and publish that first bestseller. But in September 1947 in Greenwich Village, we were all filled with enthusiastic presence and a sense of fully happy futurity.

After the two contenders for wayward Harold met and exchanged understated put-downs, we all settled into slaphappy conversation. When we had eaten, George said, "I've got Jenny's

car. Let's take a spin over to New Jersey and explore the countryside. I feel crazy tonight."

"Yes, you seem yourself," I said.

So George and I, Aliki and Helle spun our way across the
George Washington in search of wild nature. Fifteen or twenty
miles into that frontier of oil storage tanks, factories, and dim
shopping villages, we hit the open road. On finding a rolling
meadow, with ponds and odd clumps of trees, we got out. George
had his accordion with him and we danced under the stars, George
playing, singing at the top of his lungs, and hopping around. He
sang in all tongues, including songs in Russian, a language he
made up spontaneously. It hardly mattered when we realized that
our bit of wild nature was a private golf course. Finally, we drove
back to the city.

It was too late for the women to show at the place in Brooklyn
where they had been invited for a few days; at about three-thirty
I was in a phone booth, calling my mother who was not quite
awake. "Mom, I want to put up two Greek girls I met a few
hours ago."

"You what?" Somehow, the idea was not appealing to her, so
we found a room for them at the Saint Moritz Hotel on Central
Park South, not far from the Parc Von Dome, where Mother
and I were living. When they woke up, the women left for
Brooklyn and I took the subway out to see them. It was still a
sunny afternoon when I reached their place. Helle was playing
Chopin études on the upright piano—a romantic sequel to the
night in the country. Aliki was pouring out European charm in
her heroic style. The sun was all over the living room, dodging
the lace curtains. The high-spirited women were a team, smiting
me with Greek magic, ouzo, and fruit preserves swimming in
syrup served in a glass cup.

In the fall I was at Bowdoin, studying mainly philosophy
courses, though my official major was French. Because my gradu-
ating mark in a Victorian novel course at Exeter was D−, I had,
despite an A in freshman English, avoided all courses in English

literature. However, a close friend, William Cappellari, urged me to come with him to audit a seminar in recent American poetry, held in the evening at the professor's old New England house—"the Chase Barn Chamber." I went with much excitement to a discussion of the poems in Robert Lowell's *Lord Weary's Castle*, but after class, Professor Stanley Chase, gray and distinguished, took me aside quietly. "We have our quota of students. I have to ask you not to come to any more classes."

I began to read poetry very seriously on my own.

This was my last year as an undergraduate, since by putting two summer terms together I would graduate in August of 1948. My roommate during the last darknesses at Bowdoin was Bret Bare, a philosophy major. Bret was born in New Haven, the illegitimate son of a housemaid at the Taft Hotel and a Yale undergraduate. He was in a Protestant missionary family and spent his childhood in India.

"The minister never even adopted me. He kept me on as a foster child, living with his real children. So much for good religion."

Bret was often bitter—more often quiet and gentle, and though articulate when he wanted to be, he spoke little. When he did speak it was as if he were leaving some protected camp for a while; and the words, when he did release them almost reluctantly, were rinsed deep in his big horse mouth with saliva and careful meditation. He looked like a dark, young Abraham Lincoln. Bret had gone through World War II as an infantryman, unwounded, but a year after it was over he discovered he was epileptic. Often in the middle of the night in our freezing bedroom he would have a heaving, groaning attack. It was like some horrible sexual trip. Usually he didn't wake until the next morning, but he felt dry, worn, as if every bone in his body had cracked open. We lived in a dormitory named after Hawthorne and perhaps lived in his room. Nathaniel Hawthorne was Longfellow's classmate in the class of 1825. We had endless discussions about our philosophers. Although I envied the notion of being brought up in India, Bret was sullen and depressive about his past. Yet when in that cloud of darkness he felt happiness, he broke up like a big child and giggled. Before the semester was over he found that he liked to paint and that a painting offered him a tangible, sensual vision. An idea, an abstraction, a philosophical ordering of perceptions could not satisfy him any longer.

Bowdoin, 1948

Hawthorne had this yellowed room. So we share
the morning gloom of alcoholics or
nocturnal masturbators, north and nowhere,
too isolated for a date or whore.
Were you a grind like me? A dreamer slob
and weird? I sleep, the window open to
the black Maine snow, hearing my roommate throb
and scream, an epileptic getting through
another siege. He's a philosopher;
I'm lost. But he was born a bastard, he
says bitterly; my origins I shirk
from. Worst (or best?) I doubt there is a me
concocting words in terrifying blur
within. Dream, Hawthorne. Words no longer work.

The year was strange. I sought answers in the philosophers, and was disappointed when I found systems, each one plausible but in contradiction to every other. Had I read Jorge Luis Borges at the time, I might have believed that there were no absolutes, no keys to the universe, no flawless algebras for language or thought. And so the paradoxical quest, the necessary journey. Heraclitus the Obscure, as Borges called the ancient relativist, told the truth about truth's absence.

I kept a diary. I became increasingly introspective. I read many novels and was self-inspective of each reaction. Finally, I began to doubt everything—language, consciousness, and any truth. I spoke about this to a blind professor of philosophy. "Mr. Leure, what can I do? I want to get out of this."

"Go see a movie."

"I did, but it didn't work. I couldn't keep my mind on the screen. Couldn't see the film. My mind got in between and blurred away the people."

Actually, the film I saw should have held my attention—if any could. It was *Spellbound*. The theater was jammed and I stood in the rear, looking at Gregory Peck and Ingrid Bergman ski dangerously into the all-absorbing snow.

I cannot yet verbalize what I discovered that year, but I know it perfectly well. I found the mind disappear, words disappear, found the absolute blankness, noncenter of thought, the emptiness of my head, which filled up only when I stopped inspecting. And so the mind became an area of fearful detachment, almost a nightmare of nonbeing and death, with none of the colorful vision that the mystics make of such an arid night of detachment. Finally, I accepted that only by not examining thought, by not testing, not questioning, by letting the arbitrary, mechanical, learned process of thinking go on by itself, could I carry on. Only by *not* looking for a true picture of consciousness, for the core of being, could I escape into the pragmatic acceptance that keeps everyone working, walking, and managing in the world. More formally, I read Spinoza and books by Henri Bergson and felt in complete accord with the Plotinian notion of the illusions of ordinary life, its appearances, its arbitrary attributes. Beyond that incompleteness was yearning, but no finalities. When I dropped down inside myself, the winter got blacker and blacker.

How and Why I Became a Mime

Only twenty I saw darkness inside
for one year. No. I lost my eyes and came
to desolate hell, the hill of suicide
of thought. Words lost their act. I felt no flame,
a continent from eyes or passion. Who
was making talk? What polar icecap in
my scalp was me? From looking in, I knew

33

the secret hoax. Then, rocketing to the skin
I tumbled backward, lost from the dead eye
looking at me. Icepicks of light! But no
bottom or circus cannon to fly me out.
Talking, the good actor, I wriggled dry.
Am I now? Only twenty years or so
from dark, I mime the gray angel of doubt.

From the dark night of the mind, there was an escape: to be away from the geography of Brunswick, Maine. To leave the gray angel of doubt it was best to leave the place where the demon lived. Then I could forget the mind under mind where I was stuck, where nothing worked.

I began to go on weekends to Wellesley College to see Helle Tzalopoulou. In the first months I had a crush on Aliki, whom I hardly saw at all, except for one quick trip to Holyoke. When I went down to Wellesley, outside Boston, I hitched, and had the habit of not wearing more than a sport coat—no sweater or undershirt underneath, no matter how cold the weather. I had the notion that if one didn't give in to the cold the body would adjust. As I waited, sometimes for thirty or forty minutes in the snow or rain for a ride, I didn't seem to mind; and while I often reached Wellesley more as an icicle than hot oatmeal, I never got sick from that experiment in mind reforming matter. Helle laughed about how I would arrive with my jacket wide open, my shirt soaked, my body frozen.

Helle the Pou Tzalóping down the stairs. That's the title her smart literary friends, who liked Winnie and the Jabberwocky, invented for Helle Tzalopoulou, Greek English major. In 1945, the German occupation and war scarcely over, she came from Greece on the *Big Foot Wallace,* a slow cargo ship, armed with a scholarship to study at Wellesley. Helle was born in Istanbul (where Helle fell off the golden fleece and drowned in the Hellespont). Her mother came from a Phanariot Greek family, her father was an Epirote doctor who went to Turkey with the Red Cross during that brief period in 1921 when, for the first time since 1453, Constantinople was Greek Constantinople. A few years after the "Catastrophe," the 1921–22 war between Greece and Turkey, the family left for Athens where Helle grew up. After the occupation, Helle's mother had the dressmaker sew sheets and blankets together to make clothes for her daughter's trip to America. When she got to Wellesley and saw what the students were wearing, she bought a skirt and a blouse and threw the Greek "bed clothes" away.

We had fine times. I was intrigued by her foreignness, which included a good knowledge of *Paradise Lost* and the English Victorian novel. And we grew closer. I liked being at Wellesley, its Rockefeller Gothic buildings, its lake well designed and placed with Chinese care in the ample grass and wooded grounds, and all the brightness in the air of smart, alluring students. I met a stunningly attractive couple: an Israeli student at Wellesley and her Palestinian fiancé from MIT. One evening at supper in Tower Court I couldn't make up my mind what to order. When the waitress groaned at my slowness, I resorted to Helle's Milton with "They also serve who only stand and wait" to which the insulted student shot back my comeuppance: "They also wait who only stand and serve."

After a weekend at Tower Court, Bowdoin was drab. Little grace, no etiquette, which was perhaps a plus. But there was an intensity, at least in my circle of Central European friends. We laughed a lot, despite the sometime gravity of our vision. One evening Slava Klima, who was the deepest of my very deep young buddies, was on the dorm pay phone, talking, really shouting because of a bad connection, to his fiancé in Prague. The Stalinists had just taken over Czechoslovakia. He was asking her to leave, if she could, so they could get married. She couldn't or wouldn't leave Prague. He never saw her again, nor did he marry. Slava was my confidant. I was weary of my otherness. Though Slava had no easy answer, when a way came he helped make it real. Something finally did happen to free me of the obsession of introspection and doubt—and that something returned me to the visibly tangible and gave me a profession.

Christopher Isherwood wrote a novella, *Prater Violet*, in which he followed the art and personal life of an Austrian filmmaker. (Later, Isherwood wrote me that the book was not really fiction and then recounted the post-novel life of his filmmaker friend.) At one memorable moment the director wakes in the morning and decides to write a poem. It is perfectly natural. In other hands the poem and the activity would have been sentimental. Not in this instance. I remember the words as something like, "Sun at my window in the morning. Bird, you wake me with your singing. Keep singing. You make me happy."

About two o'clock one morning I awakened and wrote a poem. It was a love poem. I went back to sleep. Some twenty or thirty minutes later, I woke again and wrote a second poem, and went back to sleep. The next morning I showed these lyrics to Slava and to Olaf Hanson, a Dane. Also to a Frenchman whose name I can't recall. To my surprise, they took my first attempt at poetry seriously. Slava mentioned Rilke and Valéry and mumbled something about these poems being in a similar vein. I was overwhelmed by the association. I wrote poems the rest of the week. With no fuss or doubt or even sense of discovery I was a poet, only a poet and, like the post office downtown or night and day and the sun in the sky, I never thereafter questioned that poetry was there and my central identity. It came as a gift, unexpected. It was the luckiest night of my life.

Resignation to the Luck of Waking Out of the Night to Scribble a First Poem and Having a Czech Friend to Read it

At two a.m. in Maine, an aching night
of winter in the yellow dorm, I woke
and heard my roommate heaving, groan and bite
his epileptic tongue as if he broke
every bone in his corpse. I got up and
floated next door, sat down and wrote eight lines.

That night of moon breasts in my dirty hand
slipped into ink and I was born. The mines
exploded in the clouds. Don't worry. Though
I'm broke, can't sleep, and bumming like my son
slammed by a Boston court, we're all the same.
Groping, I stick a pen against the sun
and stain its yellow heart. Maine is to blame
for breeding me. Fail? Die? I still say no.

Twenty years old, last year in college, and only then the first poems. Wasn't that very late to become a poet? I read poetry and thought about it. In contrast to philosophy, poetry gave the particular, what Rilke in *Sonnets to Orpheus* called the *fühlbaren fernen* (touchable distances). Philosophy left me with words, jargon, and abstractions but nothing to touch. Though words—even the words of poetry—were only the names of things, inadequate semantic approximations, they were closer, as close as the mind could come, to seizing the things. Words were representations, signs, and in poems they came out as metaphors, symbols, but of course they were not the thing itself. Not even a mirror of it. Painting—at least mimetic painting—pretended to mirrors. It was not good enough to say a mountain, even a blue mountain. Sometimes the mountain was a whale, or a whale a mountain, or, as I was to discover in Patmos (the island that gave John the Theologian the Book of Revelation), the small islands in the port lay like seven whales, and this transformation of islands into whales was precious to the ancient author of Patmos and Ephesos who counted whales, horsemen, cities and churches and endowed the resultant ciphers with the mystery of holy numbers.

I began to read all the poetry, old and contemporary, I could find. In the beginning I looked too hard, as if each line should, as in philosophy, yield the truth of the universe. It was not so in philosophy nor in poetry. I was eager to study all poetry texts but felt inadequate to judge them. For years I felt I could write better than I could judge other poems. As it turned out, I felt comfortable with my own work. Not cocky. But in the beginning

I kept only a small portion. I had to go through all the styles, invent all the forms, discover and discard all the clichés that every writer comes upon. Over the years the proportion I preserved increased.

(Now, I still come to each poem with surprise. Yet, right or wrong, my judgment is more secure, and I rarely discard. I work over something until it is right. The few times I do discard I feel good. I'm always glad to be free of bad writing—really elated. Absurd as it seems, to throw away a flawed poem feels almost as good as having written a good one.)

By spring I had a collection. The only professor I showed the poems to was Robert Peter Tristam Coffin, a bard who used to recite his poems regularly at the chapel. Coffin was a sentimental Frost, but much closer to Yeats as a holy man, as a shaman of the arts. Yeats had come to Bowdoin a decade and a half earlier to receive an honorary doctorate at a time he was floating in his own oracular tower. Before a banquet in his honor he announced that he would be glad to speak to anybody, provided that he, Yeats, initiated the conversation. Robert Peter Tristram Coffin was not that elevated.

I had heard Coffin read at the George School. His ballads were haunting, like wind through a gothic window. I disapproved because they were belligerently unmodern. At Bowdoin I heard him often and was half tuned in because of his highly skilled performance of the romantic god poet; and in the end, I tuned out. He had nothing to do with the poets I then admired: the English metaphysicals; Blake's early poems, Baudelaire's late city poems; Williams, Eliot, and Auden; Rilke and Antonio Machado and the Spanish Generation of '27, all of whom I was reading with hunger. I was already reading Wang Wei and Du Fu in translation but had not yet turned to the Russians and Sappho and Cavafy—or Saint John of the Cross.

With all that, when I handed the sheaf of poems to Coffin I did so with expectancy. Although I had also heard Robert Frost at George School, Coffin was the first poet I actually spoke to. Some days later he returned my sheaf with the comment that I should read A. E. Housman (1859–1936). Strangely, I had just finished reading through Housman, trying hard to bring the Englishman's delicacy, tame meadows, and understated pain into our century. But it all repelled me, while Housman's near contemporaries, the short-lived Gerard Manley Hopkins (1844–89) and Emily Dickinson (1830–86) were fiercely there. They never failed.

It was time to change continents. In the summer Helle was gone and I planned to meet her in Europe. She went to Geneva to work as an information officer with the United Nations— under flamboyant Harold Ballou, who regularly stood on his head on his desk before going off to lunch. All for health and meditation. Harold was as eccentric as his son; sadly, however, they mutually despised their common traits. I thought of my father and how lucky I was that between us there was always love. After graduation I planned first to go to Paris in September. That journey to Europe and North Africa was to last five years.

3

IN THIS

RED ROOM

OF PARIS

STUDENT DAYS

My berth on the *Queen Elizabeth* was close to the fish. Another few feet down and we could all swim together. On the first evening the cockney steward asked if anyone wished to take a *bath*. We were a Pole, a Yugoslav, a French student, and myself. The old Yugoslav in the berth below, who had just retired on Social Security and was returning to his village to find an eighteen-year-old wife, didn't understand. The Polish electrical engineer tried to explain to him what a *bass* was. Enlightenment came. A *bat*, yes he knew all about it! You fill a tub with water and sit down in it. He had done it many times. The Frenchman and I swallowed our laughter. I was glad for the good company.

On deck I became friends with Norman Rudich, then at Princeton, on his way to Paris for a year to write his dissertation on Flaubert. Norman was legally blind—he had some peripheral vision—but he used no cane. Tall, corpulent, usually leaning a bit against the planet as he turned his face to one side or the other to pick up peripheral information, he swished around everyplace. When he danced, he was a windmill and anyone within range could be bashed by his whirling sails. Rudich was a political ideologue with an acutely intuitive literary sensibility; those two voices, his Communist rhetoric and his love for Shelley (which ironically he shared with Karl Marx), were in constant conflict and were to tie up his later writing. We took to each other immediately. I became his reader, which began in Paris appropriately with a lusty reading of Rabelais's *Gargantua*.

Norman laughed at me for liking Bergson. Wholly ridiculous. He liked my poems, however, and while he was more formalist than I—it was the times—he helped me immensely in establishing standards and forcing me to look at a poem as one without preknowledge of its meaning and intention. The first knowledge of a writer as self-critic is to know that what is in one's head is not in the reader's head—unless the author puts it there.

Ocean liners are for destinations, for changing city and life. There is the intimacy of the crossing, born of transience, given breath and candor by the solitude of the empty deck at night and the sudden friendships. I was full of aspirations. To wander, to experience, to know, to write. And there are people who open up, who speak candidly and make dogmatic declarations they would not make were these days not days of passage. Like a vacation romance or adventure, these were buoyant hours separated from ordinary life, from implications for future responsibility. After dinner the ship's orchestra played in the lounge and we tourist-class passengers had a great time. Passsengers from the more sedate, duller second- and first-class sections would invade our lounge to enjoy our fun. In late September the ship was rocking hard on the Atlantic and sometimes when the waters were very rough and tables slid from side to side, I'd rush up alone on deck to stare at the mystery of the endless ocean.

One evening I was dancing with a young Hungarian woman. Between numbers I sat down next to a tough guy from Chicago. "Too bad she's got her mother hanging around," I commented. I meant it too.

"Where you going?" the guy asked.

"France?"

"You should get over to Italy as quickly as you can. It's the hot place. They got beautiful women," he said. To wrap it up and obsess my daydreams, he added, "Big tits and tight cunts."

As we neared France, America lost its reality. A ship, especially with its days of incubation from the landed world, fosters cuts with the past and a new life. The closest I ever later experienced to an ocean liner for demarcating and altering realities was a plane trip back from Buenos Aires to New York, where in twelve hours we went from torrid January summer to shivering New York winter. And France was everything as I descended from the boat train at the Paris Gare du Nord in the midst of a taxi strike, went to the railroad station café bar, sat on a stool before the wall mirror, chose two hard-boiled eggs that sat in a brass holder on the wooden counter, ordered black coffee spiked with a shot of cognac, and took a room for the night. Next morning I was up early, put my wool ship trousers away in the suitcase, slipped into something light for Paris fall, and went down for breakfast. When I came back to the room and was about to walk out with my bags, I greeted the maid, who had already made up the bed while I was downstairs, eating and paying up. *"Bonjour, mademoiselle."*

"Bonjour, monsieur," she replied, shyly. *"Puisque c'est le premier matin à Paris, je vous souhaite bonne chance."* (Since it's your first morning in Paris, I wish you good luck.)

I was impressed by the polite formality. I went off to the rue Jacob on the Left Bank for a more permanent hotel. I was lucky. In the first old hotel, there was a fine, airy room, facing the street. On unpacking my grip, however, I found that on my first night in Paris the housemaid got my wool trousers:

Rocking on the Queen

Deep in the hold we have no porthole, yet
I gaze, X-raying whales. The greenish squall.
is pitching the ELIZABETH. It's set
the tables rolling, banging wall to wall.
I push up to the deck and wait for France.
At twenty I'm a character whom Plato
might keep for lunch—yet the Greek's reasoned trance
is not my Bergson dream. I'm a potato-
head, says my Marxist pal. Norm's blind but grins
at me. Naive! As Europe nears, wet shade
washes my eyes with reverie. I dry
my face. Europe is full of women. Inns
of smart delicious lips. We dock. The maid
at l'Hotel Flore pinches my pants and tie.

My room at the Hotel des Tours on rue Jacob had a red carpet,
a sink, was filled with light, and cheap. The sink with hot water
was the only one in five years in Europe. Fifteen dollars was all
I needed to live well for a week. The red-nosed concierge knew
one phrase in English, "no monkey business," by which she
meant no *ménage à trois* in her respectable hotel. "This is a proper
place, only couples."

"Any married ones?"

"Yes, I believe there is a proper Jewish couple who might even
be married."

Next to my room lived two painters, a Czech couple, in a
studio half the size of mine, and half of that was tall canvases
against the wall. The beautiful, sad woman, ironing clothes on
her worktable, came directly from Picasso's blue canvases. They
were good painters, with their exile experience printed on their
grave faces. Within days all my friends were foreign painters and
writers—from Greece, South Africa, India. I was enrolled at the

43

Sorbonne in a *certificat* in philosophy and a doctor in letters (like an American master's) in French literature.

In the room next to me a young Dutch woman lived. She introduced me to Bernard Citroën, a tall blond Dutch poet who was into every Quartier Latin literary activity. That winter he started an Anglo-French bilingual periodical, *Points*, in which I published my first poem. (Earlier at Bowdoin I had published a letter to the editor in the *Nation*, protesting the bigotry and racism of the fraternity system at the college, a letter that annoyed many Bowdoin people.) *Points* did remarkably well at the kiosks where disappointed women bought it up in the belief, as the French title implied, that it was a knitting magazine. Citroën, a Jew, survived the war in Holland, hiding for five years in a basement. The Dutch woman worked for KLM (Royal Dutch Airlines) and was always broke and unhappy. I lent her a few dollars. We talked a lot in her place; she lent me a current French novel which I devoured, and although I desired her and it was clearly mutual, I did not act:

Gospel of Fire

> In this red room of Paris student days,
> under the bulb drooping over the foot
> of a wood cot, my novel floods with wordplays
> of sex and existential thieves. I put
> the window down—a cement patio where
> a Dutch blonde rooms, who once looked up at me
> with young misery as if she felt the stare
> of my desire. I read on. No way to be
> with her. On the wall right behind my bed,
> wallpaper smiling lewd with its black teeth
> begins a Quaker shake. I hear the flow
> of a loud mattress, light a match beneath
> my hand (I'm smoking pipes), and Heer Van Gogh
> watches my fingers flaming on the bed.

Half a day in a train in almost any direction from Paris took you to another language and country. After I was settled at the rue Jacob, I took an overnight train to Geneva to see Helle. Although the Swiss were and remain the world's bankers for crime and political moneys, when I saw how clean and correct Geneva was, when I walked its unthreatening and charming streets, I thought of an un-Swiss incident a few days earlier in Paris.

In those days students were constantly carrying banners down le boulevard Saint-Michel only to be confronted by the police (*les flics*) who flew out of their trucks in their batlike blue capes, raised *batons*, and rushed the protesters. The students screamed "*Cochons, cochons!*" (Pigs, pigs!) and scattered, some scrambling up lamp posts before being dragged down by the *flics* and tossed in the paddy wagons. Art Buchwald, writing daily for the *International Herald-Tribune* (that paper is a European privilege like small good bookstores and delicious filter coffee), had just done a column saying the French police used their clubs on civilians' heads astutely, knowing, as a good French cook knows, that you can't scramble eggs without first cracking the shells.

I was returning home from the Sorbonne, walking by the rue Monsieur le Prince where Verlaine died drunk on a hotel floor. Then I reached the old plaza of the *Théâtre de l'Odéon*. Right near the theater is a quadrangle monument rising some ten feet; in the Paris dusk rain a student was on top the marble structure, orating to an enthusiastic crowd. The street lamps and drizzle made the upturned faces shine as under camera lighting. The young man was denouncing Charles de Gaulle—that "fascist"—for daring to represent France in a flower-laying ceremony at the Tomb of the Unknown Soldier. He yelled, "*Je pisse sur de Gaulle! Je pisse sur de Gaulle!*" (I piss on de Gaulle! I piss on de Gaulle!) His supporters shouted back, "*Pissez, donc!, pissez, donc!*" (Go ahead and piss!) And the hero took out his pecker, raised it with his hand, and a golden arc rainbowed out into the scattering and wildly cheering crowd.

As I walked the graceful streets of Geneva, I could not imagine such splendid street theater in this Swiss city.

Helle wanted to live in Paris. She spoke French. She had not yet decided to give up writing and become a painter—a definitive choice she made after we left Paris. But Paris helped her become a painter, as did Greece and Spain, and her lines and colors have never recovered from that good impact. With little background, I was already playing with the notion of studying at the Beaux-Arts, since painting and poetry for me were almost interchangeable in the dominance of image (even abstract or surreal) and in the act of translating a notion into paint or letters. I stuck to letters, except for a year in Greece when I shifted to the brush, and recently have yielded to a passion for pen and dry brush and ink. In classical China to be a painter and poet was perfectly normal and often the paintings carried lines of poetry on them—as some Lorca drawings do. The Chinese have a saying about Wang Wei, the Tang Buddhist landscape poet who was also a painter: "Wang's paintings are silent poems, his poems talking paintings." Since Paris I've moved in and out of a passion for paint and ink.

Now we were spending some days in picturesque Switzerland. We took a day's trip to an impeccably beautiful village some fifty miles away. Walking up the hill to the village square and its Calvinist church was like proving the category of Platonic harmony. Everything quietly right and in place. Later I was to work in Geneva, but my fondest association with the city is vicarious. It is through Borges's dead eyes. In later years the blind Argentine poet, essayist, short story writer was to be teacher, father, friend, companion, and, as far as my poetry and turn to fiction goes, the person who was always there. Borges had gone to Geneva as an adolescent in 1914 and remained in the city for nearly seven years. He became a writer in Switzerland, learned German there, in French-speaking Geneva, and his first published work was in French. At the end of his life he returned to Geneva and—as if sixty years had not gone by—he took up again with his first intellectual friend, Maurice Abramowicz. Borges and María Kodama, his companion of twenty years, chose an attractive apartment in his favorite neighborhood, La Vieille Ville. There in the summer of 1986, on his deathbed, Borges and María were married. Several of Borges's stories are set in Geneva, refer to a double, to another Borges, all favorite topics. Geneva was his other city and it was appropriate to find his double from Cambridge or Buenos Aires sitting on a bench by Lac Leman in his consummately peaceful and resonant city.

Wonderful as Geneva was in those days, with ghosts of Borges waiting on benches and in rooms to be reborn at his late return, Helle and I agreed to meet soon in vibrant Paris. I returned to my hotel late in the evening to get my things and take the night train to France. Near the hotel a woman in her late thirties came up to me, puckered her lips, and mumbled something about making love. I had already lost a second pair of trousers in honest Switzerland to the housemaid (it was a vice I had picked up), and in this land of cows so clean that its milk was not normally pasteurized, the very notion of love for Swiss francs seemed strange. When I hesitated, she looked at me as if I were an idiot.

In Paris I began to write poems again, now with France as the source of images. We took a bus trip along the Bretagne coast and I sat on a rock and wrote some stanzas called "Bretagne Coast." Later in the spring—after too many months in the city— we took a bus at random south of Paris till we came upon an idylic village called Vert-le-Petit. There we rented a room in a house, a plain white room with a bed and table in it, and a window facing *la douce France*. From that moment it was clear that nothing would ever be better, no house of any size or architecture is better than a plain white peasant room with a bed, table, a window onto the land, and some time. "Vert-le-Petit" was the title of a love poem.

> The bright cuckoo bird reaches out
> On sweet-France spring morning,
> And apple trees of Vert-le-Petit

Send away white sobs of beauty
And feed us with a mystic bread.

Then male smell of ox fills our nostrils.
Our love washes through us and we quiver
In the green waves growing hot and cold,
In the turfy furrows where our bodies
Hug the ivory of the young earth.

The bright cuckoo bird reaches out!
The bright cuckoo bird calls again!

The cry rises with the wood's being
And wafts through the air to our side.
We refuse to wake, and sunlight swims
Below our eyelids as a warm-water fish,
Sinking, lulling us through dreamy union.

Chips of stars hum behind the daylight,
And black-eyed pansies in their yellow folds
Stand in tender sun that like a deer
Taps across the river glaze—and halting,
Holds the pricked air on golden spots.

I wrote about the countryside in France but didn't have the
sense or ability, like Baudelaire or Blake, to bring the city, to
bring Paris, into poems. I was too young. A poem like Rimbaud's
early "Sensation" was more what I could do, although I didn't
know this at the time and had I been asked I would probably have
denied that the city was absent. Yet that year I read Baudelaire
constantly as I did for many years, and especially those late poems
of pathos about workers, beggars, and the homeless.

Norman had an American friend, Katherine Harper, whose
mother was French. By now Helle was settled in Paris, and the
four of us, Norm, Kathy, Helle, and I went to the chateau mansion
of Kathy's French grandfather for the weekend. Only the caretak-
ers were there, but they prepared wild boar for us, which we
washed down with local wine. After our country feast on forest

and village food, we went crazy and took all the pillows we could find and raced through the corridors of the castle, hurling pillows, screaming threats of murder at each other from behind columns and narrow passages. We were all alone, anachronistically, in this ancient castle with its thick stone walls echoing our American English. We also roamed the countryside that had crisp late-autumnal tastes in the air that I associated with pastoral scenes in Colette's deliciously sensual novels.

In Paris I liked going to Katherine's apartment—she was staying with her French aunt. The family had beautiful Corot paintings on the dining room walls and even an early Monet. On her American side, Katherine's relatives were in publishing. Although I had had no thoughts at all about publishing a collection of poems, Kathy came to my room one afternoon around six, actually a terrible afternoon for other reasons, and announced, "Willis, I think I can get a book of your poems published in New York."

"No!"

"Yes," she grinned.

I was lying in bed with a sprained ankle, but that news somehow prompted me to start jumping up and down on the mattress on one foot. Clearly the idea of publication was not irrelevant. It all seemed so easy. I'll have a book. Destiny. Justice.

"Stop it, Willis, you'll kill yourself or break the ceiling!"

Nothing at all came of this hint of publication, but the grain of irritant sand was planted in the oyster shell, pearl or no pearl.

I liked my hotel, liked to hear the roving musicians coming down rue Bonaparte to play and sing under our window for francs in newspaper packets that came pouring from the apartments like rain down on the performers; I liked to walk around the corner to the immaculate small plaza, la place de Furstemberg where Géricault had had his atelier; and especially enjoyed dropping in on the small galleries and bookstores at the far end of Jacob. The autumn air of Paris was blended smells of window houseplants, coffee, and smoke, and on Jacob the aromas were silently uplifting. It was enough to fill my spirit simply to look at those lighted store windows with their tasteful treasures. Yet I still moved to a cheaper hotel a few blocks away, which initiated a series of moves, each one unique. I went from rue Jacob to l'Hotel de Langue d'Oc, to the rue du Cherche-Midi, and finally to rue du Vaugirard, when Helle and I were living together. This Vaugirard hotel room faced the Luxembourg Park and had the implausible name of l'Hotel du Portugal et de Lisbonne.

One evening a gang of friends decided to go out. We began by descending into an old-style Russian restaurant, with the glamor of a Russian émigré doorman in nineteenth-century peasant garb. A rich preppie American in our group, who had been to the Soviet Union, did a sparkling Cossack kick dance. At a nearby table was a party of Hungarians who were wrapped up with drinking, laughing, and throwing empty wineglasses against the stone fireplace. As I went to the WC, for some reason the headwaiter stopped me and whispered confidingly that a famous Hungarian writer was sitting at the next table. I had been reading a streak of Koestler books, including more obscure ones such as his journal on waiting out a death sentence in a Spanish prison. I recognized the author in the group. He was unmistakable. As I came out of the men's room, he was a few feet in front of me. Without thinking, I said, "Are you Arthur Koestler?"

"No, I am not," and he walked on. I was disappointed by the denial.

A few days later I spent some hours with Tristan Tzara, the legendary founder of Dadaism. Tzara amazed me for quite the opposite reasons. Not arrogant in the least, he spent a very long afternoon chatting with me about modern literature. He was unduly interested in my remarks. More surprising, he insistently took books of his poems and other writings from a briefcase, and complained, "Everyone in the world has forgotten me. No one knows me now."

Later, Borges was to remark that Latin was a language better to have learned and to forget than never to have learned at all. But neither Latin nor Tzara is easily forgotten. It is true, however, that Tzara's name and the historic instant of his revolution are

more familiar to readers than his actual work—and that is probably what hurt him with regard to actual readership. Tzara's insecurities made me feel better, more normal. No one is immune
from doubt. With all his profession of modesty, even proud
Robert Frost at the end of his life was asking a friend whether
he, Frost, had ever written anything good.

In my irrepressible eagerness as a writer, to be a writer, I was
overly generous in laying my poems before the eyes of bemused
friends. Norman had my number and was cruelly funny. He
nailed me cold in my habits. He said to our gang that Willis was
the only person he knew who, if walking down a dark street of
some obscure city in eastern Europe happened to come upon an
old white horse standing by a door, might just edge up to the
horse and ask him if he would mind looking at a poem.

After the dancing and broken wineglasses at the Russian taverna, we went to a boîte named VENUS, which had a big sign in
the window announcing ON EST NU (One Is Naked). Inside, the
women were only half naked, from the waist up. Between acts
I danced with a performer, now clothed on top and bottom, a
tall brunette who was polite, silent, and distantly sullen as we
moved around the floor. It was midnight, we were hungry, and
decided on Pigalle and went in search of a restaurant we could
afford. We entered a largely deserted place, took over a long
table, and George brought out his guitar. He set up his harmonica
on a special stand that allowed him to stroke the guitar and blow
into the harmonica. Then began to fiddle with the turn-screws
and tune up endlessly.

"For Christ's sake, George, stop torturing us. Sing one of your
damn Russian songs!"

But George kept tooting notes into the harmonica and tuning
up. A clochard from a nearby table sat down with us, saying,
"*J'adore la musique.*" George was sentimentally impressed, especially when the man brought out an old letter he said was his
release from Devil's Island. Helle was disbelieving and disgusted.
She had seen too much during the occupation to be moved by
our guest. George kept fussing with his instruments and never

did give us a melody. Desiring perfection, he resorted to the ancient wisdom of teasing silence. But song or no, the clochard stuck with us, and even joined us when at dawn we went to the vast market of Les Halles for onion soup and breakfast.

In the '20s, e. e. cummings was still drunk after breakfasting in Les Halles, hired a hack, stood up in the back of the open carriage, and took a leak. A gendarme arrested him on the spot, but not for public exposure—since urinating in public is, or at least used to be, common—although perhaps not from the back of a fiacre. "What is the charge?" cummings asked.

"*Monsieur, vous avez pissé sur la France.*" (Sir, you have pissed on France.)

When we broke up, I had to go off to the Cité Universitaire to change money. The music lover said he was tired and asked if he could get a few hours sleep in my room. I agreed. At this Helle turned and left, disapproving of the company. I took the man to the room, and he lay down on my bed while I went off to the Cité to find my friends, a Turk and an Armenian, who roomed together in one of the dorms. Before I got back to my room, I went to a public shower house to enjoy feeling clean and fresh. Then hurried back to my room.

As I walked into my hotel, the concierge at the desk cheerfully announced, "Monsieur, you have just missed the laundryman who descended from your apartment with a sheet full of your things." I rushed upstairs. The door was open, the room empty, as if I had moved out. Gone were my overcoat, shirts, sheets, blankets. There was nothing left but books and a suitcase. He even got my shoes.

Later I calculated that my daring comrade from Devil's Island also sneaked in some sleep before descending with the laundry.

Although we went to the Bon Marché, and bought blankets and good linen that Helle sewed into passable sheets, I was still kicked out of my room—if for nothing other than my stupidity. I moved two streets away to a room with more air but where the sheets were a little short and didn't quite cover our toes. The room was fresh except when it rained. Since people regularly pissed out the window, after a rain the small inner court stank of urine steaming up. A few nights later, an hour before dawn, the police rapped loud and long on the door. *"Sécurité. Ouvrez la porte!"* (Security police. Open the door!)

Helle was with me. The police were obviously checking identity cards. Unlike Guillaume Apollinaire, who was arrested when his roommate stole the *Mona Lisa,* we were clean and our papers in order. But I didn't feel like getting up and we ignored the knocking. We lay very still. The knocker went away.

La Rue Jacob, 1948

War was fun for Guillaume Apollinaire,
sending letter poems from the trenches, yet
a bombshell came, gravely combing his hair,
but Guillaume healed in Paris, a cigarette
like a love ballad in his lips. I spied
life from a hotel room with a red rug,
hot water in the corner sink, and sighed
happy when the street singers used a jug
to catch the hailing francs. The courtyard reeked
with rising fumes of piss when evening rain
fell from the wine-blue clouds. Our sheets were far
too short. *Fin de la guerre.* Spanish flu creaked
into the poet's brain. We were young, zany
like Guillaume! who croaked with *La Victoire.*

The poets I knew who wrote in French, like many of the painters who painted, were not French. And some foreigners were of the French school but wrote in their own language—like the Conde de Monte Verde, an older Spanish gentleman who had been in Paris since the late twenties, who wrote *poesía pura,* pure poetry, like Valéry. I usually met the count at the Flore, where he showed me elegant limited editions of his books, printed in France. He always had his Waterman open and a sheaf of yellow pages filled from top to bottom with his meticulous, miniature script. He kept his little workshop between two cups of expresso. There was my pal Citroën, the Dutchman who was a French surrealist, and then there was George Jaszi Sandor de Nagy-Talavera, Baron de Rakoczy, 87 rue Notre-Dame-des Champs, as the looping gold italics on his business card revealed.

George Jaszi was striking—straight bonfire blond hair, actor's face, midnight blue eyes—but despite the titles, frivolity, and pomp, he was a very friendly, insecure, young Hungarian exile in postwar Paris. He always wore his pin-striped suit, narrow and pressed. Only his black shoes were scratched. George was not embarrassed to show me his poems, which were blatant imitations of Verlaine, exquisite, musical, and I thought hopeless. "*La musique avant tout,*" he would say. One evening George Jaszi asked me to come at nine o'clock to the back room of the Deux-Magots, which his own "Society for the Return of Music to Poetry" had rented as of midnight. He and other members of the group would be reading. George came to pick me up a few minutes early.

"You must come."

"*Pourquoi pas?*" (Why not?), I said.

We gathered our group waiting outside and went the few blocks to the Deux-Magots, where a banquet table was set up for us. George was the metteur-en-scène. He stood flamboyantly before the joyous group, making pronouncements, his straight hair flapping down over his forehead until he threw his poet feathers back into place like Franz Liszt sweeping into a piano crescendo. The reading began. It was sentimental, old-fashioned, enthusiastic. Jaszi was clearly the most talented of the group, despite his Parnassian delicacy. While the drinks and words were flowing, there was suddenly an obstreperous intrusion. The rest of the café was empty. The roar came from the street. I went out to investigate and saw two *fumistes*, practical jokers, revving a powerful motorcycle. As soon as they saw me they gunned the machine and took off. But no sooner was I back inside when the duo had circled the block and were again gunning the machine outside the door.

"*Deux fumistes avec leur moto*" (Two wise guys with their cycle), I reported.

George went outside and shouted at them and they were gone.

"Let's go on. Pay no attention to these villains," George said. The reading continued. The outside precincts had returned to silence. But suddenly two pairs of hands appeared on the top of the smoked-glass wall separating our quarters from the main restaurant, two punk heads appeared, and finally the punk heads let loose with a torrent of insults.

"*Idiots, imbéciles, petites merdes, poètes!*" (Idiots, imbeciles, little shits, poets!)

"*Salopards!*" (Filthy bastards!)

"*A la guerre!*" the baron screamed and rushed out, his cape guiding him in his pursuit of Kafka's clowns. They were gone. Maybe for good.

It was about two, I was pretty drunk (and I wasn't used to that), so I decided to leave. As I was going out, George was on his way back in, flushed with victory.

"Where you off to, Willis?"

"To bed."

"Wait for me. Can you put me up?"

"No problem, pal."

We strolled back to my room on Cherche-Midi. The night concierge was a stout man with dark horn-rimmed glasses who sat impassively with a black cat on his right shoulder. He looked up from his book and greeted us. Once in the room, before I put the light on, George found the sink and puked into it. Taking the clue, I threw up next, into the toilet. I took an extra pillow and a blanket and said, "Franz Liszt, try these over there on the floor by the window." In a few minutes we were dead, sleeping it off.

As the year went on Helle and I were spending most of our nights at each other's place. Our favorite street name was rue du Cherche-Midi (Street of Seeking the Midi). In the mid-fifties I was to spend a year as a soldier in the Dordogne, which local residents like to call "*Midi moins le quart*" (quarter to noon), punning on "midi" meaning "noon" as well as "the Midi" or what is also called by its old Roman name "Provence." So even in that exquisite region of truffles, rust-colored villages, Roman bridges, blue meadows, and birthplace of Montaigne and Sartre, I was still seeking the Midi. There were street dances next to our hotel where the butcher played the accordion and the cobbler the violin. We joined in old polkas, waltzes, fox-trots; most of the people were from the local stores, and they danced with extended arms and grasping fists while rocking up and down like innocent *apaches*.

   Helle and I met in New York and later that night danced to an accordion on the golf pastures of New Jersey, but it was in Paris that we met in the hotel rooms we shared, in the arts we would each follow, in the permanence of our futurity, in the Chinese arrivals, departures, and loss and discoveries that are a couple's destiny. In Paris I also met the permanence of Helle's Greece. I was reading the poets, pinning pictures of the islands over my desk, looking at the statues, which like the Mexican Olmec wrestler and rain god statues were heavy, sometimes buried by time and alien moments, but could never disappear.

Two Souls Meet on a Windy Night and Worry about a Marble Face

After the war when we were young and gray in heart,
I went to Paris to get exiled, kiss a soul, and hear
   the wind
blowing the urine fragrance along Bonaparte.
Stiff black coffee and warm bread were my early co-
   pains.
   Wind dozed among the linden trees. I spread it on my
   bed. The bed was bare;
a torn red blanket under a gray bulb of maybe
   30 watts, if I can count,

sputtered high on the ceiling, blinking at my underwear
dripping and wrinkled on the sink edge. I read
   the philosophy of Auguste Comte
hard as I could at the Sorbonne until my prof,
Monsieur La Porte, dropped dead. *La Porte est fermé*
was cruelly scribbled on the door. I met a soul
one windy night. Paris embraced us with her laugh.
She was a Greek. She gave me an ancient statue that hurt
   my arms. The cheekbones almost pierced the skin.
   It's so heavy, where can I put it down? I say
to her.
   Don't ever put it down, she says. We Greeks wake
   with a glaring
marble head in our arms. Hold it up or it will roll
   away.

At the Sorbonne, in my course on the French positivists, I got close to Emiliano Malive, a Spaniard from Madrid whose passion, like mine, was modern Spanish poetry. He was a friend of Vicente Aleixandre, the single major poet left in Spain from those extraordinary generations of poets. Federico García Lorca was executed in his city of Granada in 1936, shortly after the uprising; Miguel de Unamuno died in his sleep on New Year's Eve, 1936, while under house arrest; Antonio Machado died in Collioure, France, in 1939, driven out of Spain, as Juan Ramón Jiménez wrote, through the back gate; in 1942 Miguel Hernández, the youngest of the great poets of Spain, was dead at thirty-one in a Spanish prison in Alicante. The other leading poets—Rafael Alberti, Luis Cernuda, Jorge Guillén, Pedro Salinas—were in exile in the Americas and Italy.

Emiliano gave me two precious first editions from the early thirties of Aleixandre's poems, which I still have: *Espadas como labios* (Swords like Lips) and *La destrucción o el amor* (Destruction or Love). The Spanish poet was a revelation. A world of surrealism much more compelling to me than the automatic writing experiments of André Breton or the love and political poems of

Paul Eluard, then the most revered poet in France. (Robert Desnos, who died three days after being liberated from the Theresienstadt concentration camp, became the poet I cared for most among the French surrealists.) Aleixandre shared that moment of Spanish surrealism with Lorca in *Poet in New York*, with Pablo Neruda in his *Residencias*, and with Miguel Hernández in the surreal sonnets of *The Unending Lightning Ray*. After Aleixandre won the Nobel Prize in 1977, I did a volume of his poems with David Garrison, *A Bird of Paper*, 1982. We included one longish poem, "Aliki," which Vicente had written for my daughter, whom he already adored when he knew her in 1962. She was then only five and a pupil at the Colegio de Estilo in Madrid. I like to recall that Aleixandre, the poet I was closest to in Spain for more than thirty years, I first met through Emiliano in philosophy, the kindest and most sensitive of students in France.

The Sorbonne was a rallying place for many causes. One evening there was a "Réunion des Intellectuels" to protest recent activities and statements by Charles de Gaulle. At the jammed classroom auditorium, the poet Louis Aragon was haranguing an enthusiastic audience. On stage were several speakers including a priest in his robes, sitting grimly holding a rifle in his lap. When he stood up to speak, he continued holding onto the rifle. At one climactic moment, he shouted, "*Et s'il faut lutter, nous lutterons!*" (And if we must fight, we will fight!) And he jerked the rifle up over his head as everyone cheered. When it was Paul Eluard's turn to speak, we anticipated a few poems. He read no poems nor made a speech. He said soberly: "These are the names of the strikers who have been wounded and died in the national coalminer strike in western France." And for the next ten minutes or so, he slowly read the names of each miner and what had happened to him. Then he sat down.

These were strange political days. Albert Camus, a resistance hero, had come out against the Stalinists and their tactics of taking over Eastern Europe. Jean Paul Sartre was an enigma. His reputation during the occupation was as a resistance leader, but even it was strangely blurry. He was increasingly Marxist in his political ideology, later paraded in the street with a poster of Mao to show his enthusiasm for the Cultural Revolution, yet in 1948 all Paris was talking about *Les Mains Salles* (The Dirty Hands), his latest play, which seemed to condemn Communist dirty tactics for political purpose.

Paul Eluard had no ambiguity in his politics. During the occupation his poems were published clandestinely by the "Midnight Press." His most famous poem is *"Liberté."* He writes her name on his schoolboy's notebooks, on the wings of birds, on the walls of his weariness, on the steps of death: Liberty. Milan Kundera, however, gives us a bleak portrait of Eluard in *The Book of Laughter and Forgetting*, in which he describes the French poet's visit to Prague in 1950. One of Eluard's old surrealist friends from Paris days, the Czech surrealist poet and intellectual Zavis Kalandra, was about to be hanged as a dissident member of the parliament controlled by the hardline Stalinist regime. Eluard was being feted in Prague as a special guest of the government. He marched in the street with his admirers, read his poems to large audiences, and gave prestige and legitimacy to the new leaders. André Breton wrote an open letter to Eluard, imploring him to intervene to save Kalandra, but "he was too busy dancing," Kundera wrote. Eluard refused to do so, recounting that it was sometimes necessary to take one step backward in order to take two steps forward. "In the crematorium they were just finishing off one Socialist representative and one surrealist, and the smoke climbed to the heavens like a good omen, and I heard Eluard's metallic voice intoning, *Love is at work, is tireless.*"

One of my close friends in Paris was Robert Payne, who had just come back from China. It was Robert who took me to Tzara, and foolishly I missed an opportunity to go with him to Brancusi's studio. Payne was already a prolific writer when I first met him. Thirty-nine years old, he was an old China hand. He had taught in Chinese universities, was a British naval officer during the war in the Far East, and had been married for five years to a sister from the extended Sung family. In those days his companion was Jamie, perhaps a decade younger, and they were a romantic pair. Jamie had a daring freshness in her stand, a dancing smartness in her eyes, and I did lust after her, all quite secretly, hidden almost to myself. In later years Robert's fame and wealth cast him in a more conservative light. But these were days of freedom and writing and verve. The adventures of the preceding years were still invigorating in his ways. Paris was his café and hotel room. We had some of the most poignant and intimate conversations of my life, dramatized by his ability to come up with dogmatic but reasonable statements on the essence of each problem and how to take decisve action. I mentioned three words about Helle, and he said, "Marry the Greek." Robert was expert in giving himself fully to the moment, to enjoying himself with no apparent stops, while at the same time retaining an English resolution of discipline. His paradoxes even pertained to his eyes, which twinkled with diversity, strength, but also a glint of doubt, even sadness, which his display of character usually masked.

Robert insisted that I translate Lorca, but I felt happier with the landscapes of Antonio Machado, and began to do English versions of his poems. I owe my first experience in translation to Robert Payne. In 1973 when Harper & Row published my volume of the poems of Mao, the dedication read: "**For Robert Payne** who years ago when I was a student in Paris spoke with enthusiasm about a Chinese poet, Mao Tse-tung, when no one else seemed to know or care." Two years earlier Payne had been with Mao in the caves in Yenan and translated the first batch of his poems, including "Snow," into English. Now in Paris he was very excited about his poet holed up in northern China. Payne didn't speak of the Long March, the terrible civil war, politics—though later he was to write a biography of Mao—but about this talented Chinese poet, with superior calligraphy and fearful politics, whom he had discovered living in a cave in Yenan.

The first American author I knew in Paris who earned his living from his writings was Bernard Freckman. A tall, tormented, generous man, given to mild snobbery and dramatic candor, he lived upstairs in a room scattered with manuscripts, books, and coffee cups, just above my own place in a hotel opposite the Jardins du Luxembourg. I don't know why he was tormented, but he carried it with dignity. Freckman was a pro. His work had been published in leading periodicals. He translated books by Jean Paul Sartre, but his center was his translations of the novels and plays of Jean Genet. Jean Genet in 1949 was serving a life sentence in a Paris prison. Bernard read my poems and suggested publishers. He introduced me to literary friends. Although I took my work seriously, I was not prepared to find an older writer to show belief in it. When I left America six months earlier, I knew no writer my age or even close. Now in France, and soon in Greece, Spain, and England, most of my friends would be poets. We were the gypsy Jews of the world, under every carpet, in a nearby room across the street, as a guest at a quirky supper.

One evening Freckman came downstairs with some black-and-white art photographs of Genet. Innocently, I remarked that the author of *The Thief's Journal* had a handsome, striking face, as indeed he did. The following day Bernard was there, all smiles.

"Hi, what's up?" I said.

"I've just come from the jail. Jean wanted to tell me that he was very happy that you, a young American writer, thought that he, a common thief, was good-looking."

Sartre along with André Gide and Jacques Cocteau was working to get Genet pardoned, which eventually they were able to do. For the moment, though, Genet wanted to get his hands on some good books. Freckman explained a little conspiracy. Sartre chose the volumes and gave them to the warden. The warden cooked up an enticing delivery plan—perhaps only a literary French warden could be so mad. Rather than present the books to Genet as a mere present from Sartre, since the inmate was a thief by profession, he, the warden, would put the books in the prison library, make Genet a library worker, and so place him in a situation where he could steal the books, thereby giving him much more pleasure and also allowing him to practice his life's trade.

Freckman and I had become pals. His friendship, encouragement, just his presence was important. When I left France, we
exchanged letters for some years, and then it stopped. A decade
later a French writer told me a long story of a break-up Freckman
had had with a girlfriend, a depression, and then an ugly end. I
asked what it was, thinking it must have been some terrible
disease.

"No, he took a gross rope and hanged himself over the
staircase."

One evening Helle told me she was pregnant. We were too
young to have a child, we agreed, but abortion in France was
illegal. I asked people, who probably knew, but they were tight-
lipped, wary. In Denmark abortion was legal. The Greek Consulate in Paris was completely unwilling to make her passport valid
for Denmark on the grounds that the civil war was still raging
in Greece. Incomprehensible as the Greek position was, it was
real, and we had no options inside or outside France. Some weeks
later I said to Helle, "Let's get married."

"Good. How about in the *mairie* of the *sixième?*"

That was it. We did what had to be done in those days, which
was to obtain thirty-three signatures and documents. The assistant
at the American Embassy who gave us the checklist marked the
places where a bribe was proper; the suggested currency was
American cigarettes. We called our friends—my two best men
were Norman Rudich and Robert Payne; Sophía, Helle's Greek
aunt in Paris, was her bridesmaid—and on June 1, 1949, we were
married by the mayor of the sixth *arrondissement* in his office
across the street from Saint Sulpice Cathedral. The mayor was
full of verve in his rough Marseillais speech and pronounced his
wish to see us in a year, pushing a perambulator in the Luxembourg Gardens. (Our daughter, Aliki, did not come until seven
years later, in New Haven, but at least she was conceived in
Periguex, France.) Our friends gave us flowers. Like the fool I
often was, that same day I lost the key to my hotel room; so
after celebrating at the Cité, around midnight we took a cab to

Helle's room that now was in a proper bourgeois apartment. In the morning I brought the locksmith, got a new key for my own room, and left for class at the Sorbonne.

When we met at my hotel in the afternoon, Helle had a story for me. Her dignified landlady had confronted her formally with, "*Qui était ce garçon avec qui vous avez passé la nuit?*" (Who was that boy with whom you spent the night?)

"*C'était mon mari.*" (It was my husband.)

She was asked to leave that very day, which was not at all inconvenient. We laughed a lot.

Initially I was not happy about marriage, although I didn't convey this. Helle was wonderful, her Greekness a fable; she was a person who knew no subterfuge. Fully frank, intelligent, and irrepressibly cheerful. Her beauty only increased over the years. She cared for me as I did for her. But at twenty-one I had romantically thought of wandering for years in Europe and Asia, getting lost someplace in India, knowing many places, women, adventures. It was the duty of a writer to know the world, to be alone. I never got over some of those feelings. From now on we would do those things together. Precisely because of the early marriage, perhaps we wandered more, adventured more, experienced more deeply. Soon we were to experience the worst.

Jack Sanders lived in a hotel across the street. Jack was a novelist, in Paris on the GI Bill as a student but really writing his first novel, which he was to publish a few years later. Jack was my buddy. He told me one day that he had talked about the abortion matter with Jeannie, the maid in his hotel, who was his girlfriend. Jeannie knew a Lebanese doctor who could do the operation. We'd been married a week, had no plans to do anything but go soon on a honeymoon to London, and then go off to Greece. We decided on the abortion. The place was way out on the outskirts of Paris. The doctor was cold and nasty. He asked for the cash ahead of time, which we gave to him. Then with minimum anesthetic he performed the operation, which was painful. His only words afterward were, "*Voici votre chef-d'oeuvre, monsieur.*" (Here is your masterpiece, sir.) We went back to our hotel. Helle was in bed a few days and recovered quickly. We went to the park often those days. Soon we would be in London, cheerfully lost in the Scottish lowlands, and hitching back to London again on an English lorry carrying blankets, taking us Pullman to our destination at the home of Peter Russell, the English poet with whom we were staying in the city.

Years later, when I wrote about the operation in the sonnets, for rare reasons of discretion I changed the nationality of the woman who had the abortion from Greek to Polish. In fact I had a very close Polish friend in my class, on a scholarship from Warsaw, and we did go to secret meetings in hotel rooms where there were reunions of Poles in Paris with Free Poland war veterans, and she did love the delicate nineteenth-century Spanish poet Gustavo Adolfo Bécquer—but I never had romantic ties with her. By changing the name and nationality, the poem took on an artistic independence from the actual event, combined outside material, although in a deeper sense it did not stray at all from its meaning and spirit:

In a Paris Faubourg

My Polish classmate at the gray Sorbonne
loves the romantic poet Bécquer. She
wears heavy wool, is Chopin thin and fun
in Paris rain. One night she secrets me
off to a grim free Polish Army party
up in an orange room. We're comrades and
march behind banners down Boule Miche. Hearty
and generous in bed, she takes my hand
a Sunday morning, we go to a faubourg,
a sleazy house. I don't guess why. "It's clear,"
she says. "I'm pregnant and abortion's not
a legal act in France." Up in the morgue
the foreign doctor cuts her up. "So, here
is your *chef-d'oeuvre*," he tells me. We are rot.

4

GREEK

CIVIL WAR

AND ISLAND

FIG TREES

A year in Paris is good to have when one is twenty. Ernest Hemingway went there when he was twenty-one and stayed five years. He was married, poor, earning a living as a writer. He had some good things and some bad things to say about Gertrude Stein, who accused him of being a member of a lost generation. I also stayed five years, but shared it with other countries. I could have happily stayed another year or two in Paris, my French was good, I was writing. But I was just married and wasn't a newspaperman to support my wife on newspaper articles. And so I went to Greece where I could get a job. I suppose I could have hung on in Paris, as I did in Mexico, and each day in Paris the city and the friends meant more to me. But Greece was not only a job. It was a light. I didn't know what kind of light, but it was a light I knew. And it was good to live in and with that light. As for Paris, it was not only education, writers, a marriage. It was an atmosphere, a smell, a rain, and a delicate spring both in the Jardins du Luxembourg and in villages we explored at random, only to return to the deep air of the Paris atmosphere. Hemingway said it definitively in his letter to a friend in 1950: "If you are lucky enough to have lived in Paris as a young man, then wherever you go for the rest of your life it stays with you, for Paris is a moveable feast."

In Paris I had made such a pest of myself at the Greek Consulate that the director outright refused to issue me a visa to enter Greece.

"What can we do?" I asked Dr. Vassilios Tzalópoulos,* my father-in-law. There had to be some way around the bureaucracy.

The phone connection from Athens was good. Vassili said, "Go to Genoa." Then we were cut off. So we took a train to Genoa, where with no difficulty I did get the proper entry visa. All to the good, for it gave us a chance to walk around the stone streets of that beautiful city, to eat in its *trattorias*, to sit back in the kitchen and talk and listen for a few hours to the cook and maids of the *pensione* where we were staying. In the morning we boarded our Italian ship that stopped for a day in Napoli. From the city of Napoli, with huge gloomy city buildings and unknown sunny side streets, we took a bus to nearby Pompeii, a mirror of the Bronze Age city in Thera/Santorini, which had not yet been discovered and uncovered from its lava blanket. In the Pompeii Museum a guard took us aside, as apparently he did everyone, and revealed the erotic decadence of those early Roman inhabitants by showing us a statuette of six naked men facing each other in a circle, whose erect penises upheld a bronze plate.

We boarded the ship again and sailed for Athens.

At first daybreak I woke as we were rounding a turbulent

---

*In modern Greek, the stress falls most commonly on the penultimate syllable. Where it falls elsewhere I have placed an accent mark. If the word is repeated, I usually drop italics and the accent mark.

Peloponnesos. That turbulence I could see through our water-level porthole. I climbed in the half-light to a place on the portside deck and looked with amazement at the water a few feet below. The color and texture were like no water or liquid I had seen. Its uniqueness made me struggle to find a comparison as a way of identifying it. Only through metaphor, by likeness, by indexing, does the mind leap to the next meaningful perception. Finally, the image made sense. The water was like the inside of a purple grape. It had the pulpy thickness, the soft glow, the sweetness. Its brine must have been only an illusory surface attribute, for under it all the water was grape. Then I realized that others were forced into the same simile. There was the first writer we record in the West, Homer, and he anciently called it the "wineblue sea."

By midmorning we edged into the port of Piraeus. The brightness of the morning even softened fumes from the "satanic mills" contaminating the atmosphere with poisons. To either side of the city were the bay islands and the dry green coasts of the mainland, always with their underlay of marble dug out by the sun. As we got to a sign-reading distance of this industrial base, it was thrilling to see the frenetic waterfront speckled with little vans, some pulled by smoky motorcycles, others by respectable small-truck motors, but each bearing a similar logo boldly scrawled on the side panels: METAFORA. The sign in modern and ancient Greek means TRANSPORTATION, or literally "to carry across," as well as "translation" and "metaphor." So metaphor and translation are really moving vans. How good to arrive at an ancient port where even motorcycle trucks carry signs promoting the jargon of literature.

In September 1949 Athens was still a beautiful city. Antiquities were everywhere and everywhere seen. The splendid medieval section called Plaka lay alongside the Agora, and under Plaka another ancient city (which still can be unearthed only by destroying the oldest living section of Athens). Downtown was eighteenth- and nineteenth-century small mansions and town houses.

As in most cities of the ruined world, the earlier centuries have given way to tasteless apartment houses that age disastrously. But Athens in the fall of 1949 was still beautiful.

While the buses poured their black smoke out then as now, one could still see the mountains of marble Penteli and honeycombed Hymettos every day of the week. A few minutes outside of Athens was all olive trees amid wheat fields, and every day I drove a half hour through those fields framed by the changing mountains and Greek skies. Although the olive trees have now been axed and all those wheat fields have turned into cement, giving way to small industry and urban housing as Athens exploded and darkened in order to take in fifty percent of the nation's people, every day then was another gaze at beauty.

In 1949 Greece was coming out of ten years of world war, German and Italian occupation, and civil war. Italy had attacked from the west in 1940. It was a farcical invasion. The Italians had the dignity of being disinterested in warfare, and the Greek army drove them back deep into Albania. Then Germans invaded continental Greece and Crete. When I arrived in Greece the postage stamps still showed Cretan peasant women catching descending German paratroopers on their pitchforks, and in the countryside many houses still had numbers scrawled on the walls in witness of the hostages executed at that spot. The year 1942 was a time of famine when the food stocks of Greece were sent north to the German armies. Athens starved. Helle's family hid a young Greek Jewish girl for a while. A week later her father came to take her away to another safe house. After the war her father came to thank the family. She survived as did most of the Jews of Athens. However, some 70,000 of the 75,000 Jews of Greece, mainly Spanish-speaking Sephardic Jews living in Salonika, were murdered. With the end of the war came the December Athens rebellion of the EAM–ELAS Communist guerrilla forces, which Churchill crushed with British tanks. By 1946 guerrilla warfare had become civil war. Some 35,000 Greek children were taken to the Socialist countries with the aim of reeducation and return to Greece as future rulers. When Tito broke with Stalin, at least the kidnapped children in Yugoslavia were sent back to Greece. The other "socialist" countries kept their future janissaries. By late summer of 1949 the war was essentially over when Markos's army made a stand in the Atlas Mountains and, with no sanctuary to disappear into, was defeated.

When I reached Greece, there were just a few sporadic mopping-up operations. The closest I came to a war zone was on a trip to the Byzantine monasteries at Mount Athos in the north, when I went on muleback through the forests and up the mountains, escorted by a military patrol guiding us through the December snow. The front walls of Helle's Athens house on Tzortz Street were riddled with bullet holes from the December 1944 rebellion. Vassili told me that guerrillas were popping in and out of their house, firing from the front living-room windows or shooting down from the roof.

So Greece in that autumn was a country recovering from its wounds, and it showed in the most obvious way: the unusual number of amputees one saw in the streets. Greece was exhausted, poor, ruled by the right-wing Tsaldaris gang. Yet there was plenty of food and Greece was at peace. The common people dressed poorly in patched gray clothes. Having described the hardships of the people, I confess that it was a wonderful time to have there. No tourists at all. I was part of a Greek family. There is a saying in modern Greek that a husband comes from the village of his wife, so my village was Athens. I felt similar excitement when I spent much of a year in Buenos Aires with writer friends and Borges during their "dirty war" and more dramatically when I was in China during the Cultural Revolution.

White Island

Though Greece is blue I think of gray
and one-armed men after the War,
the Civil War, smoking and poor,
crossing Omonia on their way
to some raw cold cafe. No more

spears of the Persians; no more Franks
or Turks burning up towns. The pranks
of history mute, some pigeons soar
barbarous and WHITE! Now only gods
lurk on the islands. Artemis
and her gray lions fire the night
of terrorists and gleaming cheese,
her moon. Meanwhile, blue Theseus plods,
threading our village maze with light.

But Greece was something else. The arts were flourishing as
never before. The poets Nikos Gatsos, Yannis Ritsos, George
Seferis, and Odysseus Elytis were in their prime. The latter two
would win the Nobel Prize. There was wonderful theater, Greek
and international theater—more lively and varied than New
York. In one week you could see John Steinbeck's *Of Mice and
Men*, Lorca's *Blood Wedding* (both in Greek translation), and *Oedi-
pus at Colonus*. Very soon I knew the painters, poets, and composers. I have never felt so completely integrated in the artistic community of any city or country as during those first few years in
Greece.

The language I used with Helle's family was French, even after
I learned modern Greek. Helle's mother, María, went to a French
lycée in Constantinople, and though she studied piano for two
years in Vienna, French, not German or English, was her second
language. Vassili had studied medicine in Paris. It took a few
days to settle. One morning in the sumptuous living room of
the Athens house with its eighteenth-century French furniture
and oriental rugs (a room María normally kept locked and allowed
access to only on worthy occasions), Vassili asked me, "What
do you want to do in Greece?"

"I want to write poetry."

"I mean, what do you really want to do?"

"I want to learn the landscapes of Greece and a language of
symbolic images for poetry."

"How do you want to earn a living?" he said impatiently. Vassili had published a small volume of stories and poems about his region in Epirus (and a medical book on nutrition), so he wasn't unsympathetic to the arts.

"Maybe I could teach. I did that in Mexico."

We went to the American College at Psihikó, which is really a good high school. They had filled their positions, but they suggested I speak to the director at Anávrita, a new school near Kifissiá. This would be perfect, since in a few days we would be moving to the country house on Mount Pendeli, outside Maroussi, which was a five-minute bus ride from Anávrita. That same morning I saw the director of Anávrita Academy, a school of thirty-two students, including Crown Prince Constantine, then nine years old (for whom the school was established), and I had the job. I was to teach French and English.

It was a good job. The director was English, the teachers Greek, except for myself. They were obsequious, almost reverent, to the prince and even to the secretly adopted German prince Karl, who also attended the school; by contrast, you usually heard the pupils screaming, "Get over here, Your Highness, or I'll bust you in the mouth!" *Ypsilótate*, Your Highness, was for them just another name like Dimitri or Fálena, meaning "whale," which is what they called the school's fatso. I didn't teach Constantine because he already knew French and English, but I did eat lunch with him each day.

The Queen would drop in on my class and we would chat about poetry. She lent me the *Faber Book of English Poetry*, which I was very glad to study. Frederika was the granddaughter of the Kaiser and a cousin to Queen Elizabeth. Her accent in Greek was German. Her English was much better than her Greek. She was married to King Paul, Pavlos Glücksberg, a member of the Danish royal family. It was commonly said that dynamic Frederika was the power behind the throne, and sometimes he was called "O Frederikos," which is not only Frederick but Frederika in the masculine gender, implying that not Pavlos but a masculine Frederika was boss. Publicly she was on many charity committees

and initiated a campaign to raise dowry money for poor women
without dowries, so helping to perpetuate the repugnant tradition
of women as negotiable marriage property.

Morning in the Schoolyard

As always I was late. Nevertheless.
the king was standing by the cypress trees.
They pushed me forward. On this lemon morning
    at Anavrita estate where I was
    teaching, Pavlos, King of Greece,
a tall heavy Dane, was shaking hands. The squeeze
I felt made me look up into a glare,
an iron look on the fat metal face of a weak
and sickly giant. Wind lifted his hair
just as our palms embraced. I smelled the Greek
oregano and basil by the wall
and body odor of the guards. The king
grunted a phrase, a kind phrase. The press made
    fun of him,
O *Frederikos,* a dumb stand-in for a crafty Queen
    Frederika. But all
I knew at twenty-one was that a slim
disputive queen gladly lent me her English books,
    and she, the loathed daughter of the Kaiser,
    pulled a palace on her string.

For a while I started to grow a beard—not an unusual practice
in Europe. When I had lunch one day with the Queen, she told
me that she had been instructed by her son not to look me directly
in the face because I was trying to grow a beard and it might
embarrass me to be stared at.

The Greek government was as bad as the guerrillas in the
treatment of prisoners. "Why do you execute prisoners of war?"
I asked Frederika.

"They are not prisoners of war. They're thieves."

"But they're human beings, and Greece has had enough death."

"They're just common thieves."

"Do you execute common thieves?"

"There are thieves and there are thieves. These are common thieves who are killers."

"If I answer you we will have gone full circle again. So let's talk about Louis MacNeice."

When we finished lunch, I began to think of the islands and how good it would be to live on one of them. In my room in Paris, I had put up large photographs of the islands, of Mykonos, which came from a set of twelve black-and-white photos in a boxed edition, taken by some German photographer before the war. I knew the houses in those photos so well I felt I had lived there. And I began to count months until we could go and live in one of the white buildings.

When Frederika spoke about the rebels as thieves, she was translating from *klefti*, thieves, the common Greek word for guerrillas, a title the Greek Communists proudly assumed, since the word goes back to eighteenth-century rebellions against the Turks in which the Turks called the heroes of the Greek uprising *klefti*. On a personal level I liked talking to Frederika. And to dispute politics with her was after all a privilege. She in turn, I think, liked the fact that I did not feel the inhibitions of her Greek subjects, though I wasn't sure I knew when to stop. (I don't think I've ever learned that.) Politically she represented the source of many of Greece's problems, which is to say, its history of disasters.

My father-in-law, Vassili, was a strong antimonarchist and fed me his ideas about the unpopular Greek monarchy. At the end of World War I, Constantinople was liberated by the Allies (it had fallen to Ottoman Sultan Muhammad II in 1453) and Allied forces occupied the city from 1918 to 1923. Crown Prince Constantine's grandfather, Constantine II, pro-German during World War I, managed to muddle Greece into what Greeks call the *katastrophe* in which Constantinople and Anatolia were again and now definitively Turkish territory, confirmed by a huge exodus of Greeks from Asia Minor, including that of my family-in-law. The last move of the Greek monarchy was in 1936 when George II, King Paul's older brother, dissolved parliament and appointed pro-German General Yannis Metaxas dictator of Greece for life. After the war the English engineered the return of George II and his blemished monarchy, in part as an instrument against the Communist rebellion.

After the transition period from civil war to peace in 1949, there would be a series of increasingly liberal governments, which engendered an extreme reaction by the right, culminating in the successful coup by four colonels who ruled Greece from 1967 to 1974. By then this crown prince was king. He sided with the colonels. The day after the putsch, there appeared in all the papers a picture in which the king is standing with his arms on the shoulders of the colonels. Once in power, however, Colonel Papadopoulos had no further need of the young king. Constantine tried a coup of his own. It failed and he fled into exile, leaving his monarchist aides behind to linger in Greek prisons. During the period of the junta, I was involved in the resistance to the dictatorship to the extent of editing an antijunta book, *Eighteen Texts*, published by Harvard in 1970. When the colonels fell and democracy returned with Karamanlis in 1974, there was a referendum, and Constantine and the institution of monarchy were banned from Greece. Constantine's sister Sophía was married to their cousin Juan Carlos. Unlike King Juan Carlos in Spain when the Spanish generals threatened, Constantine did not prove to be a good king.

Louis MacNeice arrived in Greece in October of '49 to be the new director of the British Institute. In those days in England there were four poets from Oxford who called themselves the "new poets" and who said they were writing the "new poetry." They were Stephen Spender, Louis MacNeice, C. Day Lewis, and W. S. Auden. When a few years later Dylan Thomas came on the scene, very young and marvelous, with his *Eighteen Poems* in 1934—he was only twenty—it took the new poets by surprise. In his review of the book, MacNeice said *Eighteen Poems* was the confused work of an author out of control, who reeled out images like a drunk. For the rest of his life he praised Thomas and publicly lamented his mistaken review.

MacNeice was a classical scholar from Ireland, a member of the "new poetry" four from Oxford, less politically committed yet more of a social observer than the others. He published books of poems, translated *Agamemnon* and *Faust*, was a producer for the BBC. His wry understatement and ironic humor gave his poetry popularity. He lacked Auden's killer punch and doggerel brilliance or the fullness of Spender's Spanish Civil War poems, but many in England preferred MacNeice's newspaper eye. Greece was to give him a new imagery for his late book, *Ten Burnt Offerings*.

Louis MacNeice called me one day for tea, and I went to his apartment. Constantine Politis, a young political scientist, was there. I said, "What do you think of the political situation in Greece?" I might just as well have said, "What do you think of the planet earth?" His answer was stupendous. A gesture of futility accompanied by a weary, contemptuous sound I wish I could reproduce: a nasalized "eeenhhh," followed by *"Plus ça change, plus c'est la même chose."* (The more it changes, the more it's the same.)

It was not the French cynicism but the Greek "eeenhhh" that cracked us up.

"Why don't we go to the Acropolis," Louis proposed. "I haven't been there yet."

"That's a scandal," Kostas scolded.

So we took a cab to the hill dominating Athens called the Acropolis, "high point of the city." Since it was a weekday, the site was deserted except for a few guards. There were no fences, no admission booths, no tourist buses. The Pelasgian walls were gone. We started up the western slope to the Propylaea. The breeze from Hymmetos carried with it wild herbs and honey and the sun was sweet. The climb was not made easy by regular steps. Louis, tall, handsome, one of the black Irish, seemed to be drinking the air. Suddenly he stumbled, fell face forward, and hit the ground. He cracked his forehead on a piece of marble lying about. As he pulled himself up, he wiped the blood off his face. With a tremendous smile, he said, "What luck for a Greek teacher! On the first day to mix my blood with marble and sun!"

We reached the Parthenon. It stood there in marble patience. Pericles's buildings have been much abused by Persians, Turks, Venetians, Brits. The last massive indignity was in the eighteenth century when a Venetian general lobbed cannon balls at the Parthenon where the Turks had stored munitions and gunpowder. In the nineteenth century the British Museum safeguarded Caryatids and other Acropolis sculptures by placing their loot in the polluted London air of their grand building, only to sandblast them back to cleanliness in the twenties, thereby altering the marble patina of sensitive Greek skins to coarse Roman brutality. Unlike the Brits, the Turks didn't steal the women. In fact they added some of their own, turning the Erechtheum into a harem.

The Acropolis is monumental art on high. In the Near East, "high places" among the Babylonians and Canaanites are associated with adoration. The traditional site for Baal worship was on a hill or upon a monumental structure. The Sumerians, who are said to have come from the hills, worshiped hill gods on high places or on ziggurats that they built, and in I Kings 3.3 we read that "Solomon sacrificed and burned incense in the high places." That the Greeks also chose all over Greece to place their sanctuaries magnificently on high places should not surprise us. Often we find a temple between bullhorn mountains.

As for the great monumental aspect of the Acropolis, I felt uncertain, since I have usually preferred less to more. Of course the collective, major statement is impressive, in art as in government, but I usually favored a piano over an orchestra, a trek through intimate rhododendron forests in the Himalayas rather than one in the Grand Canyon, a brook in a Wang Wei poem more than the splash and thunder of Niagara Falls. But the Parthenon is a victory for calm grandeur. Above the city and gazing out on the far Aegean, the Parthenon is the surviving god of Greece on that Athens hill; and even in its mutilated state it has, in keeping with its name "purity," immense harmony of proportions and imposing peace. It is a symphony, but each instrument is heard with clarity. Moreover, the irregularly tall columns deprived of their roof—in contrast to the almost intact and therefore gloomy Temple of Apollo at Didyma—harbor the sun and clouds and even all the translucent winds. The air over the Acropolis—at least until the diesel buses poisoned the atmosphere—as over the sea around the islands, has an intoxicating logic. It is ecstatic. There is no indoors on the Acropolis, except for the small museum with its select pieces.

A few days later, at lunch, Louis was raging against Stephen Spender—his person, not the poems. When I began to read recent poetry, I read everything Spender wrote. I liked best his first book, *Twenty Poems*, and then the volumes grew increasingly rhetorical and sentimental, and always with a struggling, uncertain ear, until he gave up altogether as a poet. Yet some extraordinary poems about Spain, some lines here and there were enough to make up for the weaknesses. Louis blamed Spender for bisexuality, for pettiness, for arguing about every single piece of furniture when he divorced his wife. Having thought of Spender, Auden, MacNeice, and Day Lewis as a quadrumvirate of harmony, of social conscience and personal ethics, I was forced to understand that all people have their frailties. The Spender tirade was in part in anticipation of a visit by the poet, who had once published a book of stories, many of them set in Greece. A few evenings later Louis asked me over for an evening with Spender. They were old pals again, genuinely so, and surely what was constant and significant in their old friendship took over. Spender's wife, Natasha, played the piano. They told intriguing stories about Eliot, Barker, and Dylan Thomas. It was a good evening.

As soon as I went into the barber shop, I realized I didn't know how to say how I wanted my hair cut. Sure enough, the barber smiled and said, "How do you want your hair?" I knew he must be saying that and accepted that even if I were deaf and dumb, but at least a Greek, I could have explained myself perfectly well with at least half a dozen different gestures. The few words I'd picked up in these first days I learned at cafés. I had it. I'd make the barber tell *me* the word. When he asked me again how I wanted my hair, I resorted to a newly acquired language of how to order coffee, "*Ohi pikró, ohi varí glikó.*" (Not bitter, not heavy sweet.)

The barber said, "*Metrio!*" (Medium!)

"*Málesta!*" (Yes!) I shouted.

In Europe the café is where you carry on much of your social life, and in Greece the cafés are everywhere. If there is one house on a remote hill or farmland or beach, there are bound to be a few round marble tabletops (or humble aluminum ones) perched on metal legs, waiting for a customer. I saw the pianist Yannis Papadopoulos in his apartment. Then we would go to a café and chat with the composer Manos Hadjidakis. We did this regularly for two years. Manos tended to stay up all night composing and so we could never count on him showing up before late afternoon or early evening.

In those first years in Greece, Yannis Papadopoulos was our closest friend. He knew languages, speaking Greek, French, and English natively. His father had been the Greek ambassador in Washington and Yanni lived seven years in Johannesburg when married to an English-speaking South African. I had turned twenty-two when we met and so his forty years seemed to me the age of a prophet.

Yanni was a Byzantine mosaic, and perhaps a prophet. He had the large dark eyes of the Ravenna saints, his hair was very black and conservatively parted, his nose thin and slightly bridged. When he laughed he showed his front teeth, which were not bucked but seemed big and made the smile bigger, and then, in slight embarrassment about the fun of a good story, he would shut his mouth, but the smile still showed through. Sitting or standing, Yanni had the calm and erect posture of the Buddha. He was a Buddha, an idiosyncratically spiritual one, which combined

78

nicely with his endless doctrine of anecdotes in Greek, French, and English. When he started on a story, he savored every dramatic twist and each event was worthy of the *Arabian Nights*, but he gave a wise, ironic curve to every turn of phrase so that the tale became a parable. All this wealth of aphoristic experience came out whether he was recounting what happened to nation, world, or friends—who were usually in the arts or in diplomacy, or sometimes in both. The best example of the Greek poet-diplomat was George Seferis, but that combination was not uncommon in Greece and Europe—and even in Latin America where critical examples were Carlos Fuentes and Pablo Neruda, ambassadors to France, and Octavio Paz, ambassador to India. As the son of a diplomat, Yanni carried the burden of worldly behavior, which he had put aside in order to carry out his personal existence as a pianist and original thinker.

"Have some yogurt," Yanni offered. The rituals of food and drink offerings were very important to him. "I mean the good kind that we make in a *sack*. And by the way, *sakkos* is an ancient Greek word given to us by the old Phoenician merchants who carried their things around in a Hebrew *sak*."

"So a *sack* is a *sakkos* is a *sak*. Sounds older than Gertrude Stein's triple rose."

"Things haven't changed much, you see. Even when you think so. Words are disguised but they go on forever. What changes is the recognition of the masks we put on words or that we wear ourselves."

"How do you know so much about words?" I said.

"I like to browse in dictionaries. They are my newspapers. Dante is also a good newspaper. He gives you all the gossip and national doings of popes, scholars, and villains, who are often one and the same. At least in Dante's editorial."

"If you come from the East in America they say 'bag' where the rest of the country says 'sack.' We'd say 'a bag is a bag is a bag.'"

"But you know, Willis, 'sack' is more appropriate, at least for yogurt, since we in the Balkans, including Turkey, make the best yogurt. And it's best when you let it hang up and drain thick in a heavy sack. Then it's like cheese, but better, and better for you. Yogurt is one of the few things we peoples can claim after Plato and Greek Fire. And at least 'sack' also comes from our part of the world, from the Near East, while 'bag' is an Icelandic word. You need real sunlight and a marble table to enjoy sack yogurt with honey on top of it. Iceland won't do."

"Let's find Manos," I suggested.

Manos Hadjidakis was already a great composer, and then as now, Yanni kept his music in his head and wrote it down for him. It wasn't that Manos couldn't score his works. He did when he had time. But he didn't like to find the time, since he preferred to talk to friends till one or two in the morning, go home, and compose. So when was there time, with rehearsals and concerts, for writing things down? When his first ballet, *The Enchanted Serpent*, was to be performed in Athens, the piece was choreographed *en scène* while the composer played the piano. The afternoon preceding the evening performance the orchestra was there waiting, but all the instrumental parts for the orchestra were not yet completed. Manos arrived right after lunch, early for him, went to work scrawling the remaining parts while the orchestra tuned up, smoked, and enjoyed itself; by five he had completed the missing instrumental scores, in time for an hour-and-a-half complete rehearsal, an early supper, and a splendid, flawless premiere at eight.

Yanni the mental note bank, Manos the mad inventor. Variations of the ballet scene occurred regularly. Once Manos was in Paris and wired for a piano suite only Yanni had in his head (Yanni learned the pieces as they practiced together on two pianos). Yanni sent it and the concert took place on schedule. Manos the outrageous—who always came through. When he wrote the music for the film *Never on Sunday*, it was more of the same. Manos was overweight, smoked between words, wore heavy dark lines under his eyes from his casual sleep habits, and was a man of endless energy, wit, and poetry. The words he wrote for his songs were as significant as the music. As Federico García Lorca went to Andalusian popular song (folklore) to find lost words and melodies, Hadjidakis, like Mikis Theodorakis, went to Greek popular song. He was singular in reviving the *taverna* songs from Smyrna and Constantinople, the *rembétika* (solo man's dance), and *hassápiko* (the butcher's dance from the medieval butcher's guild). These city songs and dances (*zembékika*), like the blues, are distinct from the regional folk songs, usually line dances by both women and men, performed for *paniyiri* (festivities) of baptism, saint's day, marriage, or whatever pretext there might be for a party. The city songs can be love songs, some macho-proud—the Greek macho is a *palikari* (a young hero) which rhymes conveniently with *fengari* (moon), and so many heroic acts take place at night with the phonic connivance of the moon; others sing about thieves, drugs, prostitutes, death. One of the most beautiful songs that Manos rescued is "Sinefiazmeni Kyriakí," whose refrain begins: "Cloudy Sunday, you are like my heart, which always has clouds in it. Christ and my Vir . . . , Christ and my Vir . . . , Christ and my Virgin."

Before Hadjidakis and Theodorakis, the rembetika songs were very much alive, and after World War I, as a result of the massive influx of refugees from Asia Minor, they had spread everywhere in Greece, including to the islands. Masters of rembetika, like Nikos Tsitsanis in Piraeus, continued to write new songs, which gained national popularity, but the music was still associated mainly with the city down-and-outs and could be heard live mainly in the taverns in the poor neighborhoods or among the fishermen in the islands. It was purer then. Yet when the artists discovered their popular song heritage, they did so with taste. You heard and hear "Europeanized" commercial songs. But the music that brings stadiums of people together now, from all classes, is the popular music. Greece is unique in authentically joining the popular and the sophisticated. Spain's Falla went to the same popular sources, but the beautiful suites and operas are classical, not popular, and so are the audiences. On the amphitheater on top of Athens's second hill, Lykavittós, the poems of Elytis, Gatsos, and Seferis are sung in compositions by Greece's composers. There is no compromise. It is a Greek art.

"Mano, I hear Greek music, and immediately recognize when European elements enter it. Sometimes in your music I hear Peru or Paris. But mostly I hear Turkey, North Africa, India, all those places Greek music came from. . . ."

"We did come from the synagogues and mosques and temples of the East. Although now we invent our own music. We *are* our own music and are not European. Not yet. There is a difference. Even flamenco music, which at times seems to be Moorish or gypsy, meaning northern India, is European—with the exception of the Holy Week *saeta*, an almost pure Arabic chant. Almost. But Greek music is different."

"What's the magic difference?"

"It's not magic. Magic is quick and sudden. And we're patient. You see even the flamenco comes to a climax, it peaks sexually, and then the song dies. Our music doesn't die. It persists. It endures. Our orchestra (we give our three or four musicians that lofty ancient Greek title) may play a song for five minutes or an hour, and people may dance for an hour. Time in southeastern Europe is still horizontal. We have a timeless memory. It endures. But it is not historical like the Chinese. It is only eternal like India, where centuries of imitation are indistinguishable."

"You mean a Greek musician is really an Indian holy man?"

"Yes, a holy Indian with a lewd secular look and a sense of humor. Our dirges from Crete or Epirus are pure ancient drama, choral song, and timeless."

"What's your dream project?" I asked.

"To go to the Andes, lie on a hammock, and listen to the birds playing the flute."

"And after the Andes?"

"I want to write a musical drama called *The Street of Dreams*."

"I'll bet on the latter."

"Yanni will collect your money, if I don't come up with it," Manos offered.

"Don't be stupid. Yanni will have it in his head before you even dream about it."

There were certain cafés, bookstores, and yogurt shops where writers hung out—in the back of Ikaros Bookstore and Publisher, the Brazilian (a coffeehouse), and one big yogurt establishment that reminded me of the classic New York Horn & Hardart Automat on West 57th, which had a balcony where I'd go for hours to read novels. Upstairs on the balcony in the Greek establishment, I used to sit with Nikos Gatsos and Odysseus Elytis, and sometimes Katsímbalis, Henry Miller's hero in *The Colossus of Maroussi*, would also be there. Katsímbalis was indeed a wild-speaking colossus. I had a run-in with him once, and he said some nasty things I remember with pain, but later, on the islands, we spent an afternoon talking, and there was no sign of anything but adventure. In fact he lay flat on his lounge chair and spent some hours telling me about a trip he took on his back, floating in a boat down the Blue Nile.

Nikos Gatsos was very tall, his face sculptured and severely handsome, big features, including a nose excessively noble. He sat draping back in his chair. It was difficult to know whether he was deeply bored or meditative. I'm sure both guesses are right. I was told that Gatsos came from a titled, rich Greek family and that as a young man, after receiving his inheritance, he went to Monte Carlo and gambled it away in a few days. What I know for certain is that he wrote a major poem in modern Greek, "Amorgós," a 3,000-line surreal poem about the far Cycladic island of Amorgós (which I later included in *Modern European Poetry*). In late '49 and the early '50s when I met Gatsos, his friends lamented that this most promising and perhaps most accomplished of the new Greek poets had abandoned poetry. It disturbed me. When we spoke, he was courtly, kind, and weary, though he could not have been more than forty. He did give up poetry. There have been no later books, at least none that have been reviewed. But to my great surprise, this most wonderful and difficult poet, whose images were clean shots of island Greece, beautiful as they were, in their totality, elliptically obscure, began a new career writing transparent lyrics for popular songs. Gatsos collaborated with Manos Hadjidakis in his musical *O Dromos Onirou* (The Street of Dreams), and the lyrics are amazing. My judgment is so passionate when it comes to the good lyrics in Greek popular song that I fall back on John Steinbeck's lame excuse in *Travels with Charley* when he comes upon the beauty of northern Maine. He has no words for it.

Greek gods and goddesses are fashioned after men and women. So the gods are imitations of humans who are their makers. Angelos Sikelianós was a model for that imitation.

The revolution in our century in modern Greek letters occurred when the poet Kostes Palamás championed the demotic language, *dimotikí*, as opposed to *katharévousa*, the purist language—a mélange of ancient and modern Greek and the nation's official language. A generation later, Sikelianós, the first great modern poet of continental Greece—I say continental so as not to forget Constantine Cavafy, 1863–1933, who lived in Alexandria—also wrote in the demotic language, which comes directly from koine and Byzantine Greek. In keeping with his notion of seeing a continuum in all periods of Greece, in 1927 Angelos Sikelianós and his American wife, Helen, revived the Delphic games and drama festival at the ancient site of Delphi. It continues to this day, now moved to Epidauros and Athens, where ancient plays, usually in ancient Greek, are each summer performed by the leading actors of Greece.

Helle and I had been translating poems by Sikelianós into English. Mainly as a result of my teaching job, where I used Greek most of the day and had to know the Greek grammar for each lesson before I could teach the equivalent English or French forms, my Greek was getting reasonably good. We translated about seven or eight longish poems, including a brief sensual vision of Aphrodite surrendering, whole and naked, to the sun's embrace. (Eventually we gave them in Spain to the English poet

Laurie Lee, who had them broadcast on John Lehmann's BBC program "New Soundings.")

Aphrodite Is Born

In the happy fire of daybreak, look, I'm rising
    with outstretched hands.
The holy ocean calm summons me to step out
    into blue regions.

But sudden earth-winds ram against my breasts
    and shake my body.
O Zeus, the sea is heavy, my loose hair like stones
    weighs me to the bottom.

Breezes, hurry! O Kýmothoe, O Glauke, come, lift me
    by the hollow of my armpits.
I had not foreseen such quick surrender
    to the sun's embrace.

One day Helle said, "Why don't we see Sikelianós?" So we called and went to his house.

Sikelianós had just come back from the hospital. He had had a stroke and his right side was partially paralyzed, enough to force him to use his left hand for writing new poems. He lay in his bed like a god, and not only in face and expression but even in the posture of the reclining figure. He was not a severe, authoritarian deity from the Middle East or Mesoamerica, nor an itinerant rabbi-magician like the verbally mysterious Joshua the Messiah, but a contemporary, humane figure, whose transcendental qualities spread, like Walt Whitman's generous voice, into the modern world, waking us to observe the world and ourselves. He couldn't help the godliness. He had walked too long on the soil of Greece with his head in antiquity to be free of divinity.

Constantine Cavafy also re-created the past and, like Sikelianós, saw Homeric, Periclean, Alexandrian, Byzantine, Modern

Greece as many faces of a changing statue. But Cavafy restored his gods and heroes with outsider's irony, and he favored the demigod, the deformed in spirit and body, the bastard and step-child. He urged an Antony, weak, courageous, susceptible to love, on the eve of his defeat outside the gates of Alexandria, to go to the window, for the last time, to confront, to hear, and enjoy the mysterious singing of the troupe passing in the street. And Cavafy avoided mainline classical Greek figures. Rather he would speak about Greeks in a Roman satrapy in Syria or Anna Komnina, author of the *Alexiad* and daughter of Emperor Alexios I Komninós. Like Sikelianós, Cavafy made the past indistinguish-able from the present. Sikelianós in his classical and mythological realm, Cavafy an Alexandrian in his perverse profundities, Seferis in his Homeric world, Ritsos in his political and aesthetic merging of classical tragedy and popular Greek culture couldn't do other-wise. They were Greek and their memory and identity of a few millennia were no different from what they knew or learned about their great-grandfathers. The fall of Constantinople in 1453 or 1921 is a learned fact to most Greeks, and both losses occurred indistinguishably yesterday.

E. M. Forster, during his years in Alexandria a friend of Ca-vafy, carried word of Cavafy's restoration of history back to England and specifically to Eliot and Pound. By contrast with Cavafy's integration of his Greekness with earlier periods—and I use Cavafy as the earliest major example though Sikelianós, Seferis, Elytis, Ritsos all share Cavafy's exploitation of all Greek worlds—the Anglo-American modernists explored and exploited the past as a paradigm for comment on the present, yet always as strangers in the past. They are not even, like Cavafy, exiles, but true strangers, with citizenship elsewhere. Indeed, when Eliot, Pound, or Joyce re-created or alluded to a past, it was to show us that there was a past, to contrast the ages, but not make the past present—and this despite Eliot's frequent meditations on time past and present or Pound's lively depiction of Chinese, Ancient Greek, and Anglo-Saxon figures. The time gap is not obliterated but emphasized through exoticism. This is not a defect in Eliot and Pound, simply another approach by authors who were not, and could not be, of the times they described. Joyce, who even continued Roman linguistic imperialism by calling his Greek novel *Ulysses*, Eliot, who despised the Smyrna merchant with currants in his pocket, and Pound, who was so full of loves and wraths as to belong everywhere and nowhere, were not Greeks, Romans, Italians, Provençals, or Chinese. They were well-read, English-speaking writers, who came upon good ancient stories.

Sikelianós gave us a colossal smile. The Sicilian (which is what Sikelianós means) knew we had translated his poems. He beckoned us over to his bed and somehow managed to reach out with his one functioning arm and pull us both on top of the bed in order to embrace us. What do you say next?

"What are you writing these days?" Helle asked.

"The last book of a poetic drama trilogy. Do you have the earlier ones?"

"No. I'm afraid we don't."

"Take these," and he took two books from the side table and handed Helle two magnificent editions of the plays.

I hesitated. "Do you have copies for yourself?" I said. "They're not your last ones?"

"Don't worry. I have friends with copies." And the other people in the room nodded that he was safe.

"You're being very stingy to Angelos Sikelianós," I said to the poet. "I mean to yourself. You're throwing away your last books on strangers. Have pity on the Sicilian."

"No, no. That's what they're for. For strangers," he insisted. "My friends won't read them with honesty. It's always the stranger that counts." And the god winked.

Two years later, Sikelianós was back in the hospital for a routine treatment. The attendant gave him the wrong medicine, actually a cleaning solution, and though as soon as the mistake was discovered they pumped out his stomach, it was too late and he died.

A month before Christmas the director of Anávrita Academy called me to his office. The Englishman was not going to renew my contract for the spring semester.

"What's wrong?"

"Nothing's wrong."

"Let me ask you again. Why aren't you renewing my contract? Why are you firing me?"

"If you insist . . ."

"I do."

"You are an antimonarchist. It is not appropriate. There's nothing more to be said."

"There is nothing more to be said."

I wasn't happy. Here was my first job, and I was out. I was always a spontaneous person, which is a way of saying I couldn't keep my mouth shut. But in Greece and at that age I couldn't have done otherwise. I also got into hot water when the sculptor Dimitri Hadzís, then a Fulbright student at the Polytechnion, took me along to a party at American Ambassador Purifoy's house. In the receiving line I asked the ambassador why the American government didn't support the democratic forces in Greece. The gentleman was furious. Hadzís later told me that he got rebuked for bringing me and Helle along. Within a year a moderate government actually prevailed in a national election and the old gang was out; and since then, except for the seven years of night under the colonels, Greece has not had extremist governments. Purifoy became notorious a few years later as ambassador to Guatemala when he openly directed a coup against the reformist government of Jacobo Arbenz Guzmán, leading to the rule of Colonel Carlos Castillo Armas. Castillo Armas, whose last names, meaning "castle arms," were a wise, well-chosen title for the military leader or for the series of governments that for the next three decades would decimate its people.

I had saved some money from my job and was still dreaming of those black-and-white photographs of the islands. We left for Mykonos a month after the new year.

Mykonos was not visited by Greeks or foreigners in 1950. The islanders called both Athenians and foreigners *xeni*, so we were the only *xeni* on the *Eleni* that crawled and rocked through the winter seas to reach the island. The ship interior was stuffy and fascinating like a small village square: chubby peasant women with bandanas in their hair, many in mourning black; old men in wool waistcoats and leggings, and carrying solid crooked canes which they used to walk around with and to keep their goats and chickens quietly in place. There was no "nylon" prosperity in their dress—"nylon" being the word for the most costly polyester clothing of the coming generation. When the sea was rough, with each long rocking there was a communal moan, retching, and a lot of vomit on the deck. But no one complained. We spent most of the day topside, enjoying the passing islands, the cold whale clouds overhead, and the intimate fury of the untamed February sea.

It was dark when the ship dropped anchor a hundred and fifty meters from the dock. The harbor was too shallow for us to come in closer to the amphitheater of white houses lighted bright for the two-time event of the week: *Eleni*'s arrival. Big rowboats with glaring headlamps began to pitch toward us through the windy sea. Sailors were shouting orders to the boats, and boat captains were shouting back their version of the argument. We descended into one of the rolling craft, under screaming orders to hurry and be careful, and before the cheerful noisy chaos diminished, the *kapitanos* was rowing us to shore.

Theódoros, age twelve, was waiting for us. His mother, Kyría María Hartopoulou, had a place for us. And who were we to argue? Theódoros grabbed our suitcases, and while the wharf pelican monitored us we hiked by the dog chapel into the twine of alleys on the eastern side of the island toward the great eyeball dome of Paraportianí. We passed through the darkened igloo streets, under a loggia crossway, and in a few minutes the cobbled paving led us to Kyría Hartopoulou (Mrs. Daughter-of-Paper), who was waiting for us on her second-floor door stoop.

"*Elate mesa.*" (Come, inside.)

We obeyed. We went inside, passing through a maze of geraniums potted in white-painted cans.

Without any negotiation or questions, María took our luggage to our room, showed us the washbowl and the pail of water to refill the water cabinet over the bowl, the closet for our clothing, and the toilet, which was a miniature chapel facing the sea. Into that chapel came a cutting smell of brine and urine rising from the hole at the bottom of the red toilet bowl, and another current of briney sea air came blowing in through the paneless chapel window. All the floors were covered with blue Mykonos-woven rag rugs.

Our supper was soon served. We would eat with the family— Katarina, Theódoros, María, and Captain Andonis when he came back from the sea.

"*Ávrio* (Tomorrow) we'll talk about finances, but they'll be no problem," María shouted in the particular singsong of the Mykonian speech. And there was none. María tended to shout even when she was whispering, although she was a mild, even-tempered lady. At our late supper that night we consumed stewed lamb, boiled carrots and tomatoes, country green salad, and plenty of good bread and yogurt. The retzina was harsh and tasty and it washed the food down with perfect authority. I ate about twice what I normally eat. Seeking our sea legs, we gobbled everything, including the creme caramel in honor of our arrival. In a few days Captain Andonis would be home from the Dodekanese Islands, where he ventured during much of the winter as long as the local *melteme* winds were dangerous. Spring was only a few flowering almond trees away.

"When Andonis returns, we'll hear good stories," María promised. "Now, go to bed," she ordered.

Very quickly we passed into deep island sleep.

Dawn was tentative. It broke the darkness with a few rays. Then it dropped into clouds and night returned. Some gulls began to alarm the sky. Their screeching called the sun and Apollo slowly came up from the Aegean, icy and dripping dew across the stone back of Mykonos.

I slipped out of bed, went quickly into the freezing toilet chapel, then walked down into the street to see this whitewashed village whose only reality had been pinned on my Paris hotel wall.

Minoan Crete was far to the south. Here in the Cyclades the statues were far more primitive, geometrically plain and modern than anything found in that ornate Minoan civilization. But Mykonos shared one phenomenon with Crete: a labyrinth. The Mykonian labyrinth was not underground with fearful mysteries of a Minotaur who fed on virgins, but outdoors, under the sun glazing every irregular boulder shape into whiteness. It was only 5:00 A.M. yet the whiteness quivered. Some black cypresses stabilized the streets. Intermittent small churches poked the sky with half circles and triangles of ice. Astonishing peace. I stopped and the island halted. As I walked about, the perfectly measured shapes of the labyrinth contracted into hard fire.

Wandering lost in circles, I got used to the fire and it calmed into a constancy of ordinary light as full morning diffused the maze of iceberg sculptures. Light shifted to fishermen carting nets, black widows carrying water in clay jars, donkeys loaded with trash, a cheese peddler, my own steps. As the orchestra of noises grew, the building settled back into magnificent passivity.

Nearing María's again, I paused near the cupola of the white globe of Paraportianí, with its five churches connected under that stucco eyeball dome sending its rays to the entire firmament. Amid the acacia I heard the morning priest singing a cappella from the chapel.

The Small White Byzantine Chapel

On this island, nude, and nearly treeless
(But for the few acacia trees in bloom
In the small white plazas of stone and sun
With their zones of salt and seaweed aroma),

On the far side, across the island rock
(And the dry wind and fresh donkey dung),
The cupola of the white chapel stares:
A stucco eyeball brightening the sky.

Inside are sparks and fumes of incense,
And candles flames before the iconostas
Where a slant-eyed virgin leans in grief:
O points of mystery in the finite space!

Through the black air (within the whitewashed dome),
The priest leads the orphans in prayer and song.
O lifelong darkness of the finite vault,
And the white dome vainly searching the sky.

"You can make money teaching the grocer's daughter, and the postman, and the teacher can find you other students," María was telling me. "Yes, talk to the grocer, but be careful. He'll want something you won't be able to give to him. The grocer Assimomitis (Silvernose) is cunning, but you can teach his daughter. Have absolutely nothing to do with Zoakos, the *horofílakas*. The town policeman. His name 'small animal' means he is small, though he's fat as a pig, and a vicious animal. I've told you so. When you come back I'll have carnations for Hellitza." María was fond of Helle. Not only didn't she mind that my wife was Athenian but she was clearly pleased.

After breakfast I set out to find a job on the island.

By nightfall it was done. The mailman, the teacher, and the grocer's daughter. I would give all of them English lessons. And there would be enough money for us to live on. Just about. We wouldn't starve in Mykonos. When I announced the good news to María, she told me Andonis was back.

"Then let's celebrate."

"Of course, we'll celebrate. Right here. I'll go for Cyclops and for Frangisko who plays bouzouki."

"Who's Cyclops?"

"Ah, *Kýkoples*, my one-eyed friend. You'll get to know him. And his old mother he lives with."

"I guess Cyclops and I are old buddies."

"It's okay, Wilaki, you can meet his mother some other time."

Andonis was a serious man. Built like an unbreakable spike. He wore his black captain's hat most of the time. When he spoke it was worth listening to, though he didn't speak much, unless he had a few drinks and you might cajole him into telling a story. Then he was an artist. Andonis was also an artist as a dancer. He had a reputation in Mykonos. He didn't dance often, but all his seriousness came out stoically in the *rembetika*. That was another story.

We drank and ate a lot of bread and goat cheese. Andonis made me dance first. He corrected me when I slipped into something *xenos*. I sat down and Andonis began.

The captain stood very straight and paused a very long time. Then he began moving toward a fire, which wasn't there, in the center of the small living room. He looked at that fire, he studied it intensely. He circled that fire, slapping his thighs lightly. Stooping like a drunk, a controlled drunk, he hit the side of his shoe, leapt to the ceiling, and began to dance. Andonis was captain of all his gestures. He circled, drawn into himself, and, a hundred miles from the island, slapped the floor. His steps were delicate and rhythmically powerful. He spun, studied, shuffled, dropped to his knees. It went on for about ten or twelve minutes, ending with a leap to the ceiling in which somehow his whole body turned like a high-tower diver. The bouzouki stopped. Andonis sat down. Gave the slightest smile, took a drink, and then gently began to make conversation.

"How long are you here for, Kyrie Willi?"

"Not for long. Ten years, I suppose."

"Not long enough. You need a few more to get used to the water. The well water's very harsh. It takes getting used to. I think you need at least fifteen years. Then you can be a Mykoniatis."

"I don't think I can stay more than ten. But I'll return."

"*Kalá*. But you mustn't fool us. It's your word that you'll come back. After tonight, Kyría Helle, you must never let him go. Who will I dance with?"

White Island

My first day at the school for Constantine
I meet a peasant father with two hooks
(wounds from Albania) and the German Queen
of Greece who loans me her blue *Faber Book
of Verse*. But soon I'm fired and so begin
to loaf and write on islands. Mykonos,
the iceberg. I'm the only *xenos* in
the village, living with a Greek, and close
to getting jailed for working without papers.
The ship comes twice a week. Down at the pier
we all watch who comes in, but lemon vapors
of broiling fish seduce me. One white night Captain
Andonis slaps his heels. Austere,
he teaches me to dance, to live on light.

Once we were settled, Helle put a cloth on the small table in our room, made it into a desk, moved the glass with gardenias to one side, and wrote short stories about Epirus. She used her father's half brother, Apostolis, as her narrator. He was a village storyteller. At Wellesley she had written a book-length memoir of her Greek childhood, including the occupation when a German motorcyclist roared toward her, running her off the road and causing her to crash her bicycle; when her father was picked up as a hostage by a military truck in Athens, held incommunicado, and released by the Italians on Christmas Day; when her mother grabbed their clandestine radio, went upstairs and crawled with it onto a neighbor's roof while the Germans downstairs searched their house; how she dreamt that when it was all over she would have a cord around her neck with cheese and bread hanging from it and anytime she was hungry she would eat the cheese and eat the bread, and as often as she wished. Despite hunger and executions, the occupation was a period of hope and people lived on that hope. Issues were clear. The confusion, the new groups killing each other, came after the war. Cavafy said it in 1904 in "Waiting for the Barbarians":

> What's going to happen to us without the
>   barbarians?
> Those people were some kind of solution.

I envied Helle's fluency. Although I wanted to do a book about our life on the island, none of my attempts worked. I had neither the discipline, language, or mastery, and most lacking was the confidence or courage to do it even with fear. If I had persisted in my failures I would have found the form. Even if it took years of rewriting and reworking, which it would have. But poetry was the only center then, and enough. I worked through many stages in poetry. Although I published a book in Greece, and it was essential to do so, it was only later in Spain, and in New York and New Haven, that I found (or thought I found) a way to speak through the landscapes of Greece. Seferis and Cavafy helped of course. Greek cypresses in cemeteries, whitewashed villages, city streets with smells and newspapers were clear when the experience was selected and intensified in memory. So in New Haven I finished the first book of poems in America, *From This White Island*.

Much later, after a lot of drafts, I learned something and a time filter wasn't necessary. I could write on the spot about the immediate.

The day began before breakfast with a walk to the Three Wells, under the windmills. I drew water from the the good well for the whole family. On the way back, just before Paraportianí, I went across a small bridge where the island jutted out and Kyría Galina, the Russian yogurt lady, lived. I was often waylaid by Kyría Karpouzi (Mrs. Watermelon), an old lady, crazy as a bat, who always told me some wild story. Staring at me through her silver wire rims, she enjoyed her extravagance and knew I was a willing victim for her harassment. At the yogurt shop, Kyría Galina, married to a Greek fisherman, taught me a few words in Russian. She was plump as a bowl of honey, with small, blue Slavic eyes, and a smile that didn't let up. I liked our exchange, especially the big "*spasiba*" (thank you), as I balanced the clay water jug and red bowls of yogurt while crossing the bridge to go home.

We were the only foreigners on the island except for an elderly English gentleman I rarely met. There was a snarling formality to our brief exchange of words. Unhappy, in gruff, upper-class speech, he warned me about someone or other. His name was Mill, and he was said to be a grandnephew of John Stuart Mill. A starkly lonely man, widower of a Mykonos woman, the Englishman was a smuggler by profession. I never learned what he smuggled or whether his title was just flattering gossip, but he was Mill the smuggler like Stelios the barber.

As a reward for our writing labors, if we hadn't trekked across the island to one of the deserted beaches where it was still too cold to swim but a perfect place for reading or scratching down passages, we would have a meal in one of the harbor restaurants. With spring only just coming on, there were not yet the pyramids of watermelons built outside the eating places. One afternoon we had been glancing through a big, new book, a Greek thesaurus, and came across a word Helle didn't know: *ksekolomenos*. It was under insult words and literally meant "the man without an ass," or more freely, "the man who had lost his ass." In the evening we wandered down to the port and went into a restaurant where the fish was grilled over charcoal and doused with lemon and then touched up with local herbs. Fresh fish from the wharf, beans baked in their own sauce, island bread, and a glass of beer was the meal of your life.

Stephanos the waiter was a boy of thirteen or fourteen, school-shaven hair, and staring black eyes. Very smart and funny. I said to him "*Ksekolomenos!*" Because I didn't use the vocative but the nominative case with the final "s," the boy knew I was not addressing him personally and identifying him as assless. He squinted, looked all around the room with great intensity, checking it out carefully to see who was the guy who had been screwed so much he had lost his ass. Then he turned back to us, seriously, and said "Piós?" (Who is it?). We burst out laughing, we couldn't help it. We also knew the thesaurus had given us a living word.

The place was crowded, dense with spirit, noisy. Greeks like to emphasize their words with mock-angry outbursts even when they're being most friendly to each other. Most of the island restaurants don't serve coffee. That's the work of a *kafenéion* or a sweetshop with a long name like KAFEZAHAROPLASTÉION (Coffee-Pastry-House-Establishment), where men, mainly men, sat playing vigorous games of *tavles* (backgammon), or just sipped coffee while fingering a *kombolöi,* a string of worry beads. So after the grilled fish, we went to the kafenéion right in front of the pier where the evening ship from Athens came in. It was fun to be with everyone else inspecting who emerged from the sea on those little rowboats to join the island.

When our evening was over, everyone went home. At such moments I liked to walk the wharf alone. The island was asleep except for the lighthouse and a few bits of fire on the hills that looked like low stars. I could think, feel the drama of the island's distinction from the ordinary world. And by that difference I could define myself as a transient renegade, as clearly separated from what I had earlier known, a piece of pie in a dish suddenly cut off from the rest of the pie by a knife. The difference in me was a whole zone I had swallowed, as discernible as the taste of the briny air over the wharf. It didn't matter but I didn't have the words to define it, nor the experience to make it into poems I would keep, nor into prose I could link together. These abilities I wished, but I had to wait.

Wait, yes, but actively follow the life and verbal attempts of the writer. Otherwise the wait would be futile. Time must be actively filled in order to lead to a later time of difference. Without the constant preparation, time will lead only to increased age. So the Mykonos night was a laboratory. And even when I feel anxiety today, unable to escape the moment, incapable after all these years of moving into a philosophy or spirit to gain me peace or perspective, I look back to Mykonos night and my ignorances, filled with fire, if not words, with immediacy that also relished its future of inner and outer ventures. On the quay I got into the habit of spending an hour or two just walking and thinking. Although Wittgenstein might have protested, I seemed content at times to think perfectly well without words.

An Island

By white walls and scent of orange leaves,
   Come, I'll tell you, I know nothing.
     By this sea of salt and dolphins
I see but fish in a dome of sun.

In stars that nail me to a door,
   There are women with burning hair,
     And on the quay at night I feel
But hurricanes and rigid dawn.

On cobblestones at day I watch
   Some crazy seabirds fall and drown,
     And as the bodies sink to sand
I know I pay my birth with death.

I only see some plains of grass
   And sky-sleep in the crossing storks.
     I know nothing and see but fire
In the crater of a cat's eye.

Sometimes intruders with miracles in their pockets walk right in the door. The trick is to recognize the thief, before he gets back out with the rubies and sapphires. When I woke in the freezing bedroom of my dorm in Hawthorne Hall to write a poem, I saw the thief with his pockets bulging with loot. I went back to sleep but only to dream up a second poem within a half hour. Then I had some help. My friends convinced me that I had rubies and sapphires, or at least fragments of those stones, and I could have a lot more. So I was lucky. If I were a believer, I'd say I was blessed.

But the opposite can happen too. Just when you have the fire in your hands (using another metaphor borrowed from Federico García Lorca's words about knowing what poetry was as he knew what clouds were or the feeling of fire in his fists), some blasted thief walks in and blows it out. For now, let me recall the man who delivered the treasure. It was a Swiss.

Albert Schüpbach was a painter from Geneva, who, despite his typically Swiss-German name, proudly knew no German at all and, despite the Swiss school system, claimed he could not even pronounce his name correctly. (Many years later, in his own studio-house in southern France, he settled his Swiss nationality problem by Gallicizing his name into Chubac.) The painter came in that night on one of those pitching boats. We all spotted each other.

"*Bon soir, mes amis,*" Albert greeted us.

"*Bon soir.*"

"*Je cherche une chambre. Peut-être. . . .*"

"*Entendu.*"

I grabbed his dufflebag, Helle took his portfolio, and we disappeared into the back streets of the village. Cyclops had an extra room, a spacious bachelor's lodging, and Albert was delighted with both the room and the notion that he had found Cyclops on a Greek island. Then we returned to the harbor and spent hours talking about art and hearing how Swiss order and correctness had turned him into a wanderer, which was good and impossible for a painter who above all needs a studio.

"*Si le soir j'invite des amis chez moi, le lendemain je reçois une amende de la police.* (If I invite a few friends over for the evening, the next day the police slap me with a fine.) *Tapage nocturne.*

(Nocturnal racket.) Only my countrymen can dream up such silent evenings."

Albert knew no Greek but refused to see this as an obstacle. He spoke to everyone in French, and in most instances he managed very well. By speaking slowly, he drew people in. They listened carefully and guessed what he was saying or needed. In a few days, on his own, he set up a studio. And almost invisibly he acquired two disciples—Helle and me. When he ran out of supplies, we did help him order things through Zaharías, the local general store merchant. But he went to the butcher to buy his own paper supplies. He discovered that the butchers of Greece wrapped meat in excellent paper for his gouache paintings. Paper that withstood blood was perfect for absorbing his colors.

Helle gave up writing stories. She didn't think about it. She simply began to draw and paint. Before long she too had a studio, with easel, acrylics, gouache, inks, and a big supply of butcher paper. (I think it was her early work from Greece and Spain, the colors, that got her into Yale as a graduate student where she studied with Josef Albers.) I also began to paint, but it was back in Maroussi that I set up a studio. Albert was behind it all, though I don't remember him telling us to begin. It was his example. And a few words of encouragement.

Albert was then twenty-seven years old, which seemed a very advanced age. He had been working in his profession for years and in Geneva earned his living as a painter. He had hilarious habits. While we were all eating and he was sitting to Helle's right, he had the malicious skill of placing one finger on her wrist just as she was about to direct a forkful of food into her mouth. He'd say, "*Tu disais, ma petite fée.*" (You were saying, my little sprite.) And the fork halted in midair, an inch from her mouth. In Athens when a beggar came up to us, he tapped the gentleman on the belly with the flat of his hand, intoning "*Bonjour, mon vieux. Vous êtes un grand comédien*" (Good morning, old fellow, you're a great comic actor), and guffawed. The beggar's face flashed from misery to involuntary laughter. But the smile remained. "*Je vous dis, mon vieux, vous êtes vraiment un grand comédien*"

(I tell you, old fellow, you're truly a great comic actor), Albert insisted.

One morning Theódoros ran upstairs to tell me that the *horofíla-kas* Zoakos wanted to see me down at his office at the harbor. María had warned me that he was a rotten bully. I had an early lesson and then walked upstairs at about noon to the policeman's hideout. Zoakos, a chunky, ugly man in his forties, was broadly smiling.

"*Ti kánete?* (How are you?)

"Just fine," I said. "Kyría María treats me like an older son."

"You're doing a fine job I hear teaching English to our people."

"Thank you. Before coming here I was at Anávrita."

"Yes, I know."

"A small village, isn't it?"

"How would you like to teach English to my daughter?"

"How old is she?"

"She's eleven."

"A good age to begin. What's her name."

"Aglaía."

"Let's work something out." I didn't really need any more hours. A small inheritance had just come through, taking the mystery and adventure out of the next meal. But I thought it would be a good gesture.

"Of course I would expect you to do this as a courtesy to me."

"You mean teach your daughter for nothing?"

"If you wish to put it so crudely."

"I'm very sorry."

"You cannot be sorry. You will have to give her lessons if you wish to continue the other lessons. You have no working papers."

"I have temporary working papers, and they were enough for me to work at the king's school." I was angry and not at all diplomatic.

"They won't work here."

"They'll work just fine." I turned to leave.

"You're breaking the law."

"You're crazy!" I had had enough.

Zoakos seized my arms and tried to shove me into the barred room next door. I wrestled his arms off me. I wanted to say something insulting, but I didn't. I turned very slowly, walked even more slowly to the door, and descended the stairway. At the public telephone, I called Vassili in Athens and said I was expecting trouble.

That afternoon I gave my lessons to the grocer's daughter.

There were difficulties. It wasn't pleasant to be at war with the local policeman. Zoakos sent me a threatening letter, which I sent on to Athens. Vassili made a legal complaint against Zoakos for trying to force me into giving his daughter free English lessons, and filed the document with the Ministry of the Interior. A higher officer from the island of Syros, we were informed, would come to investigate the dispute.

Spring was everywhere and the sea calm. After two months, it seemed good to take a few weeks off to wander the islands. Of course we had been to Delos, a kilometer away by *kaiki*, where Apollo and Artemis were born. After Leto became pregnant by Zeus with Apollo and Artemis, Hera, Zeus's formal consort (and sister), was furiously jealous and Leto fled across the Mediterranean, seeking a place to receive her. Only Delos at the center of the Cyclades—those islands floating on giant tortoise backs— had the courage to offer Leto a sanctuary. Zeus stepped in to steady Delos for the birth of the sun and moon gods by attaching the island to the sea bottom with adamantine chains. Sun and Moon were born and thereafter Delos was a holy island, and also a treasury. One night Xerxes, a Greek general (not the Persian emperor), came to Delos on the ship *Parábola* with an offering. He brought with him a huge statue of Apollo and in the night he extended a gold bridge out from the *Parábola* on which to carry the statue to the shore. But in the morning as he set it up, lightning struck and a tall palm tree fell, bashing and cracking its chest, and today the Apollo still lies on the sand, with his chest fractured, not far from the row of archaic marble lions.

Each island has its gossip about ancient gods. We decided to go west to Ikaría and Samos and then way out to Patmos in the Dodekanes.

I gave my students some extra lessons to do on their own. On the evening of our departure, our friends were at the wharf, at the sweetshop, including the faithful students who saw my struggle with Zoakos as their contest between civilian and military authorities. We heard the dramatic foghorn announcing the ship and scrambled to carry our few things out to the end of the pier where the passengers from the *Eleni* were arriving, under spotlights, in the rowboats.

"*Elate mesa!*" (Get in!) Albert, Helle, and I stepped into one of the boats that spun around and began to row us out to the steamer. There was a five-minute stretch between the harbor spots and the ship searchlights in which we were in an open sea of darkness, as in a cave with fires at both ends. It was suddenly peaceful. Spring had quieted the surf and only the gentle lift and dip of the oars was heard. The stars descended to be closer to the unlighted precinct. Another space, a transition, time for another perspective. It was good to be alone in the darkness, to have this minute of freedom before setting out on the most exciting activity in Greece: wandering the islands.

As we reached the midnight *Eleni,* the sailors shouted at us and vigorously pulled us up on board. *Eleni* would take us to Ikaría where Ikaros had his agon with the sun. And then *Eleni* would go on as far as Amorgós, Gatsos's island, with its great Byzantine monastery like a white pancake wrinkled against the cliff over the sea. Amorgós lay at the outer circle of the Cyclades where, tugging against the adamantine chain, the last tortoise lay below the surf with the white island on its back.

Ikaría was not in the Mediterranean. It was Gauguin's Tahiti. At dawn the village of Evdilos was well-watered green. Then more pastel colors on the walls appeared until the full range of the French painter's palette was shining under fresh greenery everywhere along with the taste of honey and radioactive springs. Water had visited this island. The women carrying water on their heads from the wells were clearly from the Asia Pacific. As we moved closer to shore, however, we heard the surprising sound of Greek. It was Hellas after all, another of the many Greeces I found from Alexandria and Crete to Aphrodisias in western Anatolia and Cappadocia deep in Asia Minor.

Albert had a hard time accepting this different beauty. "*Où sommes nous?* (Where are we?) Till now I thought we were in Hellas." We settled into a café and no sooner were we eating our bread, butter, and lemon marmalade when he had his gouache pad out and was wetting the paper with colors. Helle took out her sketch pad and I mine. Helle liked to do both landscapes and portraits. We had a camera with us, but the pad took its place.

In voyages, figuring the next step is critical. Often it's the immediate conversation. In the woods there are two roads to take, or three or four. After Ikaría we were going to Samos, just off the Turkish coast, and the ship would leave from the city of Ikaría, on the northern coast. We decided to walk slowly across the big island, stay overnight in some village, and reach the southern port city of Ayios Kírykos the next day. After stocking up on figs, tomatoes, cheese, sardines, and bread from the *fournos*, we walked up into the high center of the island.

Unlike Mykonos or Serifos, whose beauty is its stone aridity, its starkness in houses and fields, where the few trees and cultivated meadows stand out like flowers, Ikaría is lush with water and fertile fields. And mountains are not burnt ochre and rust but Vermont green. As all over the Mediterranean, olive and fig trees grow amidst the wheat. We walked a few hours on high slopes between barley and wheat fields. The wind cooled us.

"Watch where you're going, idiot!" Albert warned me, as I stumbled.

"You need a woman to put you in a better mood."

"I can afford so many tubes of paint, so many canvases and

brushes, and right now, my quota of pretty women is very low. I'll have to sell a few more pictures before I can afford films and kisses."

"You Swiss miser."

"That's the Swiss. You see why I'm in hospitable Greece."

"I bet you count the hairs on your face so you can somehow make a razor blade last a day longer," I insisted.

"Not bad. Not good either. But I'm a meticulous counter. A champion."

"Do you think we can afford to eat some figs?"

"If I'm a miser, you're a criminal," Albert contended. "Trying to beat up on a Greek *flic*. The Greek *flic* is going to turn you into a jailbird poet and clip your feathers," he warned me. "And if you get out, you'll still tumble into the sea and drown like Ikaros."

"*Tai-toi.* Your eloquence about my demise is sickening me."

"Don't get upset. Once you're safely in jail, Helle and I will bring books and paper to your cell. A real poet needs a few months in a prison cell."

"So does a real painter," Helle said.

"If it's that good," Albert offered, "I'll volunteer. But will they take me? Will they waste good Greek food on a Swiss?"

"Greeks are generous. You never know when a stranger is a disguised god," Helle said.

We walked much of the day, stopping for food breaks. In the evening the stars came out very big. There was no moon. According to our map we had still a few hours to go to the next village. We were in a very isolated center of the island. Helle couldn't find her glasses, which were lost someplace in one of the packs. Albert was very solicitous. "Don't fall, *petite feé.*"

"She's a Byzantine and nimble," I said. "She won't fall."

As a matter of fact, despite her myopia she was very nimble and danced along while Albert and I were clumsy, sometimes tripping as we crossed through fields in the dark night.

"I see the village!"

"Where?"

"To the right, over there."

"Over where?"

"Just over there," she said, pointing. "On top of the mountain."

"Those are stars."

At midnight we did find the village. In those days there were few hotels and in villages there was always one way to find a bed. Knock at a door. Greeks are hospitable beyond reason. And they enjoy the ritual of the stranger. It was impossible to walk down a village street without people pulling you into their houses to offer you coffee and fruit preserves with a glass of cold water. Especially in those days when with little money, years of disaster immediately behind them, people acted humanely and with curiosity. We knocked and asked where we could find a place. The sleepy woman said, "*Kalós írthete.* (You arrived well.) Forgive me while I kick the children out of the room."

Before sailing to Samos, we went by *kaiki* to a very small island named Fourni (Ovens). It was just a happy afternoon trip to a place no one goes except the people who live there. We were walking by a blacksmith's shop and walked inside. A giant of a man was pounding a square of white-hot iron. His undershirt was sweat. Out of the blue, I said to him, "*Den fovase to sídero?*" (Aren't you afraid of the iron?)

"The iron's afraid of me!" the giant said, and he smashed his hammer down on the burning block.

Next morning we were on the coast of southern Samos. We decided to spend the day walking to Vathí, the capital. One beach where we swam was marble-smooth pebbles and stones and there was a small river feeding the shoreline. The wind used the sun to sweep and purify.

We were all in the water. Albert said, "This is like fresh water. No salt."

"The sea's a lake," Helle shouted.

By nightfall we had hiked and swum our way across the island to Vathí —the deep city. As we explored the neighborhoods, we came upon a French monastery with a sign stating: WINERY FOR

BENEDICTINE MISSIONS IN EQUATORIAL AFRICA. I rapped on the door
and a sallow Dutchman appeared.

"*Un moment, s'il vous plaît,*" and he disappeared. A few seconds
later the father superior came to the entrance and, addressing
Helle and me, asked:

"*Vous deux, vous êtes vraiment mariés?*" (You two, are you really
married?)

"*Oui,*" I said.

"*Pas de blague.*" (No kidding.)

"*Pas de blague.*"

"Then you stay here with us."

Turning to the sallow monk, Father Alphonse ordered sternly,
"Martin, prepare the rooms for our guests and then fix the sup-
per." Addressing us again, he said, "Please, join me in a drink."
And he brought out a bottle of muscatel wine.

Samos is the island of wines. "Drink deep the Samian wines,"
wrote Byron. The English poet, a hero in Greece, died at Misso-
longhi in the cause of independence and even today Byron remains
a common given name. His poem on rich Samian wines, however, assumes one period of classical glory and blackens out the
rest. As for the sweet, rich Samian wine from the muscat or any
alcohol, for me a little goes very far. I anticipated a long trip in
the French mission.

The mission had two monks, Father Alphonse, a jovial Breton,
and his gloomy slave, Martin, the Dutchman. After twenty-five
years in the monastery, Brother Martin had lost his fluency in
Dutch, he told us pathetically. The people had laughed at him
when he went home a few years before and they heard him
struggle through his native language; he never learned much
Greek, since he left the mission only for shopping; and he spoke
imperfect French. He was the jovial Breton's cook and house-
keeper. I liked Martin for all his sad fate.

Alphonse was a *bon vivant*. He drank, had many Greek friends,
and his main purpose during our visit was to keep us drunk.
"You must drink. Water rusts the soul but wine renews it," he
told us rhetorically. "Drink."

Being three weak-willed visitors, we obeyed. The muscatel was heavy, delicious, and lethal. Even the muscat grapes seemed to add to our stupor. I never before had wine at breakfast, a full breakfast that Martin laid out on a fresh, white cloth and decorated with flowers in a Greek pitcher. He did his work well. As we sipped some sobering coffee, Alphonse sent Martin into town on an errand. With us there alone, he settled down to serious talk.

"I confess I cannot stand Brother Martin. It's a sin, I know, but I don't feel it as a sin. I'm a happy man, and he makes me disgusted. I despise him. I should be a man of charity and he makes me stingy and cruel. But I think I will outlive him."

"You always struck me as stingy and cruel," I commented. "Look how wretched you have been with us."

"You're right. I'm a profoundly abusive person and have no desire to change. God is writing it all down in his notebook."

"I'm beginning to feel sorry for you too."

"No, no. I'm not worth the pity," he struck back. "By the way my superiors in Paris sent me a big parcel of French classics. It's very depressing. I won't live to read them all, and don't want to read any of them anyway."

"Why not, *bon père*," Albert asked.

"They bore me. I like solitaire and bossing Martin around. I'm so good at it, recently I've got the Dutchman to pick up a stutter. But these books, you have to take some away."

And the master of the monastery pressed Corneille, Balzac, and Proust on us. "They even sent me a book by Jean Paul Sartre. Those Fernandels in black dresses must think I'm a Communist."

After these days on the sea of Ikaros and of monastery wine, it was time to float back to the icebergs of Mykonos.

Hapless sea captains were routinely halted in mythical days by sirens of the sea. The ships drifted while their captains were quizzed about Alexander the Great. Where was Alexander the Great? Have you forgotten him? Any wrong answer, any forgetting, would earn the crew the immediate sinking of their vessel.

María's son Theódoros had his own versions of antiquity, which he retold in a family way.

"So what happened to your papoús when his fishing boat was sinking?"

"Well, Kyrie Willi, you know my grandfather used to go back and forth between Mykonos and Delos, and one afternoon there was a terrible storm and it flooded his boat with water and he was swept away from it."

"What happened?"

"He was a great swimmer but he was in the middle of nowhere."

"So he drowned?"

"If he drowned, how would I know what happened?"

"So he was saved?"

"Shut up, Kyrie Willi. I'm trying to make sense and you're killing me."

"No, just torturing you."

"Anyway, Papoús saw a dolphin swimming near and he asked him to let him hang on to his back till they got to shore. The dolphin said sure, but when you reach the shore, you must remember to give me a push so I won't choke on the beach. Well, he swam with my grandfather to Delos and when Papoús reached the beach he was so happy he started to shout and ran into the middle of the island hoping to find someone to tell his story to. By the time he came back to the beach the dolphin who saved him was dead. Since then dolphins are very friendly, talkative, you can swim with them, but if you are drowning they will no longer take you on their backs and carry you to shore."

"Theodore, when you grow up, what are you going to do?"

"I'm going to be the cook for the president of Greece."

"You'll always eat well, huh?"

"The president will eat well."

Needless to say, in 1974 when Constantine Karamanlís came back to be prime minister after the fall of the colonels, Theódoros was his cook. It was quite a few years, however, before Karamanlís became president.

The investigation of my working papers was at a standstill. But slowly the bureaucracy kicked in. The officer from Syros came to investigate. The charge now was not the working papers. That wouldn't stick. It was more extreme. Lieutenant Karkavitsas was serious, but he skillfully avoided a confrontation by interviewing us separately. Zoakos had filed a charge that I had insulted his office by calling him *agrámatos*, a word I hadn't heard before but which I immediately understood to mean "without grammar or education." Worse, I had attempted to steal his handcuffs and lock him up in the cell next to his upstairs office. I talked to Karkavitsas about other things, our recent trip to Ikaría and Samos, and he wished me and Helle a good time in Greece. He was proper and clearly embarrassed. It made me feel very good. Either by design or accident on both our parts, we did not allude to my crimes. We parted.

I had some lingering doubts. Should I have defended myself against the outrages I committed in Zoakos's eyes? It was a long beautiful summer. I carried the water jugs for Kyría María each morning, read, wrote, and with summer came some visitors to the islands, Greek writers who became close friends. But nothing came of the conflict with the police chief. Through enlightened neglect, there was no official report. I escaped the Greek jail. The teacher told me that Zoakos was still threatening and cursing me. The teacher was cursing Zoakos. And one evening all my students celebrated at the grocer's house, since the bully was being transferred—routinely perhaps, we had no information—to some place in northern Greece.

"May he eat shit and mayonnaise for breakfast," said Mr. Silvernose with the big belly.

"You're a grocer and want to make sure he has a nice healthy diet."

"Yes. My recipe should fit his constitution. He could live to a hundred on it."

So we drank to shit and mayonnaise and his being gone. I had lost a few nights sleep over the mess, but in those days, while emotions were deep—and that was good for the well of poetry—

experience was neither cumulative nor wearying. Today, a bit of bureaucracy (an IRS audit or even waiting to hear from a publisher) leaves me less philosophical and prepared than I was in those days under the eye of the police chief who vowed to get me.

Greece was Helle. She gave me Greece. Not only by leading me to her country, but by being herself ancient, Byzantine, modern Athenian. And I loved her for being herself and a civilization. Greeks took me as American or Greek-American (most often) or, since I am from my wife's village, Greek. The latter Greek connection made me happiest. I adapt quickly to new cultures, learn the languages almost as quickly as a child (I should get some benefits from incorrigible childishness), and feel at home, not estranged. The immediate merging is especially right in France, Latin America, and Spain, where I "look" French, Latin American, or Spanish, but it has also held up in China. In China I knew many poets—Beijing's poets lived in our rooms during waking hours. That we were all of one clan gave us a commonality superseding origins and nationality.

Helle also gave me a blood identity with a culture, later fixed by having children who are my Greek blood relatives. The initial identity was not for having picked up ethnic prejudices—I had no desire to hate Turks or wartime Bulgarians as Serbs traditionally despise Croats and Croats Serbs. My obsession was with Greek history, ritual, Greek Orthodoxy, popular music, popular dance, the poetry. I felt like a European poet, and specifically a Greek poet who wrote in English. My ideal reader was a Greek thoroughly fluent in American speech, who would also be a reader of the Greek poets. By extension, even now, as I think of having lived eleven years in Europe, the secret reader I would be grateful to meet on the page would know the work of the poets of Europe. Such feelings probably led me to do the Bantam volume *Modern European Poetry* that appeared in 1967.

Helle also gave me the open identity with a people that, as a Jew, was not so simple to have with Jews. I wish, in a nonrestrictive sense, it were possible to be a Jew as I am a Greek. (Given this good age, in my own mind I am improving at naturalness.) I know that when I translated for New Directions the volume of the mystical poet Saint John of the Cross, son of a *converso*, or translated the Song of Songs (*Shir Hashirim*) with an Israeli linguist (in a book published by Kedros in Athens), or did the Harper & Row *The Other Bible: Jewish Pseudepigrapha, Christian Noncanonical Apocryphya, and Gnostic Scriptures,* I was discovering, as I do with Philo of Alexandria, Yehudah Halevi of Toledo and Córdoba, Franz Kafka, or Paul Celan, an identification with a literary word used by Jews. And that word has given me the clearest sense of kinship with a possible Jewish ethos—more than any vague memories and inventions of blood kin from Eastern Europe. I am an outsider. In a rare moment when I hear Kaddish or look at texts that I barely decipher despite seven years of inefficient childhood Hebrew or hear snatches of wild Yiddish klezma music, then do I discover any deeper cello chords that I hear constantly because of my Greek connection. A fortune in my life has been to turn into a Greek.

Helle and I, a wandering Greek and a wandering Jew from the Western rim of Asia, we joke about our imagined earlier wanderers. For good or bad, they left in Europe and the world much of their civilization.

Athens in the autumn was literary, but by now I was very committed to painting. I had a fine studio in our Maroussi house and worked there every day, doing large paintings worthy of a child's vision. (Even in recent years when I have returned to dry-brush ink drawings and have illustrated some books, my work is meticulous, quick, and primitive. Color planes in painting and poetry lure me, and I feel them in my veins.) To wake each day and go to a studio was a good life. It could be done and had all the attractive impossibility of a poet who could sit down each morning, turn on the spigot of inspiration, and write.

In that same autumn of 1950 I also began to translate fiction. Helle introduced me to Rita Liberaki, an excellent novelist whose books won literary awards in their French translations. She was Albert Camus's love in Greece. Camus also wrote a fully deserved, extraordinary blurb for her second novel, *Three Summers*. Helle and I began a translation of her novel *The Other Alexander*. We worked on it in the winter and spring of 1952–53 in Andalusia, the next year in London with Rita, and then again with Rita in Paris after she had moved to France. Nine years after we began the novel, Noonday Press brought it out.

One bright fall morning I was rushing around the Monasteraki area in downtown Athens—named for a small Byzantine chapel, but not nearly so small as one in Mykonos. When a captain, sailor, or fisherman came through a perilous sea storm, the Mykonian family erected a white chapel in the village or in the countryside. One poor family could afford only a small one, a few feet high, and they built it down at the harbor by the pier, adorning it with good icons and hangings. The islanders called it the dog chapel. Just as I got to Monasteraki itself, I saw Kimon Friar walking toward me, arm in arm with an older, stout gentleman. Kimon stopped and said he wanted me to meet George Seferis.

In Paris I had read the poet's *The King of Asine* in translation, strikingly rendered by Bernard Spencer, Nanos Valoritis, and Lawrence Durrell. I told Seferis how much I liked his poems in translation. And they do lend themselves as few poets do to the hand of master translators. Philip Sherrard and Edmund Keeley have done the complete Seferis and one can read the entire corpus in English with confidence in their English incarnation. One summer I read the collected poems in Greek three times through just because I cared so much for Seferis's poetry. That day, that first day, we spoke just a few minutes. I remember his smile.

The first day you meet a poet you love—George Seferis, Vicente Aleixandre, Luis Cernuda, Octavio Paz, Theodore Roethke, Jorge Luis Borges—stays with you forever. In the case of Aleixandre, who also had a romance with the child poet Aliki, we were in Madrid in 1952, in gloomy early-Franco years when the gray *policía armada,* the armed police, with their heavy tommy guns, were on every corner. The book Vicente Aleixandre gave me had a vanquishing title of his own darknesses and light, *Sombra de paraiso* (Shadow of Paradise), and on the flyleaf he wrote: "*A Willis Barnstone, en el primer día de amistad.*" (To Willis Barnstone on the first day of friendship.)

I'm not sure the kindnesses of older poets persist into our time. I hope they do.

Later Kimon told me that Seferis was very cheerful that a young American poet already knew his work. That was touching but silly. How could I be in Greece and not read him? I was not that crazy. In *Mythistórema* he wrote:

> I woke with this marble head in my hands;
> it exhausts my elbows and I don't know where to put it
>   down.
> It was falling into the dream as I was coming out of the
>   dream
> so our life became one and it will be very difficult for it
>   to separate again.

> I look at the eyes: neither open nor closed
> I speak to the mouth which keeps trying to speak
> I hold the cheeks which have broken through the skin.
> I haven't got any more strength.

> My hands disappear and come toward me
>   mutilated.

Seferis had served as a diplomat in cities of the Near East, in Europe, and in Washington. His last post was as the Greek ambassador in London. In 1963 he was awarded the Nobel Prize in Literature. I think of Seferis in the period following the coup by the colonels in the late sixties. The poet was in New York and had just given an extraordinary reading at the Poetry Center. After the reading some members of the audience volunteered questions about the colonels and the Greek dictatorship. Seferis refused to respond, stating it was not the place to make his opinions known. He would do so in the proper place. There were some boos and much discontent. Seferis returned to Greece and called a news conference for foreign journalists, denouncing the junta, and asking for an end to oppression. From the outset he had joined the artists of Greece in their moratorium on publication, exhibition, and performance. As a result of his declarations to the foreign press, he was put under house arrest. When Italy accorded him its highest literary prize, he could not go to pick it up.

The last period I saw George Seferis began in December 1969, on the first evening he left his house publicly. It was at a private party in Athens and he had an introverted gaze that night—not the great smile. Though he was with friends, much of the evening he leaned over a big dining-room table, saying nothing. People were shy about interrupting his solitude and he exchanged only a few words with them. But he was a mysteriously important poetic presence and his silence spoke.

A few months later Seferis called me at noon and was a joking mortal again. He wanted to talk to my daughter, Aliki, to talk over her poems with her, and say goodbye to us, since we were leaving Greece. When Aliki was ten she had her first poem accepted by *Poetry*, and two years later *The Real Tin Flower* was put out by Macmillan. In the preface to it Anne Sexton wrote, "Everything is within her range from Greece to El Greco to bubblegum." And she cited lines from a poem about her Greece, which was blue and white:

> Blue is Greece
> where fishermen tame their boats
> and islands stand
> like white monastery birds
> on the Greek flag
> of spinning blue.

(I suppose my happiest moment as a writer with writer friends was when my daughter began as a child to publish her poems.

Then I had a writer friend in my family, soon to be followed by Aliki's younger brother, Tony Barnstone, who did a volume with Wesleyan. I've always felt a mixture of gloom and calm in regard to the fate of my own work—but as for my children's things, I've been an insufferably proud collaborator.)

Seferis's call came less than a year before his own death, resulting from a botched ulcer operation he had been putting off. But at that moment in Athens, the poet had only one thing in mind. He was taken by my daughter and her *Tin Flower*. In his deep voice he said to me, "I don't want you to leave Greece before I say hello to Aliki, to the girl who wrote "purple makes me want to blow my nose."

Distant Color

Purple is a funny color. It's maddening
and I hate it. It's icky. No one ever
    cares for it

but El Greco. Sun is yellow and in Greece
I saw boats and the sea and white temples
    and sweet air

but purple makes me want to blow my nose.
I only like it growing in the grass
    as violets

yet feel sorry for purple, a very good friend
who paints lilacs and horizons and beards
    like far mountains.

I published Seferis's poems in Friar's translations in *Modern European Poetry* and "The Cats of Saint Nicholas" in Keeley's translation in *Eighteen Texts*. "The Cats of Saint Nicholas" was Seferis's last major poem and was an allegory for Greece in its period of darkness. The story of the cats is based on a book published in Paris in 1580, which tells of a monastery that the

Duke of Cyprus built on a promontory in Cyprus in honor of Saint Nicholas. The duke imposed one condition: that the monks of the order of Saint Basil feed at least one hundred cats a day. In a period of drought the cats fought snakes and reptiles that were devastating the island; though the cats saved the island, they were themselves overcome from having taken in so much poison. At the moment of Seferis's poem, the military junta was devastating Greece with snakes and reptiles.

I, George Seferis, This Friday of Barbary Figs, Say Hello to Blood

> Two horses and a slow carriage outside
> my window on the road in Spetsai where
> I walk when everyone has gone to hide
> under the cypress shade of sleep. The air
> is salt, a gentle wind of brine and smells
> from the old summer when a woman said,
> "I am no sibyl, but your asphodels,
> Antigone and blossoming seas are dead.
> So let's make love." I am a diplomat
> and poet, taste the archeologies
> of old statues weighing me down, yet think
> before I'm under house arrest I'll chat
> and sleep with her. Help me, cut me. The sea's
> live blood is better that a glass of ink.

Kimon Friar had become my friend a few months earlier when I spent a week on the near island of Poros, where he was living in a small house on the estate of Mina Diamantopoulou. He was engaged in his seven-year translation of Nikos Kazantzakis's epic poem *The Odyssey: A Sequel,* which was to make Kazantzakis a world figure. Kimon was born on the island of Pringipos in the Bosporus as Kimon Kaloyerópoulos ("good old man" or "friar") and came to America when he was two. He taught at Amherst, fostered the poetry there of James Merrill, whose first book, *The Black Swan*, was published by Ikaros in Athens. Kimon was always pleased to tell me that *he* was the black swan. In New York he founded the Poetry Center at the 92nd Street Y, did a seminal anthology of modern poetry with John Malcolm Brinnin, and then moved to Greece, where he has remained for more than forty years, making known the poets of Greece in English translation. I remember one evening in Kimon's small studio house on Poros—the island off the coast of the Peloponnesos whose orange trees fill the sky like the sirens' song. Mina had it built for him for his work. Kimon showed me correspondence with Ezra Pound, who had refused to correct the mistakes in Ancient Greek words in the *Cantos*; so Kimon printed them with the errors but noted the correct spelling in his annotations. He was clearly pleased by his own censorial scholarship, and it would have delighted Jorge Luis Borges, who was less generous than Kimon in regard to Pound. Despite his nippity corrections of Pound's grammar, Kimon was a prince of generosity. His place in Athens was a home to me.

One word was said to me in the next days that altered what I have done with my years. Accident shapes our lives. Initially, we determine very few circumstances in our lives—not our birth, nor our parents, nor most early decisions. We work, and then there is chance. Our lives are a roll of the dice of luck and failure— whom we meet, where we are, what is said, or not said. Having said this, I still think it essential to assume responsibility and, as far as possible, to struggle even with chance, with lightning, flood, and the telephone. Philosophy speaks of kinds of will or the lack thereof. Although I was given a birth name that is a homophone of will-less, I am not will-less and perversely praise my failed actions. That helps me not to give up.

In Mykonos, arriving in the afternoon from Athens, as some of the summer ships did, was Geoffrey Graham-Bell, a South African with the famous acoustic name. We were friendly. Albert had very funny things to say about Geoffrey because of his parodic snobbery. One long evening at a party in Maroussi Albert dozed off in his chair. He was in the corner of the living room and he woke for just long enough to shout to Geoffrey, "*Chante, barbu.*" (Sing, bearded one.) On the fatal day of chance, Graham-Bell walked upstairs into my studio while I was painting. It was about noon. I remember the moment sharply like a dog bite I once got in a Mexican village by the volcanoes. The evening before the Graham-Bell incident I had been reading the surreal love sonnets of Miguel Hernández. I wrote a poem in Spanish that same night that later appeared in *From This White Island*. Geoffrey really didn't enter the studio. He stuck his nose in, looked at the painting I was doing, and said "Ugh." Nothing else. Not even a complete word. "Ugh" did the trick.

I don't remember thinking about the comment. It was enough to reach me, however. I ceased painting. Of course there were regrets. And I cannot blame Graham-Bell for what should have concerned *my* will. I could also have regretted that after enthusiastically translating a novel I did not immediately write my own rather than wait thirty years to do so. And another hundred second roads not taken. Regret is worth nothing. I return to my original fortune in finding, at the age of twenty, the center of a life, poetry, and sticking to it. Every good or terrible journey has fed it. Joy and pain instigate it. I have no complaints. Painting lost but writing found. A fair exchange. Whatever questions there are of publication, recognition, and all the literary hocus-pocus in a writer's years, I have had another kind of luck. I wrote and did so with faith, and do so now. Beyond that are perhaps nice public rewards, but not paradise. If there is one, it resides only in the creation and an invisible friendship with a secret reader.

So my sometime pal from South Africa helped to center me, to give me one. I thank him.

(And by curious irony, I'm back with the brush, the dry ink brush, and book drawings.)

Winter was here. Despite the weather, we decided to go into the heart of the Peloponnesos and work our way up north. Winter adds another layer of reality to Greece, a working harshness fed by bright light while Persephone's cries are still heard from the underworld. We took a ship to the castled port town of Byzantine Monemvasía and a dawn bus toward Olympia. After we got on the road, the ticket collector sat in the back and he and the driver sang antiphonally while most of the riders slept. The bus was a chapel. Those old postwar songs had an Asian Minor melancholy and pathos that later better times could not engender.

"Where are you going?" said an old, smiling lady.

"To Olympia."

"You have relatives there."

"No."

"Business?"

"No."

"Why are you going to Olympia?"

"To see it."

"Strange things."

Our alibi was no good. No one on the bus believed we were going to a village, in winter, at dawn, just to look at ruins.

There was no hotel anywhere near Olympia. We walked an hour to the site and had the columns and the River Alphaeus to ourselves. Pindar's odes sang resonantly about every event of boxers, charioteers, discus throwers, and sprinters before the gaze of the supreme referee, marble Apollo, but his athletes were now bones scattered under the black earth. Some have been there since 776 B.C. when the first Olympic games were held. Not far from the temple of Zeus, I found an enormous lion head with its face pressed into the ground. It was ignominious. I spent the whole morning shoving and rolling the lion head about sixty feet to a marble base next to erect columns of varying heights. Using the genius of Archimedes's levers, we succeeded in sitting the lion head up on a marble pedestal so it could observe the frozen solitude of Olympia.

(Twenty years later in summer Olympia, jammed with guests staying in new nearby hotels, it was good to find postcards in the shops, displaying transposed our lion still sitting on its newfound base. Next to the temple columns the guardian beast remained constant, peaceful, and sanctified in place through untold centuries of residence.)

That evening we found a peasant house not very far from the site. It was the first house we knocked at. Kyrie Stratos let us in, and as soon as he saw us, we had to stay. No arguments.

"Like to play cards?" our host asked the three of us.

"Sure," I said, speaking for the team.

"It's been so cold lately, even my goats are bellyaching."

"Roll a few cigarettes and let them light up. They'll get them warm."

"I'm a rare converted Greek who doesn't smoke."

"Yes, but you can be sure my goats do."

Stratos didn't ignite tobacco but he filled the fireplace with a formidable fire. Then he gave us animal hides as blankets and we slept a long deep night on the floor, in a primeval forest, next to the flames.

There was no paved road to Hosios Loukás. In this Byzantine monastery on the way to Delphi, the two-hour walk from the highway to the monastery was divided into two paths two hundred meters apart: one for going, on the left; and one for leaving, on the right. The way traversed meadow after meadow, and the walkers and those on donkeys or mules called greetings to each other as they came near and passed by. We were greeted with "*Na pate me ton theo*" (May you go with God), a hymn which hung in the air as it drifted from path to path. We picked mint and sage on the way. Nothing is as invigorating as walking in sunny winter in the Greek mountains.

Hosios Loukás has a great Pantokrator Christ in its main entrance, a very Greek God who would do well as sea captain of a vessel in the War of Independence. His spirit is worldly and severe, a mosaic man accustomed to giving orders and having them obeyed as he glares down on his mortal flock. And yet there is some Apollonian beauty in his face. The marble of antiquity always penetrates the Byzantine paint and mosaic chips.

Only the Pantokrator's human attendants and disciples, Saint Peter, Saint Mark, the Archangel Gabriel, and the Virgin Mary, are all mind and only modestly corporeal. As we moved around the eleventh-century church, the monks eagerly waited for conversation with us. There were very few guests in those days, and in the winter none.

"You will stay with us?"

"Of course."

"You will stay with *me*, in my cell," said Brother Petros, "and I will cook you a good meal and you will teach me how to tango. I have records and a player." And indeed he did.

We were sitting outside in the patio. The most energetic of our hosts was Mitsos, the cook. He engaged us in conversation, although the other monks tried, good-naturedly, to shoo him away.

"*Trelós einai, ma kalós*" (He's crazy but good), Petros said to me in a low voice, which Mitsos could probably hear. "We felt sorry for the poor devil, so we took him in to cook for us."

I agreed that Mitsos looked a bit mad, but then Petros was no boring saint.

"We have been through war after war," the friar cook began, "and all the generals are still alive. So we will go through another war after war, everywhere in the world. But I have a plan and you must take it to the United Nations and threaten to kill everyone there or at least have them eat wood if they don't put my plan into operation."

Albert nudged Helle to ask him for the secret plan.

"It can't fail."

"But what is it?" Helle queried.

"It can't fail."

"Okay, it can't fail. Now what is it?"

"You want to know?"

"Brother, Mitso!" I shouted. "Stop and talk!" But I wasn't at all impatient. We had to play the game or the story would be no good. Mitsos drew us into his conspiracy masterfully. Finally, he saw he had worked us up enough to be worthy of the revelation.

"Here's my plan. Catch every word of it, since you must report it accurately. You begin by getting all the bombs in the world, every single one of them, and every bullet in the world from every country and hamlet, even from the Eskimos, electricians, and orange pickers, and then ship in every sword and rocket and warplane and tank and battleship, old and new, from Russia and America and the seas of Bolivia, and put them all in one huge pile, with dynamite and TNT and gunpowder and gasoline, in a pile so big it reaches above the holy clouds."

"Yes?"

"You look at it," Mitsos said. He was so excited by his own story he could hardly control himself. He started to walk in swift circles, yanking at his belt, and pulling his hat down over his braided hair. Mitsos's eyes now were as ferocious as the Pantokrator's.

"What do you mean, you look at it?" I said.

"You look at it and think what it all means."

"But you must do more," I said.

"Of course you do more, you idiot, pardon me, my dear guest. Of course you do more. Do you think I would bring you this far just to look at a pile of gigantic destruction. You call on me and I take out a match, light a rag torch, hurl it as far as I can into the pile, run like a demon, and BOOM, an explosion big enough to blow a hole through heaven, and we have peace!"

After Mitsos, no one could compete. But Petros was very eager. He was kind and absolutely obsessed with learning the tango from these foreign experts. Helle was from Athens, which also made her a *xeni* today. So at nightfall we went to his rooms, his cell, and after dolmades, retsina, and powdery kourabiede, we briefly looked at his precious personal library, photographs of his brothers and sisters, and danced. Following his instructions, Albert and I danced with Helle first, and he observed, diagraming the steps so they would be permanently in his notebook. Then he would dance with our authentic Argentine female.

"Now it's my turn," Petros said. He was very short, and as he seized Helle's waist he bent his head very low, looking down intensely at their feet so as not to miss one magic movement of the tango.

Brother Petros was happy and excited. Well, we were tango masters for several hours. The mountain evening was cold, and his coal brazier didn't do much. But we were dancing, dancing Argentine. He had the volume as loud as the poor machine could shoot out the 1930s voice of Carlos Gardel.

After Hosios Loukás, Delphi, which we reached by way of a perilous road through blue mountains, was peaceful antiquity. At the site there was a guard in the museum and Patrick Lee Fermer, the English novelist hero, who during the occupation had captured the German general in command of Crete. Fermer, who had been living in Crete, took the general down to a secret rendezvous on the coast where a British submarine spirited the German off to England and safety. An English aristocrat, Fermer spoke and sang Cretan dialect songs like a native—as we soon found out. During the occupation he was able to capture the general by passing for a Cretan peasant. Fermer has lived his life in Greece, now in the Mani, the austerely beautiful southeast of the Peloponnesos, near Monemvasía.

Whenever I go to Delphi—and these days of crowds have deprived Delphi of its peace—I think of its Bronze Charioteer, now in the Athens Museum, who is preserved in his entirety because of having had the luck of being toppled and lightly buried by ancient earthquake lava. Since the Charioteer was a victory statue for a Syracusan prince and the sacred property of the god Apollo, he merited a worthy burial and thereby escaped the iconoclastic wrath of the Christian emperor Theodosius II, who in A.D. 426 ordered all pagan temples destroyed. The Charioteer was not a god but a professional athlete. Yet no athlete could win a race with his poise. His dark eyes of bone and semiprecious stone are not glancing at the competitors. And no statue of Aphrodite or Apollo has deeper grace. What is a Greek god after all? They are modeled entirely on human beings—idealized, yes, but their model could be the Charioteer. If he were not holding the reins but a sceptre, wore less clothing and had a less beautiful headdress, this handsomest man of antiquity could have been standing on Mount Parnassus, adding tales to Homer's books. As it is, he is a challenge to the gods, not because he is like them, but because they are like *him*. The gods, however, are stained by immortality and myth, reducing that total humanity that is his.

In Thessaloniki (Salonika) we rested from our hiking and wandering. We had climbed the steep steps at Meteora to reach the monasteries on their stalactite summits. Albert was outrageously irreverent to an El Greco Saint Jerome-like father superior with whom we shared our provisions one stormy night in high Meteora. As we entered the fabulous building, perched in isolation on nature's tower mountains, we were greeted by the tall white-haired saint. Albert smiled and said *"Bonjour, mon père,"* tapping the stern patriarch on the belly. After a flash of severe hesitation, the patriarch burst into laughter and we were set for an evening of history and reminiscence. I recall the monastery toilet, a tiny room that extended precariously over the mountain. The whole room trembled as you entered it. As I flipped open the cover to the wooden box toilet, the howling night rushed up at me. Sitting on its wooden box was like riding a gale of thunder and darkness.

Here now in Salonika, we were in the city with the old Spanish ghetto. Before the war most of the Jews in Greece lived in Salonika. As in Warsaw the Nazis built a wall around the Jewish quarter and killed all but a few. The Jews were all Spaniards. Borges has a sonnet on old Spanish Jews who remember Toledo and the Romans.

A Key in Salonika

Abarbanel, Farías or Pinedo,
Hurled out of Spain in an unholy sweep-
ing persecution, even now they keep
The doorkey of an old house in Toledo.
At last, from hope and terror they are free

And watch the key as afternoon disbands. Cast in its
bronze are other days, far lands,
A weary brilliance, a calm agony,
Now that its door is dust, the instrument
Is a cipher of diaspora and wind
Like the other temple key someone flung high
Into the blue (when Roman soldiers bent
And charged with dreadful flames and discipline)
And which a hand received into the sky.

In Salonika the Jews spoke Greek and their maternal tongue,
Ladino (Latin), which is a Spanish cut off from Spain after 1492,
the year of the expulsion. Before the war, only in Epirus were
there about one thousand Jews from antiquity who had not been
Hispanicized. These were the descendants from the earliest diaspora, which began after the dispersal of the Jews into the Near
East following the end of the Babylonian Captivity in the sixth
century B.C. It was they who invited Paul into their synagogues
of Antioch and Thessaloniki to preach to them and make them
into the new sect of Christian Jews who were to multiply and take
over Europe. Four survived of these original diaspora Semites. A
few years ago, when I saw the Auschwitz tattoo on the arm of
the guardian of the Yánnina synagogue in Epirus, I said to him,
"How did you survive?"

He looked at me severely and declared, "*Dioti O Theós ton
íthele*" (Because God wanted it so).

Our next destination was Mount Athos.

Helle went to Kastoriá, Albert and I to Mount Athos, the
holy mountain at the southern tip of the Halkidikí peninsula in
Macedonian northwestern Greece. We had to split since no fe-
males, not even female domestic animals, are permitted in Athos.

The way to Athos was an odyssey. A small *kaiki* took us there.
Each morning the gales threw our black sails against the sun and
we slid ahead, almost invisibly. With bad weather we made only
short distances, and from Salonika to the peninsula required four

days on the sea. At night we anchored in tiny harbors or camped on abandoned beaches. One night we slept in a lodge. At dawn the sky took on the colors of a bloody Barbary fig.

On our *kaiki* there was a village storyteller and all through the trip he told his tales to the passengers. On deck, under a black-and-red wool blanket, I shivered and listened to the war adventures, the village dramas, the comic and dirty stories. He was a one-man playhouse. Even today when I find a blanket at all resembling my Greek wool one (which I lost in France when it fell from the back of my motorcycle), I'm back on the boat, wet, cold, happy, with my ears filled with oral drama.

The boat left us a few hours from the mountain area of Athos. Although the civil war had been formally over for more than a year, here and in parts of Crete there was some guerrilla activity. We were on mules and horses in a convoy through the snow into the forested area above us. The lead horse and rear horse each carried a soldier with his automatic weapon held in readiness. I didn't think there was any danger of an ambush, yet I saw faces that appeared from nowhere and disappeared. We reached Daphni, a small port on the coast, and climbed very high into Athos.

Albert could stay only a few days, but I remained there a month. Before he left Athos, we stocked up on provisions at the general store. It cost nothing. The monks refused to accept money. There were no visitors in those days. And then we went to a nearby Romanian monastery. Athos or Hagion Oros (Holy Mountain) is the center of medieval Orthodoxy and has sketes and monasteries representing Bulgaria, Romania, Serbia, and Russia scattered on the Holy Mountain. Some are poor, others rich. The monks have their plots of land to grow vegetables, fruit, and olives, and they are largely self-sufficient. The monks chop wood in the forests that slope down the peninsula into the northern sea. The first night we spent in Zografou, a Bulgarian monastery castle hanging over the sea like a mountain in Tibet leaning over an abyss. Our hosts treated us to cold beans, bread, and vinegared wine, and we opened sardines of our own to share with them. Sleep came early and mountain deep. My bed was a thin straw mattress on a wood bench.

On the first day of wandering Athos, I met a Russian hermit prince as I walked around a tall hedge. We exchanged greetings. The prince looked like Tolstoy (on Mykonos I had been close to Tolstoy's grandson Alexander, the French linguist), and he spoke impeccable British English. We went to his little hermitage and shared some bread and liqueur. It was all strangely matter-of-fact. He was perfectly at ease in his hermitage and had no regret for lost estates or homeland or sophisticated company. I wondered what lay behind his imperiously good manners, his cheerful resignation and wisdom. As in a story by Borges, when the seeker finds the jaguar with the invisible script on it or the Indian god in the desert or the poet with the word in the Chinese court, the author, Borges, stops, since no one can sanely blurt out words of truth. The unknown, if it is worthwhile, must remain unknown and not be cheapened by explanation and summary. So I assumed there to be that huge spirit, with its keys and enigmas, into which the Russian hermit might retreat or experience at will. Perhaps it was my desire that the spirit be there. In any case, here was a man serenely himself. He was a prince in his own room.

In the evening there was a ceremony at Vatopedí. The monks were in magnificent vestments. The chapel was incense, ikons, gold brocade, silver chalices. It was very dark and yet brilliant, the singing faces lighted as in a Mannerist tableau. My eyes fixed on one beardless monk with gold hair who sang like a bullfrog or angel-woman to the Pantokrator. In his orange robe and the long uncut hair characteristic of all Greek clergy, he was clearly a shining intruder among the dark-bearded friars. His eyes were fixed on the ceiling as he and the others sang the Byzantine hymns for Christmas.

Entranced as I have rarely been by ceremony, by the sonorous illumination of the singing monks, I thought of a much more extreme form of utopian community: the Essenes holding out on their mountain retreat at Masada by the Dead Sea. These Greek Orthodox monks, mainly of the order of Saint Basil, had gone as far as they could: to a mountain at the bottom of a peninsula in order to shun the world. The Essenes chose a mountain in the desert. The renunciation of monks at Athos, however, was tempered by centuries of their acceptance and the accumulation of art and instruments of comfort, while the Essenes and their Dead Sea scrolls and their Teacher of Righteousness fell before the long Roman assault, though not before their literate guardians deposited scriptural scrolls for storage in tall clay jars at Khirbat Qumran near the Dead Sea. Many writers must wait a long time before they are read. The Gnostics and Essenes, at Nag Hammadi in Egypt and Qumran by the Dead Sea, waited two millennia for light to pick up their words and deposit them in books and museums.

Going Muleback in the Snow on the Holy Mountain of Athos after the Civil War and Thinking Back to Masada

Going muleback in the snow to the monasteries on the holy peak, I see
some rebel *kleftes* hiding from the drawn
weapons of the soldiers. When they spot me,
they fade. The forest groans. Once with the monks
they give me vinegared wine, bread, a bed
of straw on wood, and guide me to the crypt
where oil lamps by the icons show the blood
of converts sworn to parables and script
about some Essenes from the wilderness
who scorned the Roman weapons and were drunk
with faith and towering awe. Light gilds the hair
of one young beardless monk whose gaze and dress
mark ancient Zealots in their rebel prayer.

Albert left and I went to the great Russian skete.

The skete was a major monastery in Russian Orthodoxy, but since the monks were largely prerevolutionary *kalógeroi* (good old men) from before 1917, there were only sixty there, most of them old, except for some Greek monks who began to fill the uninhabited cells. There was a large stone wall surrounding the skete, and just as I was about to go inside I saw a strange Greek monk, pissing against the wall. It was cold in the snow and he was wearing torn, flapping galoshes, with no stockings, which I took to be neglect rather than poverty. When he eyed me, he turned around, shoved his penis back into its proper shelter, and said, "Come to my hermitage. We'll eat fish."

He saw me hesitate. To assure me, he said, "Don't be scared. It's close by and the fish came right out of the sea this morning."

I went with him. This hermitage was a mosaic gem. The walls were rich with Christian mythology. When we entered, Brother Spiros yanked open the door, looked to his right, and shouted, "*Siko epano!*" (Up on your feet!) to a sleeping monk, his room-mate. The man popped up like a mechanical toy, his feet remaining straight on the stone slab where he had been sleeping while his torso and head moved mechanically and quickly into a vertical posture. "*Vrey Yanni, aftós einai o fílosmou.*" (Pal Yanni, this is my friend.)

We shook hands.

Yannis seemed to match Spiros in wit. After the Russian cosmos, we were back on earth. Spiros went to work preparing the meal, and Yannis rushed outside into the snow, forgetting to put on his galoshes which he had kicked off into the corner, but he came back almost immediately, slush on his toes, with a pail of water. In the cold water were his fish.

Yannis stuck his hand into the water, pulled out a thrashing fish, and said, in English, "Good fishes. My friend catch them. What's your name? My name is Jim. I washed dishes in Detroit."

"Why did you come back to Greece?"

"The crash. Many come back 'cause of the crash."

"Why Athos?"

"I got a brother here. And I like good life. He got me in. He got me this house and this servant monk who's my friend and he listen to me. I like good life."

I couldn't shut Yannis up after the explosion in English. But I did show rare discipline and soon went back to the Russian skete to ensure my lodging. They gave me a very fine room in their own quarters, where I set up the books I had lugged with me but had not been able to read, and took a nap. I was glad to know I had a place to stay for a few weeks. In the past weeks I had seen so much, I needed to stop. I wanted to walk, but walk nowhere except for the walk, wanted to read, and perhaps to write. I guess those have been my real activities. Walking, reading, writing. Borges told me once that being blind gave him the opportunity to think. He could now sit on a bench or a chair and wait and think and not feel the need to fill his time with doing and planning other things. I had or haven't reached such a plane of undirected meditation. Sometimes in the shower I think I am just thinking, with no necessary purpose. And I stay there until the hot water threatens to turn me into a peaceful rag.

At three in the afternoon there was a knock at the door, and a tall courtly monk in red-black robes, with a Tatar face, set a glass tray with food, including black bread and wine, down on the table in front of my bed. I was honored. I didn't dare say I had just eaten lunch. In fact I couldn't say much, because he spoke no Greek, French, or English, and in Russian I could only utter *da* and *nyet*, "yes" and "no." Clearly we were destined to be famous friends. When he smiled all of Central Asia spilled from his mouth.

When the Tatar left, I ate the second meal with no trouble, relishing the black Russian bread, and began to read the collected poems of Emily Dickinson. By eight o'clock I was a little hungry but my friend had not returned. There was no one in the halls. I heard snoring from many rooms. Could they have all gone to bed so early? Indeed they had. There was some misunderstanding perhaps. I could find no dining room and no one awake. Then at eleven thirty, there came the tattoo waking the faithful to prayer in the cellar. The player had a wooden stick that he hammered against a wood block in musical rhythm, a beat that came near and faded as he moved near my room on our floor, and then, far but piercingly, on the floors below and above. The beat was once explained to me by George Gabor, the percussionist with Pro Musica Antiqua, who assured me that its complication was real, intricately good, and important in the history of sound. I found it haunting compensation for my hunger. I read all night.

In the morning I needed the sun again. I roamed about, found one of the Greek monks who lived in the Russian skete, and he explained that my supper would come at two-thirty or three in the afternoon because by four everyone went to sleep so they could wake and be ready to descend into the crypt by midnight where they would pray until eight in the morning. As at most of the twenty cenobitic monasteries at Athos, the monks ate separately, not communally where the gospel is read aloud from a central table to silent-eating monks.

For the next few days I tried and failed to convey to my Tatar friend that we should find some other time for supper. I tried to say with gestures that I could perhaps go elsewhere for supper, but there were no restaurants on Athos, or way of paying someone to leave me something. *Nyet.* Yet there was understanding. On the third day brother Mihaili came not at three but at one. He had a big smile and I expected the worst. He led me to a grand banquet hall. Then he gave me the key and explained that he would leave the food for my supper, which I could eat at any time I wished, at the central seat of the U-shaped banquet tables, under large pictures of the tsar and the tsarina. I was thrilled. Suppers at three in the afternoon, unless we were in Lapland, were problematic. They were treating me like a Russian prince, though I had had no conversation with any member of the monastery other than Mihaili the Tatar and that was restricted to *da, nyet,* and gestures.

I read Dickinson. I read John Hersey's *Wall,* and then, for liberation from walls and rooms, I read the Greek poets. For reading all night I had been prepared during those months in the orphanage in Mexico, behind the gate or in the street restaurants, and now, unwise of course and impatient, I was adding to the book of memory at least one winter peacefully amid monks and snow.

A Winter on Mount Athos Long Ago

Recalling Athos I am time's freak, one
who grabs the past and will not feel or show
his age. Outside Plato's cave the good sun
is drying off stunned hermits. Lilies grow.
Time hasn't wasted me that much. So far
I've copied memory's images, but lost
the words. Under the portrait of the tzar
and the tzarina, oblivious to the frost
on the great banquet table where the monk
left me black Russian bread and wine, I ate
my supper, happy and alone, and froze.
That happens in a monastery. Junk
I owned back then is gone. Cheerful, I wait,
remembering light beyond the cave, and crows.

One morning before my regular supper there was a knock at the door. A Greek-speaking monk was there. After a week of speaking to no one, being forced to spend much time thinking, not just filling time with worthy activities, here was someone speaking Greek, my language. (Curiously, despite years of study and fourteen months of China, my spoken Chinese was never marvelous. Yet in Turkestan and Tibet, where I cared for the people immensely, when someone could speak Chinese it was again almost as if there were the communication ease of English.)

The Greek monk told me that a Russian novelist wanted to speak to me. He had heard I spent my days reading and writing and was curious.

"I must warn you about Brother Sasha, however."

"What is it?"

"Kyrie Willi, he's a clubfoot."

"What do I care? I don't care if he's a clubfoot or a hunchback together. So much the better. Now, he's not the local hangman?"

"You are joking and I am serious."

"I'm sorry."

"But he has something else wrong with him."

"Let's have it."

"He will ask you to send him things when you get back to America."

"What does he want?"

"He'll ask you for a Baby Ruth. He misses them, he says. Before he became a monk he visited your country and ate Baby Ruths."

"I'm glad you warned me."

The next afternoon I was escorted to Brother Alexander's cell. I went inside. The door closed behind me. I was sitting before a very sour-faced Russian monk who spoke excellent English. He had traveled everywhere, had several lives, and these last years of exile were on Mount Athos.

"I'm Sasha."

"I'm Willis."

"I do not like my fellow monks. They are for the most part ignoramuses. But that's my fate." As he spoke, his face fell into an ugly mold that spoke the truth of his unhappiness.

"I wish you could be happy."

"But I am happy. I am a novelist." And he showed me a shelf of some eight or nine thick, bound, book-length manuscripts. "This is my life's work."

"Have you published the novels."

"I am a Russian exile and now a monk in Greece."

"So what will you do?"

"God is my publisher."

"You mean he's your reader?"

"My publisher too. He will not let these Russian works turn into worm food."

"What will happen to this monastery?"

"There will be more Russians, but we must wait another thirty years. After another thirty years there will be nobody in Russia to pull a trigger. Not even the police will do so. And the Kremlin and the Secret Police and the army will flatten into nothingness. Listen to me. It will take thirty years, but then it will be gone as if it had never been there. The statues will disappear. The city names will change. I will be dead. But new monks will come. Though I will not be sad, especially in my grave, even if new Russian monks do not come. It's lonely here."

"Do you know the Russian hermit prince?"

"He is my one reader, apart from that one," and he pointed to the ceiling. "And to tell you the truth, I prefer the prince, since the one up there makes me nervous. I've never known for sure what he thinks about artists."

At this point, I felt I owed Sasha something and didn't care about the warning. "Is there anything I can do for you?"

"You can't publish my Russian novels, I know."

"Anything else?" I was asking for it.

"They have told you, I'm sure, about my fetish. Some people like shoes, some adore women's breasts. Mine you already know."

"Baby Ruth."

"Yes."

At the end of January we were all back in Athens. By February bureaucracy had caught up with us again. Helle and I were married civilly in Paris. The American government recognized this marriage and gave Helle a visa in her passport to enter the United States. The Greek government also recognized that I was married to her; but since we did not have a religious marriage in the Greek Orthodox church, and Orthodoxy is the state religion, it did not recognize that she was married to me. Therefore, they would not issue her an exit visa for foreign travel. In those days only Greek students and businessmen were granted exit visas. This onerous restriction was an attempt to prevent hard currency from leaving the country. It succeeded in reducing foreign travel by its citizens.

In our case the most obvious way to circumvent the visa problem was to marry in the Greek Orthodox church. I had reservations, but if this was forced upon us, what else could we do? Vassili called the Athens bishop, who had once been his patient.

"My son-in-law, an American, wants to marry my daughter in the Church," I heard him saying on the phone.

"How can he be your son-in-law and marry her again? Isn't that bigamy?"

Vassili laughed. "No, my bishop, they were married in a civil ceremony in Paris. Now we want a church marriage."

"Very good. I will do it myself for my doctor friend."

"Thank you. Oh, by the way he's a Jew."

"No thank you. It's impossible." And he hung up.

"That was short and sweet," Vassili told me. "So much for the bishop." Vassili had no more love for the clergy than he did for the monarchy.

"What next?" I asked.

"Go to some other city, as you did for your visa to get into Greece. But not as far as Genoa."

Helle and I talked over every angle. I was glad to have to stay in Greece longer. A second year was already getting language, friends, and places deeper in place. But we had to have the option of leaving. Crete was the most tempting destination. I longed to go to Amorgós and the Dodekanese, not to mention Mani and Epirus. But Crete had many cities, and one straight road connecting everything horizontally. Besides, there was the labyrinth at Knossos and the Minoans. So we took an overnight boat and rocked our way like Allan Bates on his way to meet Zorba.

Hanniá is one of the most attractive smaller cities in Greece. Náfplion and Náfpaktos are others. Relentlessly Venetian, it is a port with snaky and Greco-Italian mansions. Red is the color of many buildings, another memory from Italy. Lingering in Hanniá—in its harbor cafés and walking the cobblestone amphitheater curve of the port itself—is a distinguished occupation. But we left the lovely city quickly, for we had a mission, and took a bus going west.

After a few hours we were both dozing. Even the beauty of Crete will not keep you awake all the time, although to shut your eyes when traveling through that land is folly. Suddenly we heard gunshots and pellets came flying into the open windows.

"What is it?"

"Walnuts," Helle said.

"Walnuts?"

"Everyone out of the bus," a man was ordering the driver. He was carrying a rifle.

"What's going on?" I asked the driver.

"A baptism."

"Do they make war when they baptize?"

"No, they eat and they dance."

So all of the passengers on the bus got out, joined the circular Cretan dances, made lots of noise, sat down and feasted, and an hour later we were on our way again. No one complained.

Crete was so lovely in that moment when spring comes. It comes not quite as early as in Andalusia, that is, in December when the Málaga almond trees blossom, coinciding with the coldest moment of the year as well as the winter solstice, but we were in Greek February and all the fruit trees were frolicking serenely. In late afternoon we asked the driver to let us out at some small village. We stopped at one that looked nice. We didn't know the name.

The road lay above the village, which extended down a long fertile valley and eventually to more meadows and the sea. We started along the sloping main village road. Before we knew it there were cries from women: *Xeni!* "Foreigners! Who's going to put them up?" We didn't get very far, since people insisted on drawing us into their open doorways and feeding us mezedes, coffee, and water. As in China, water is a fundamental drink, though in China it comes in thermoses and is hot. Greece is the country of cold fresh water.

Three sisters in black finally cornered us. We had to stay with them. We couldn't argue. We went inside. The bareness of the living room, the large white wall spaces with a few choice pieces of furniture make Greek houses beautiful. The nakedness of the outer white geometries is repeated in the interior. There is a natural taste. The interiors of Greek peasant houses and sophisticated new ones are designed to make plain internal sculptures of light and wall space match the exterior play of lines. In this house, however, there was a dramatic digression. The living room mirror was covered, a black cloth draped over it. A death in the family.

The sisters' brother had been through ten years of war, from 1940 through 1949, and was never wounded. At last he came home for good. One day while picking olives from their olive trees, he slipped off the ladder, fell to the ground, hitting his head against a rock, and was killed instantly. So there were three sisters and the mother, already a widow, all in black. But we had a good time. They prepared a special chicken dish for us. After supper we played *tavles* at which I was no good but for which Helle had an avid talent. We didn't tell them our mission of marriage and how we were already married. Yet if we had explained that the government was obliging us to do something ridiculous they would have been in sympathy and fully believing.

In the morning the sister who was silent was up earliest. She brought the ironing board into our room and began to iron the family's clothes. Her name was Elektra. She had an amazing beauty. Her eyes were large and peaceful. Her classical nose fashioned by Phidias, strong but more gentle than the Parthenon sculptor's faces. The black dress set off her marble features. And when she smiled there was a quiet eroticism of the sea.

Elektra said nothing. We didn't speak to her but we did exchange glances. One of her younger sisters told me casually when I stepped outside to eat an orange for breakfast, Elektra didn't speak. They didn't know if she was smart or dumb, but she had never really spoken. She was not deaf and had no apparent speech

defects. At the market she pointed at what she wanted and pronounced numbers, very clearly and naturally, and calculated with
no difficulty. Numbers were her only spoken words. The family
was so adjusted, as was Elektra herself, to the beautiful woman
who was unspeaking that they scarcely noticed, or didn't appear
to notice, anything out of the ordinary. We left this family reluctantly. Elektra kissed us both.

We took a bus to one of the towns and stopped at the first
church. Everywhere it was the same. You must spend six months
studying how to be a Christian and then come back, or nothing
doing, or we don't know what to tell you, or wait till the bishop
comes and we'll ask him. In Greece there is negligible anti-Semi-
tism compared to most of Europe. A boy may hit a donkey with
a stick and shout *evréo!*, Jew!, to make the animal move, but have
no idea what the word in that linguistic tradition means. Such a
boy on the island of Spetsais had rented me a donkey for the
afternoon and was helping me to get it started on its walk by
cursing it with *evréo,* which I'm certain he felt was a courteous
way of helping a stranger. But the Church had no experience,
or didn't in my uncomplicated case, in marrying a Jew to a Greek
Orthodox.

So after reaching Irakleion and the museum housing Sir Arthur
Evans's restorations of the Minoan wall paintings and, in
Knossos, the labyrinth itself, the work of Daedelus who had also
fabricated the fatal wax wings for his son Ikaros, we gave up and
went back to Athens. As before our journey, I remained, in Greek
eyes, legally married to Helle, and she remained a sinner living
unmarried to me. As Cavafy might have said, as he did say about
Odysseus and Ithaki, Crete gave us the trip and we were not
cheated, and now we knew what journeys to Crete were all about.
Moreover, we had seen the labyrinth, chatted with the bull and
with its horns in the maze's very center, and learned that laby-
rinths are constructed, even by masters like Daedalus, primarily
for purposes of escape.

Now we could return technically empty-handed, rich in experience, and free of worry from dark meanings of the labyrinth.

To have seen the labyrinth should have been more extraordinary than walking around the Parthenon. Not so. While the Parthenon is historical, the Minoan maze is a passage in mythology and, moreover, as proved by Evans, the discoverer of its reality, an actual place where religious rites of the monarchy were practiced. Both the Athenian and Cretan sites are roofless. Yet the unblocked sun enhances the glory and beauty of the Parthenon. As for the labyrinth, to sit at its center, by the bull horns, not in the fearful dark but under the autumn sun, reveals that light can destroy dread. To know and see what is around the corner of that exposed maze deprives the work of Daedalus of its mythical powers. Young men and women may have been slaughtered in that maze when it was an intrigue and enigma, so in the memory of a myth its dread remains. But now roofless, bright, and redolent with wild herb aromas, it is simply an ordering of anciently carved stones. The labyrinth has lost its power and challenge to any visiting Theseus, with or without his thread.

George Orwell was really down and out in *Down and Out in Paris and London*. He was attracted to that life and wrote about those more down and out than he. Even then his earlier experience told him that his plight was momentary. In his terms, I've never been really down and out. I went to Mexico and sold blood, and to Mykonos with the need to pick up room-and-board money some way on the island. But I never worried about it, about food, or where I'd sleep, even though I slept on many floors in many countries. And I'm glad I didn't fret, since when you're young you should be broke, and nothing in my past, even my father's bankruptcies, had given me any fears. I shared Orwell's attraction to real down-and-outs. I also felt sympathy and compassion for them, notions I scarcely saw in Orwell's work. Their absence doesn't mark meanness in the Englishman but a quality of Orwell the writer's hard-nosed style. He wouldn't be caught in any old-fashioned sloppy emotions.

Maroussi was down the road from Mount Pendeli, where our house, with its vineyard and sixty cypress trees, was. At the bottom of the road was a small restaurant, with a roast on a turning spit, and the men sitting on a few wooden tables in front. There, sitting on the ground was Babi, a blind beggar musician from a town in Anatolia up near Trapezon, by the Black Sea. I began to speak to him. He stopped after a while and sang. People greeted him. He was as well known as the mayor of Maroussi— which then was not much more than a village.

During the two years we had been living in Vassili's country place, I often walked the few miles down Pendeli into Maroussi. Pendeli (written Penteli in Greek—*t* after *n* is pronounced *d*) still had the mines from which marble was quarried in antiquity. The island of Paros (where was born Archilochos, Europe's earliest lyric poet, and surpassed perhaps only by Sappho) and the mountain of Pendeli gave their marble to ancient columns and statues. During the classical period, marble was broken by placing water in strategically drilled holes; in the cold of winter the water would expand and crack the marble into useful blocks. Now we heard an occasional dynamite blast as the old mines were ravaged for their remaining good stone, but in the last years Pendeli was a center for sanitariums. In those days there were no antibiotics to cure tuberculosis, and men living in these hospitals near the top would stroll down the mountain, usually in their pajamas, sometimes in slacks and undershirts. Opposite our house was the Sikiaridion Preventorium, a school and clinic for children in the first stages of the disease.

Babi normally sat outside the small souvlaki restaurant, his guitar lying on the ground beside him, absorbed in reading a braille volume with his fingers. He didn't spend much time in begging. He was about forty, short, and he stared intensely, if one with no eyeballs can be said to stare.

"What are you reading?"

Answering in good English, he said, "The book."

"What book?"

"The book, the only book."

"That makes it hard on any other writer when there is only one book."

"There is only one book and one author, but God permits others to write as well."

"Yes, sometimes he's been a good sport. When did you learn English?"

"I learned English after the Red Cross in Anatolia plucked out my diseased eyeballs. I had to learn English since they had no Greek bibles in braille. The set of bibles they gave me is in English."

"And whom do you speak English with?"

"With God."

"Anyone else?"

"With the people in His book."

"And with me?"

"Yes, sir, with you."

I was soon able to break down Babi's defenses and stern biblical speech as we got to know each other. Once we met, it was easy to find him in his regular spot on the sidewalk outside the souvlaki joint, where at night he slept in the kitchen, under the sink. He also washed dishes there on weekends when there was more business. The owner was a good man, he told me.

We talked often, but the visionary speech never left him for long. Sometimes every sentence was Isaiah. The Bible *was* his English.

"What happened to you during the occupation?"

"The Lamb in his Paradise looked my way and made me happy."

"Come out with it. What did you do?"

"I chopped wood for the Italians. They gave me a regular job every day. I could work, and I slept in a bed. The Italians gave me the only full-time job I ever had. People don't want to let blind men work."

"And now?"

"I am not unlucky. Several times a week a young woman leads me around town and we even take the bus to Athens, just so we can walk. I like to walk."

"Is she a religious nut like you?"

"I think she is not a religious nut like me."

Babi was so bright, no word, however slangy, went not understood, and he would normally throw it right back at me, testing it out.

"What would make you happy these days?"

"I am happy."

"And happier still?"

"To have a safe place to store these big volumes. Braille books are bigger than ordinary books, and I don't like storing them in the kitchen with all the dampness and water spilled everywhere. Even Noah wouldn't feel comfortable when we have a flood of customers and the kitchen turns into a zoo on a lake."

"I wish I could help you."

"You cannot."

"I cannot," I agreed.

"Kyrie Willi, I like talking to you, although I know you don't believe a word of my visions." Babi wrinkled his brow.

"On the contrary I believe they are your visions. Others claim to be visionary, but yours I know are real pictures in your head. They are really yours."

"They are not mine. I take my sight from this book," and his fingers struck the Bible.

Babi was the first blind Borges I knew. Like Borges, he also had endless humor and twisted words to his individual vision. Borges as a Socratic was looking and found no answers but let his characters come upon truths—at death, in a dream, in some way they would not reveal to the reader. But Babi was convinced that all the answers were there. The Devil threw up smoke screens but Christ danced across Lake Tiberius with all the parables and their meaning dropped into language and the soul. Borges the blind man would permit no such clarity. There were no keys. Only enigmas. Of course Babi's miseries helped him to find and hold onto his truths determinedly. Both men were saved by their intelligence, which even in the instance of Babi's faith (in contrast to Borges's skepticism) led him always into speech, which is never absolute.

Blind men sometimes beg and are sometimes wise. I don't think aristocratic Borges, who had a romance with his knife-dueling *compadritos*, would have been angry with me had I compared him to Babi the beggar. In fact, I know what he would have said. He would, in total false modesty, have tried to prove how Babi was the wise man, and he Borges, well, another impostor and failure. I saw the pattern constantly.

I spoke to Vassili about letting Babi live in a largely empty storage room in the basement of our Pendeli house. Vassili, a kind man, who went each year to attend the sick, free of charge, in his native Epirote village and to supply them with medicines, would hear nothing of my suggestion. There was no point in arguing.

"I will chop wood in the forests on the clouds," Babi said to me. He was often talking about his death, though I think he could throw off any ailment. "God will replace my empty sockets with soft glass and I will see for horizons around."

Some months later I did begin to worry about Babi. I saw him with the young woman walking around the square in Maroussi, and he looked awful, coughing, feverish.

"Kyrie Babi, how are you?"

"Happy, Willis. I am going to die. I have been waiting a long time to live well again. Up there the bed is real and very comfortable. The lambs lend their wool for covers, the mulberries lend their silk for sheets."

"Babi's just a little out of his mind," the young woman said. "He's got an awful cold and a fever, and is spitting like a Turk."

"I'm glad you have someone with you who won't listen to your apocalyptic complaints," I told the musician.

"She knows me pretty well," Babi smiled.

Then for some months Babi disappeared. The restaurant owner told me he was in the hospital. He did come out again, thinner, and was back on his spot on the pavement, playing the guitar. He sang the songs of Asia Minor. He sang very well. His rough high voice was a perfect lament. It was dark, shrill, ecstatic, very low. A *rebetis*.

"We are leaving, Kyrie Babi, in just a few weeks. Our papers are ready."

"You are leaving my books? Do you realize that I just touch the pages and I hear God talking? You must come back to hear the pages again."

"I'm a bad coin. A wooden nickel, we say. I always come back."

Babi stood up. "Goodbye." He stretched out his hand. Blind men are used to touching, so he held mine quite a while.

A Blind Beggar-Musician of Anatolia

Mr. Babi's indrawn eyelids cannot move.
The watery craters scar his baby face.
They are sewn-up holes of Bible light.
Glory burns inside; yet the Devil's close.
The Devil's friends who make him trip and fall
will grovel in the burning grease of Hell.

Dogs and cats are daughters, sons of Christ.
All love him. He loves every simple being.
He would fondle lambs, bears, tigers, lions,
any furry, felted hide or flying thing.
Mr. Babi's fingers (firebirds in black space)
dance on the necks of donkeys eating grass.

Mr. Babi boasts of death. He's sick with pus
and tonsillitis. Now he cannot swallow.
Wiping his wasted cheeks with a hot hand,
he walks alone and stumbles into furrows.
Friar Francis singing for his brother sun,
he founders in a ditch of carbon flowers.

Mr. Babi's eyelids feel a blow of light
as yellow angels plummet through his sleep.
The fig trees freeze in silver candelabra,
the black moon boils up into coughing seas,

heavens open to the bright wool of summer,
and death is home, health. Dying is cheap peace.

In 1960 when *From This Island* came out, Cleanth Brooks wrote a long, extremely praising blurb for the volume—"these poems are drenched in the light of the mind"—and ended his piece with "and 'A Blind Beggar-Musician of Anatolia' is a small master-piece." "Masterpiece" is kindly absurd, but thanks. As for small, in my vanity I wished "small" were an easier epithet to receive, though I am sure that Brooks's qualification was quantitative and goodwilled. I've felt sustained by his words on a book I care about.

A writer's life and writing are always entangled in clear meta-fiction. In a conversation with the other blind man, Borges, Borges said a character is a string of words, yet a real character. "Alas, poor Yorick, I knew him well, Horatio," and with those words Shakespeare, through Hamlet, brought Yorick into being forever. Brooks's reference to "A Blind Beggar-Musician of Ana-tolia" has helped keep Babi alive for me. And now Babi is more alive, since the needs of a memoir have forced me to remember his words: "God will replace my empty sockets with soft glass and I will see for horizons around." A memoir is all about memory and its trickery. Once I accused Borges of having a monstrous memory when he had repeated the first stanza of Hopkins's "The Wreck of the Deutchland" after having heard it only once, the week before, and he replied, "There are lines harder to forget than to remember."

By a series of good events in Athens, the Institut Français d'Athènes offered to publish a book of my poems. It was paid for by the office of the American Cultural Attaché. As I look back at this enthusiastic and eclectic book, *Poems of Exchange,* I am glad I had the chance to write all these things away. From the book a few poems were preserved that appeared in my first American volume, *From This White Island. Poems of Exchange* also contained six poems by Antonio Machado, including his elegy on the death of Lorca. I feel very good about all the Machado poems and am proud to have been identified with Don Antonio from such an early age. In 1951 when the book appeared I was twenty-three.

I followed the book through each stage of its typesetting, design, and printing. It was an elegant volume, hand set, with all the care of a limited edition of five hundred copies. It helped me. Not particularly publicly. But now, had I any doubts, I knew this was my work. Borges would have said his destiny—though Borges is usually not caught uttering such pompous words. But he did say many times that his destiny was to be a writer. As I write this memoir and have added other kinds of writing to my obsession—scholarship on noncanonical apocryphal scriptures and Spanish and other poets, fiction writing, libretti—at last I too feel like a writer as well as a poet. It's a good feeling and in no way threatens the lyric. It helps.

When the book was out, it was as if my destiny in Greece for that first étape was completed. We still couldn't leave because of the visa, but then, like the abortion in France, someone said a few words and there was a solution. Instead of going through the Church, through the ministries, all futilely, we discovered that a travel agency off Sýndagama Square could obtain an exit visa in twenty-four hours if you bought your ticket through them. They knew how and had the connections. Years later, though I got into China for special reasons during the Cultural Revolution, others met only silence when their applications were sent in. But then a few people discovered the secrets of entry. Some Hong Kong travel agents could obtain a visa within twenty-four hours or less into mainland China, if you purchased your train or plane ticket through them.

So we bought a ferry ticket from Corinth to Brindisi and left for Rome, our papers in good order.

Greece was not behind us, however. For me it had begun.

5

THE OLD
PHILOSOPHER
ON HIS BENCH
IN ROME

Spain was our destination. Spain was another image of Greece. The periphery of Europe, centuries of Islam, women in black and white walled villages in Andalusia, Spain's great Greek-island province. Farm and city workers in a country then hungry and under tyranny of men in three-cornered hats, men in black dresses of a severely intrusive church, gray armed men waiting to inspect the arrival of each bus from village to village, and all joined, tight like shit and ass (to use the Catalan expression), under the fearful mystique of one man, Generalissimo Francisco Franco. Spain's lands and its popular culture and architecture were still intact by the preserving nature of poverty and injustice.

Spain was also poets in a language I knew, who would be, like the Greek poets, at my center. That center later included Chinese, and of course Russians, Italians, Germans. Though my

German was bad, the first poet I read when I began writing was Rainer Maria Rilke. Greece, Spain/Latin America, and China would be the focus of light for poets and for place. I would spend my life reading and rereading Sappho, Archilochos, and Cavafy; John of the Cross, Quevedo, Machado, Vallejo, and Borges; Wang Wei, Li Bai, and Li Qingzhao.

The late Uruguayan critic Emir Rodríguez Monegal said in a talk at Indiana University that if you want to know who from Latin America was important to American poets, ask an American poet. Even if the poet reader knows only two extraordinary lines of the poem in Spanish, the revelation is there. He was right. Two lines of Rimbaud or Machado can tilt a world. My bilingual edition of Rilke and a few lines gave me the poet from Prague. In Spain, although most of its poets were in exile or dead, the nation could not escape their words, and even the new poets lived under their cloud.

Spain was our destination, but we would go there by way of Italy and Switzerland. Italy was a voyage, Switzerland a pause. We would buy wheels in Italy and ride through Tuscany. In Switzerland I would work for a publisher, an excellent Swiss publisher in Geneva, until another Englishman fired me. That habit of mine—the French expression *mis à la porte* (thrown out the door) is excellent—made it possible for us to leave for Spain.

When we crossed the Adriatic to Italy, we were still in a remembered Europe, but we had left home, which was Greece. After home came another venture and a freedom, which in those days we took for granted. Thereafter, every place we went to was a quest, the voyage its own justification, the end uncertain—especially in the eyes of my family, which accepted our vagabond news but regretted the wasted years of my wandering. Yet life was not a timetable. I saw the world, its people and literatures, out there. Why not go to them? Why not accept them? I was too young to think of any responsible career other than writing. To glance at the evasive spirit inside—for which I had no decent lexicon—I had to go around outside, stumble, look, and be a scribe to what I saw.

Italy of 1951 is a clear moment in my mind. Alas, I have not returned to it, except for an hour, a year later, to a border village to renew paperwork on a motorbike. A country of so many human and artistic magnificences, I wonder why we were to spend only two months there. But Spain called. I began speaking Italian immediately. After Latin, Spanish, and French, and a semester at Bowdoin of Italian grammar, the language was impossible not to pick up and I was surprised by my fluency for newspapers, films, and ordinary conversation. These were harsh postwar times in Italy, conveyed in the black-and-white images of early De Sica movies—*Shoeshine, Bicycle Thief*—in unstable coalition governments, angry Communist unions, a poor south full of character and a richer north, which, as in Spain, viewed the south as primitive low-class. The flavor of that south-north collision comes out in Carlo Levi's novel, *Christ Stopped at Eboli,* a portrait of exile in Basilicata and a beautiful white village at the end of the world reached by no one. Nevertheless, in literature the masters, like Verga, Vittorini, Quasimodo, were so often from the south. Apart from his own poems and the Nobel Prize that recognized them, Quasimodo did lucid versions of ancient Greek poetry into Italian—the finest from the Greek lyric into any language with which I am familiar.

I knew Quasimodo in the last years of his life, and those ordinary evenings with him—after we discovered we had a common language in French—were amusing, profound, precious, and always dominated by his ordinary humanity.

"I went to Russia, what they call the Soviet Union, on a tour," he told me one evening at Wesleyan. We were alone in Downey House. "I met poets, drank vodka, and had a heart attack. Well, we all have to die. After all, I've read the Greeks. I know there is a black earth. But I thought this time I would recover from the heart attack. I felt good, but the Russians wanted me to feel better and improve my health. So they set up a schedule of massages, and every morning two two-hundred-pound giant nurses pounded me for my health until I was sure I would die of assault and battery. I felt if they would stop, I would live.

And I wasn't sure it was worth living if they kept beating me up."

"So what did you do?"

"To tell you the truth, I did nothing. All my Sicilian astuteness failed me. Whatever complaint I had, caused by their pounding, encouraged them to beat me more. I was not a political prisoner. I was their literary star, and they were determined to exalt me with their cupped hands and their fists. Worst was that the two giants attacked me at the same time. With their enthusiasm and charm these women could easily have turned me off women for life, made me a monk, a homosexual, or reduced me to pure onanism. I'm proud to say that while I respect all other ways of being, I came back to Italy recovered as my conventional self, a poet, a translator, a lover of women, and determined not to get sick again, lest next time I'm pummeled to death."

"Salvatore, you lived up to your name."

"It has saved me more than once."

Poor Salvatore. Before he won the Nobel Prize, he was esteemed, along with Montale, Ungaretti, Sereni, Saba, as the poet of Italy. Then with the prize he was furiously attacked because some critics thought Montale, not Quasimodo, should have been so rewarded. Yes, Montale did merit the prize and a few years later received it. But Quasimodo was not guilty of the Swedish Royal Academy's first choice. Personally, I adore Montale's powerful and usually obscure poetry and confess I am moved by his "Dora Marcus" as I am by Quasimodo's humane lucidity. Quasimodo has the breathing line of George Seferis and is also historical, although the focus of his pathos is the present. Only Constantine Cavafy reaches all periods in his "histories": his illicit loves in the dingy room over the tavern and his recreation of Antony looking out from the balcony, courageous, aesthetic, and doomed, the night before his defeat. Antony hears the mystical troupe singing in the street, and listens—as his last act of recognition. Quasimodo made the streets of new Rome sing.

The Italian poet did die soon after, not from the fists of giant nurses but from another heart attack.

As a way of knowing them, I like to compare poets to things in the world. Ultimately I must compare Quasimodo to the clouds of Italy, the clouds when he was a young and old man. Through them he knew the cities and its fields, heard the Sunday bells, the donkeys, the workers, the intellectual and artist in the village, saw the sober beauty of a brief life. Through the clouds of Italy those scenes were luminous. The author's humanity and clarity made them so. One evening he told me, "My grandmother was a Greek from Thessaloniki, you know. I had a right to translate Sappho and Alceo."

"I knew there was some genuine reason for your good poetry," I let him understand.

When Helle (with her maturely formed eternities) and I, as one team, had set out for Europe—I say "Europe" because in demotic Greek, to leave Greece for the continent is to go to Europe—we had taken the overnight ferry to Italy, passing though Greece's grape waters out into the Adriatic. The ferry took us to Brindisi where we thwarted some purse-and-luggage snatchers in a wild pulling match. After a horse-carriage ride to the railroad station we left by train for Rome.

Roma.

Red-walled and marble Rome. Between pasta shops and expensive bordellos, between old convents and fountains, George Santayana was sitting in a piazza on a bench (away from his bed in a woman's convent where he spent his retirement), reading novels, throwing each page away, after reading it, into a public trash basket, with the knowledge that he would not in this city and world reread his pleasures again under the sun and the indifferently fluttering pigeons overhead. He was "a citizen of heaven though still of Rome" as Wallace Stevens saw the old philosopher. Rome has had a thousand Santayanas—the Spaniard who circled from Madrid through Harvard back to Rome. But of Romes there is only one.

To be young and walking the streets of Rome. I had lived in Paris, married there, wore my beret, argued in the little stores, read my Colette novels. In Greece I entered Asia, antiquity, dry wild-herb fields, and the lines of George Seferis. If there is no one to see, no immediate obligation to place or official papers, to be walking the streets of Rome is a bit of glory to keep forever. Moreover, the Romans worked for millennia on those cobbled roads, ghetto alleys, iron door gates, and peopled piazzas. They did so for the great loafer, Walt Whitman. How could I not accept Walt's vocation?

The painter William Congdon, from a patrician family in Rhode Island as he let me know, was pissing in the sink. The plumbing wasn't great in the hotel near the Piazza del Panteon, and he had developed an accurate aim and it was better and cleaner than trudging down the hall to the dark little room with the public smell. Bill was of the Peggy Guggenheim crowd, shuffling around the triangle of Paris, Venice, and Rome, and had just had a full spread in *Life*, showing his Rome paintings. We were such good friends during those weeks. The natural mix of painters and poets. Bill taught us pasta as Professor Holmes had taught me calculus in the snowy mornings of Brunswick, Maine. He had his own pots with pasta boiling in them and the right pottery bowls to eat the stuff, and there were the small restaurants nearby that in those days we could all afford and where the waiters waited for him and his friends.

"I have a rich mother and she'd like to tame me in her mansion. Just write your poems."

"In cars, trains, and if necessary hidden in a tree trunk. I am a safe bet."

"Thank God you're a fool, Willis."

"I was pretty good at that before I woke up a poet."

"Will you stay on here in Rome?" I asked him.

"I'm a Roman."

"So was Rumi, but he died in Turkey."

"All roads lead to Turkey."

"What do you mean?" Bill had a way of dogfaced absurdity. I didn't mind asking.

"When you begin to live a few miles from the Pope and the

Villa Borghese and the roar of midget Fiats outside the window, you need some fresh air from all this civilization. So I disappear once in a while. And why not Turkey which was ancient Rome."

"You mean it had an imperial moment between Homer and the Byzantines," I said.

"Call it what you want, a nice month in Cappadocia, the old Roman province, which no one but a few nuts like me ever visits, is a good way to help my monkish side. I go to these places to hermitate."

"Hermitate?" I said, laughing.

"Yes, to think myself into a fury. Somehow it comes out later on canvas."

"I've been a hermit all my life. It's my split personality," I said. "But it doesn't show. Hermit's another word for loneliness. When I discovered I existed—and most people never do—I felt very lonely, even though I have so many friends and care for them. There are distances in me. And there are the two biggest, before and after. I mean before my parents bore me out of their secret bed and after all this running around is over. Death I see only as a drama but not a reality. I'm too young for that I guess."

"Have some more pasta," Bill said, as he dumped it on my plate. "When are you tramps leaving for Florence?"

"When we get sick of you."

"Leave Helle here. I'll show her my studio."

Congdon's room was not only his crowded studio but his library and dining room.

"No. You come to Spain," Helle contended. "I'll cook Greek for you."

"I'd like that, and be sure to paint my profile too."

"What a clown!" I shouted.

"I can't help it. It's my good breeding."

"*Basta,*" I said, pleased with the lunacy.

I looked at my ruddy friend, athletic, a little overweight, regular English features, some fifteen years my senior. "Bill, you seem so strangely happy and unhappy."

"Of course I am. Fuck it. I'm nearly forty, scratching out a living from selling canvases. I'm a canvas salesman, living in a jammed mousetrap with a great view. I have no children, no lover—at least not right now—yet I'm doing exactly what I want to, and the price I pay makes me miserable. But I'm super happy," and he moved to his paintings leaning against the wall. "Just miserably super fucking happy."

"I figured you were a sleezy artist monk, a common friar with a softness for a decent meal and friends. I wish I had your lonely faith," I said, sententiously.

"Willis, you make me puke."

"Have some more wine," Helle said, helpfully.

We got pretty close and sentimental, and a few days later we were on the train for Florence. Bill wrote to us for years. He recounted exhibitions and word of his paintings acquired by the Whitney, Metropolitan, MOMA, and the Vatican Modern Artists Museum. And we wrote back. He was last living on the Via Marconi in Milan. Then the silences. When I searched for him in a reference book, I discovered he had published a book of his own, *In My Disk of Gold: An Artist, His Art in a Christian Community*. So Cappadocia and the hermitage dream was not mere metaphor. I don't know whether he is alive or not. To disappear is to disappear, and to lose knowledge of a person is also to lose a right to their existence, since there is a finality in ignorance. Yet William Congdon is alive now because I remember. I am sad and happy to be with him.

Because I don't know his history, Bill is fixed in time. He is pissing in the sink and has pots of pasta boiling for his guests. Secretly he and his painting and his life, or the death he and we all carry like a set of teeth inside us may have changed. But those changes have no emotional reality. Have no time of experience. They are the mind's inventions.

"Hello, Bill."

"Dove il Duomo?" (Where is the Duomo?) The Germans had knocked down all bridges in Florence but the Ponte Vecchio.

And Michelangelo's "David," despite his being a famous Jew and a naked one at that, and sculpted by a notorious bisexual, survived the Nazi sledgehammer. His spirit gently firm, internal before all gazes, somehow survived the uniformed supermen. His reproduction stood in the quiet cobbled Piazza della Signoria.

Dante survived also. Though he spent much of his life in exile from Firenze. It is good to write from memory (and distances help), and Dante, as he wrote in the *Vita Nuova*, called himself merely a scribe of memory. Florence is the Arno with those buildings looking at it. And then everywhere the city is the ultimate catalog of paintings, frescoes, churches, public buildings. To list the names is a scary schoolchild exercise. Vasari, Masolino, Masaccio, Ghirlandaio. A facade by Alberti. Botticelli, Donatello, Piero della Francesca. The Uffizi, the Pitti Palace, the Pallazo Vecchio. Raphael, Andrea del Sarto, and Titian. Cellini's "Perseus." At least I know the real street where Perseus walked, in Serifos in the Cyclades, on the way to slaying the Medusa. He had to pass the barber shop-café and the carpenter's wire-fenced-off plot of land guarded by an angry island dog.

As I looked at all the measureless beauty of Florence and the cities of the hills, it was also good to remember Greece, where there are also many statues in museums, but where the myths are visibly alive in their recorded settings, where Ikaros's bones are still drifting on the sea bottom by Ikaría and Perseus may sit down to have an ouzo with Cyclops before he climbs the mound at the far end of the street where the shiny Medusa hangs out. I have always liked the ancient object in the myth more so than renaissance versions of it. That real object—though sometimes there is a discovered Troy, Knossos, or Bronze-age Thera— is the imagined one in the appropriate Greek landscape. Then antiquity glows. So in Epirus at the prehistoric temple at Hades I liked to climb down two flights to its ancient floor (fifty meters from the river Acheron still watering the fields) and let my mind fill in the invisibly descending Odysseus and the miseries of Achilles, king of a darkness he abhorred. So I also liked the butcher who was Apollo perfected in the flesh and lighted by his 200-

watt bulb hanging outside his shop as much as the sun-god's representation by a late sculptor or painter. Every ancient column in Greece, even a lone flat rusting one on a farmer's barley field, was more thrilling than the finest neoclassical building or an intact temple on a Giotto board or David canvas.

When an Alexandrian painter asked the Neoplatonic philosopher Plotinus to let him paint his portrait, he answered, "Why paint an illusion of an illusion?" I find those truths painful. Yet if we live by illusions, we live by them. To fill in the illusions of myths is a happy and physical activity. Greece, and sometimes Italy, animates the mind into such powers of creation. Before leaving Greece I saw Artemis come over Mount Taygetos with her lions, carrying a huge moon-white disk of feta cheese. Alkman had a similar vision.

> Often at night along the mountain tops,
> when gods are reveling by torch light,
> you came carrying a great jar
> (like one shepherds use) but of heavy gold.
> You filled the jar with milk
> drawn from a lioness, and made a great cheese
> unbroken and gleaming white.
>   Alkman (mid-7th c. B.C.)

In Florence we picked up the wheels. Two odd-sized rubber ones. We bought a Lambretta and had a roving machine. From then on, because of our Firenze license plate, wherever we journeyed all Italians were compatriots and waved to us on highways—as we crawled up the steep *route Napoléon* into Switzerland, in France, Spain, England, and even in North Africa—and if they were from Florence they not only waved but shouted. One day between the hill cities of Siena and Arezzo, an older gentleman walked out of a cafe-bar, and as he came near Helle and me in our helmets, our bike loaded with worldly possessions and ready to eat up the road to the north, he paused, looked, and paid us the compliment of our lives: *I grandi sportivi.* The great sportspeople. And we were free.

We went to the hill cities.

We had so little time for lovely Tuscany.

We loved the umbers and siennas of city walls, drank the beauty of the churches till we could drink no more. Assisi we saw as a city El Greco had captured when he painted Toledo, but we also looked, paid the alms fee, and groaned down in the awful crypt of Saint Francis, who in life had been brother to sun and beasts. We were thrown out of a cathedral—"*Senza complimenti,*" the guard said to Helle—for improper dress. Our eyes were prostrate (if that notion is not too grotesque) by the time we rolled into Venice.

In Greece we had two years to be still. In Italy we speeded through beauty on our way north. We saw too much too quickly then. While trip fatigue faded quickly, the castles and hills remain intact in a dream that has not disappeared at all. I don't know but guess the Italians have been able to preserve most of the dream as it was and keep our century's concrete trucks out. We halted our race when we crossed into Switzerland, where I had a potential job waiting for me.

Whether it is Greece, Italy, China, all realities are necessary— the bullying island cop Zoakos with his handcuffs and the saintly blind beggar musician Babi with his caustically fantastic tongue— if a place is to be known. During the first month in Switzerland, although we did have a room of our own and remained constant in one city, I couldn't get the black-and-white film of Roma out of my head, nor colors of the Tuscan cities, the irregular old walls of the villages, the woman I bought bread from in the morning, Verona so beautiful as to render English-speaking Romeo and Juliet mere actors, and the people of Italy who, like Greeks and Spaniards, were all things, a people south of the mist, in the oxygen of southern Europe, where I was never a foreigner.

6

MICHAEL

THE CROW

GOSSIPING

IN ZURICH RAIN

In Geneva an old Dutch lady rented us a room not far from the city center. Both Helle and I ended up working for Les Editions Skira, which then was beginning to publish its pioneer art books. So we had a bed, work, and also good friends. George Ballou came down from Zurich. Albert Schüpbach was living again in Geneva, and other pals from Paris had moved to this city of Borges's adolescence and formation as a writer. For quite unrelated reasons, Europe was becoming for us as Turkestan and Tibet would be for me in the mid-eighties, a place where friends inevitably showed. In western China, however, it was not the intimacy of Europe but the Asian vastness that brought friends together. The exotic cities were so remote and difficult to reach that only the same legion of resolute venturers turned up.

George Ballou and his Swiss wife, Barbara, were living in

Zurich in the house of Franz Morgenthaler, Mr. Morningdollar, an interesting, old-fashioned, and well-known Swiss painter. Soon after we got to Geneva, George came to see us. We put him up in the home of the Dutch lady who had rented us a room in her house. George thoroughly impressed the lady by speaking to her in German, French, and English.

"You are an expert in skunks?" she said.

"I know skunks very well."

"What makes them stink?"

What an opening for George! As the seriously attentive lady followed his explanation, George elaborated how a skunk squirts its stink, and exactly where in the genital area is the tiny hidden hole and hydrant that initiates the animal's vast aroma, and how, on command, it could lay a gas on the countryside a mile around. He wouldn't smile, yet while his lecture went on and on, he was clearly having the time of his life.

Although he downplayed his abilities with animals, in the years when he traveled he never crossed an international border without carrying at least a few snakes and rodents in his coat pockets and baggage, and he had such understanding with the small beasts that they never betrayed him before a customs inspector. One day he scared my Greek mother-in-law half to death in Athens when she saw a long serpent crawling up her living room curtain. George simply slid over and grabbed the snake in a friendly way and dropped it back in his deep coat pocket.

Later we would go to Zurich, where one afternoon in pouring rain we set out, at his insistence, to look for snails. The rain was to bring them out, yet they were content with anonymity. We were drenched and exhausted but George kept our minds off our failed hunt by resorting to animals. He started a significant conversation with a backyard crow named Michael Black, whom he had taught to chat like Woody Allen. Their nonsense was fluent. The two of them were Brooklyn buddies.

After George's lecture on skunks, we started out for downtown and had our only real fight. We yanked off our berets—I don't know why—but even as we were screaming at each other from opposite sides of the street in quiet pastel suburbs of dignified Geneva, we knew it was ridiculous. What proud imbeciles. We were passing through some rite. George was my oldest friend. I saw him through his three wives, his amputated leg, the failure of his writing, and his final disappearance when he lost his mind and vanished in New York City. That walk and the people glaring I remember because it was not for us to argue. We never did thereafter. We were friends from our eighteenth year till three years ago when he became a *desaparecido*; and, though he would exasperate me at times, as I must have him, he was my lifelong good brother. I always stayed with him on trips to the city.

Before he disappeared, I did speak to him from Indiana for hours, trying to persuade him to come out to Indiana and live with me until he felt better. It was useless. He was sane enough to speak about being washed up. In his apartment in New York's Chelsea district, all the jungle animals were gone, replaced by roaches and rats. Unable to trace him, I am haunted by his absence.

George Ballou Among His Animals

Oldest friend, wild in your Chelsea mud hole
where I could always crash next to the beasts
and birds inhabiting your flat, your soul
got bald, it hurt your pride, but all the priests
and brats of Salvador couldn't eject
you from your hammock in the jungle where
you slept and trapped your friendly snakes. You picked
a wife and two and three. They let you share
each child, you maddened them, they dumped you. Now,
leg amputated, books unpublished, friends
burnt out and you burnt out, you lie, a sow
among the roaches crawling on the ends
of rotting pizza. George, the ravens faint
in France. Remember rain? Animal saint.

It had been George who introduced me at Skira, where they gave me work as a translator of French art texts.

I liked Albert Skira. Sometimes he was drunk. He was always courtly and warm, and sensitive to every aspect of art. Skira created the museum without walls, more than anyone in our century, through the quality and extreme breadth of his art books, from El Greco to central Asian wall paintings. His name Skira was altered from Italian Chiera (which in its French pronunciation is an obscenity and probably incited the attractive invention of "Skira"). One day after work when the office was deserted, I was chatting with M. Skira in an adjacent room. He was restless that afternoon, standing, not sitting, but going nowhere, just pacing and worrying. We settled down to a good talk. Where had we been? Why had we chosen Greece? Who were its painters? Why Spain? He was all questions. I liked his severity and imagination, and a suppressed quality of desperation that lay not far under the attractive grimace of severity under his blondish hair. I liked the man enormously. I had with me a poetry book that had in it a drawing I'd done and I showed it to him. An ink drawing of a boat on a night sea. I was surprised when he got his serious look and said, "I like this." It is strange what praise does to a young or old head.

My job was the translation of diverse scholarly art texts. Every experience in writing is good. Translating art criticism is mainly information transfer, but there is also an aesthetic component as there should be in rendering all scholarship. It's often said that translation, because of choices, is analytical interpretation. More interesting is that scholarship, any hermeneutic, is translation. To read, to think, to speak, is a transformation. As the logo METAFORA on the Greek moving vans tells us, translation is everywhere. I have liked to translate because I like poetry and want people in my language to read the work of others as poems in English. And translation has taught me half of what I know about reading and writing poems.

Stuart Gilbert was the head of our team of translators. James Emmons, friend from Paris, who was to stay on at Skira to translate many important books under his name, warned me about this grumpy man. Gilbert had been a friend of Joyce and had written a book, *James Joyce's "Ulysses": A Study*, which connects *Ulysses*, chapter by chapter, to Greek myth. As a judge in Burma before he settled in Paris, he had had curious pleasures. One rare day of reminiscences, he talked to our group about some colonial court trials in Rangoon. "I liked to sentence those rascals to the gallows and believe me they hanged." He heartily disliked Jews and complained about how his wife had had to put up with seeing fat Jewesses at public baths in Paris. He was a bachelor when I knew him. He had translated the novels of Camus. They are plodding versions. They have since been retranslated into versions that re-create the formal ease and simplicity of the transparent French text. In all, Gilbert had translated major works by Camus as well as *Man's Fate* by Malraux, *Huis Clos* by Sartre, and *Night Flight* by Saint-Exupéry. His pompous, academic style was a tonal disaster for French fiction in English, but now he was doing his best work: his supervision and versions of formal art history and criticism. When later on the Skira books came out under James Emmons's name, they had an element of grace.

Albert had a friend in northern Switzerland who invited us to his lodge for the weekend. Helle went by car with the family, and Albert sat terrified on the back seat of my Lambretta as we floated up and down through the mountains to the wooden chateau four hours north of Geneva.

"*Willis, tu va me tuer.*" (Willis, you're going to kill me.)

The chateau lodge on a steep slope overlooking a long valley had a balcony, and after the perilous ride we sat on it, with some drinks, looking out. Just looking out was a restful warmth as your mind circled the orderly chaos of Swiss mountains and then the emotion circled back to reenter you and be a meal of well-being. It was a pleasure to do nothing. It was our duty to be happy and we were. That night we slept in the mountain air. It was the tastiest lofty air I knew outside of the night air in those mountains of Epirus where our village faced obscure Albania.

It was hard to get a fix on Zurich. T. S. Eliot, fleeing from his first wife, went to the Jung Institute to have a nervous breakdown and write most of the *Waste Land* in the clinic just outside the city. Tristan Tzara incited another revolution in literature by inventing Dada in Zurich. The world revolutionary Leon Trotsky was several times based there. His friend Mr. Bach, the Mexican economist on the Trotsky-assassin hit list, was a native of the city. And George, a professional friend of animals, instructed birds to walk on branches while gossiping in English and cursing in German.

On an earlier trip north we had visited George in his house at the outskirts of Zurich. Before we got to that house of propriety and wildness—any place with George in it was immediately otherworldly—we sat in a streetcar to its very last stop. The car was heavy steel and rolled on silence. Silence was also solid among the passengers. There was silent concentration on the Zurich newspapers and on nothing. I suppose the people of Zurich in those days were secret Buddhists meditating. By contrast we had taken a train ride a week earlier in southern Switzerland, a route that went back and forth across the Swiss-Italian border. At one moment, when the train dipped into Italy the cars emptied so passengers could make use of the public toilets. The men's toilet consisted of four very long walls, with no roof, and a slate urinal that circled inside the open grassy enclosure. After careful Switzerland this shabby structure had an extravagantly wasteful grandeur to it. Who ever heard of a semi-outdoor urinal built to accommodate two hundred souls? As I walked to my duty, I saw a tall man in a long brown trench coat whose tails the brisk wind was flapping about. The man was pissing away and singing Italian opera at the top of his lungs. As he sang, he looked up to the right side and the left side of the heavens and their clouds, which were visible from his place on the grass. It was not the Buddhist silence of the Zurich streetcar temple.

During the work week at Les Editions Skira, four of us sat around a large desk and typed out our translations. After two months of this, one late afternoon Jim told me gently that Mr. Gilbert had fired me. Nothing personal. He didn't care for my translations. In retrospect I cannot protest his judgment. I was attempting a catholic translation, but surely he was right. After a good summer in Geneva, Mr. Gilbert freed us to go to Spain.

Spain was virtually a closed country. Its main visitors were the trucks of smugglers from Gibraltar who carried their illegal, untaxed black tobacco perfectly safely throughout Andalusia, waved on everywhere by the obliging patrolling *guardias* who received payoff pesetas for their good humor. The poorest fisherman had to have his black tobacco. Now we could join those few outsiders who went into Hispania.

7

SUNDAY

MORNING

IN FASCIST

SPAIN

In 711 a Muslim Berber army under Tariq Ibn Ziyad crossed the Strait of Gibraltar. The Romans and their heirs the Visigoths under the last king, Rodrigo, were defeated, and until 1492 most of Spain was governed by the emir in Córdoba, who ruled in the name of the Baghdad caliph. And before the Romans were Greeks and Carthaginians.

In the village where we were to settle for a year, the poorest of the poor and the remnants of the *rojos* (the Reds), fished out of the mountains, were carried muleback through the main square—a warning to the impious—and buried on the hill where the beggars lived, in the old Carthaginian caves. When the village Almuñécar (a good Arab name) began its descent into a Miami coast ruin, there was built an attractive hotel furnished with seventeenth- century Spanish furniture—those austere pieces with

the plainness and translucence of late Ming tables and chairs—
and the hotel was defiantly named Hotel Sexy, Sexy being a
Carthaginian place-name for the area. It eventually gave way to
condominiums for English and Austrian retirees.

(In the '80s when I returned to the region for a few days, by
highway, the old Costa del Sol was definitively blasted off the
map. Tasteless modernity forever banned Odysseus on his drifting ship, Aeneas on a quick trip from Carthage, Paul looking for
converts, as well as tobacco smugglers from those once scarcely
visited precincts where no one and everyone had passed by. I
couldn't find the original beautiful village. The pharmacy, the
stores, the *parador* (inn), the casino, the family houses, all medieval, had vanished. But the Spain of this memory is 1951, four
decades ago, and in my memory it still smells of millennia of its
Carthaginians, Greeks, Jews, Romans, Visigoths, Berbers, and
Spaniards.)

We prepared for our year in Spain by sending the accumulation
of our years in Europe to a small village in France where the
stationmaster kept our belongings for several years in his storage
room. In that way we were able to get on our Lambretta, with
what was most precious to us stuffed in a cardboard carton on
the carrying rack, and cross *douce* France free of cargo and loaded
with spirit, aiming for the Spanish border.

The *guardias* at the Spanish border gave us no trouble. We
looked and were as innocent as the late afternoon of our arrival.
But their gray uniforms, the large omnipresent portrait of Generalissimo Francisco Franco, the gate which was really a barrier,
conveyed a gray fearfulness that did not touch us deeply as foreigners but to which we were always sensitive. Entering a new
country is always a surprise. It cannot be anticipated.

Yet Spain was like Greece, a country whose language, history,
and culture I knew, whose literature I read as I did literature in
English. I had lived with Spaniards in Mexico. There were the
great Spanish poets who had been at Middlebury—Cernuda, Salinas, and Guillén—at a time when only Vicente Aleixandre was
left in Madrid from that original generation of '27. I already had

that special identification with all things Spanish. Mexico City's center remains one of the great sixteenth- and seventeenth-century Spanish cities in grand architecture. Spain was also Mexico as Mexico was Spain. I also felt ties through my Mexican step-mother, Matilde Franco, and my younger brothers, Spanish Jews, with Marti's mother, Rebeca, who spoke Ladino, a Spanish prior to 1492. Spain is many histories and diasporas and I was happy to be there at the *fuente*, the source.

Here was Catalonia, Romanesque churches, marranos, Barce-lona, and the corridor of flight during those last days in January 1939 when the Republic fell and Antonio Machado and his fellow intellectuals left Spain, driven out, as Juan Ramón Jiménez wrote, through the back door. We followed Antonio Machado's escape route back: the frontier, Figueras (where he spent the last night in a barn with Tomás Navarro Tomás and Juan Roura-Parella, his linguist and philosopher companions), and Barcelona. So in autumn 1951, after filling out papers at the border post, we wheeled into Catalonia, stopping at Gerona, our first small city in Spain under the Caudillo.

It was nine o'clock, the hour Spaniards begin to think about supper, and the central plaza, with its hotels and *tapas* bars and *paseo,* was crowded with evening people. As we slowed, looking eager and confused, a gentleman came up to us, pushing a bicycle.

"*¿Cómo puedo ayudarles?*" (How can I help you?)

"*Buscamos un cuarto.*" (We're looking for a room.)

"You won't find any. There's a convention in town and they're all booked up, but I'll be glad to help you try anyway."

"*Vamos.*"

Antonio Puig (Puig in Catalan is pronounced "pooch") accom-panied us to four or five hotels, and when it was clear there was nothing, he smiled and announced that we'd have to stay at his house. We had been away from Greece, but now we were back. There was no way Antonio would let us reject his hospitality. Antonio mounted his bicycle and we followed him to his house, a modest but newly built stone and cement structure. His wife and daughter had dinner ready. It was surely a conspiracy.

The first Spaniards I met were Catalans, and in those days of multiple repression the injunction against the use of Catalan was absolute. Barcelona was the major industrial city of Spain, yet the language of seven million speakers in eastern Spain could not be taught in schools, used in newspapers, heard on radio or television. It was illegal to send a wire in Catalan. For the central government Catalan was a symbol of defiance against Madrid authority. It represented the subversion of separatism. The Catalans, proud of their literature, culture, internationalism, and work ethic, claimed every employee in Barcelona worked to feed one bureaucrat in Madrid.

"Come in."

We sat and talked politics and money. Antonio had been a railroad official before the civil war. During the war he was a captain in the Republican army. When the rebels, the Nationalists, the Falangists, the Fascists triumphed (the name for the winner depends on the speaker), this Antonio, like the other, the poet, fled to France. When the Germans occupied France, Puig was interned and became a forced laborer in a salt mine. In 1943 he escaped and reentered Spain in order to help his family.

"They were hungry and my daughter was sick. So I found a way back. They didn't kill me. They beat me, kept me in a cell a few months, and let me go. In 1939 had I stayed, I would have been shot."

"*Un millón de muertos*" (A million deaths), I said.

"*Sí*. We've had our magnificent Franco. For all his armies the bastard doesn't dare step foot in Barcelona. If he came, they'd first have to evacuate the city of every living inhabitant. And a few angry dead ones."

Foreign books and newspapers gave that figure of "a million dead." Even writers who were on the *blue* side cited the fearful number. Those few intellectuals who had sided with Franco—the savior of order and church—including the novelist Cela and the philosopher Aranguren, soon after the terrible war was over joined the opposition. The slaughter of revenge, the repression, the shrill anachronism of the dictatorship was too much. The order imposed by Falange blueshirts had little appeal, and the Falange itself quickly became secondary as the nation settled into rule by Franco, army, and church—and an increasing number of Opus Dei technocrats.

Falange ideology and slogans in early Franco Spain came out in parades, in songs of Scouts, in editorials in the newspapers, which had not the slightest independence. Local news had moral purpose, national and international news was propaganda. Dominating the papers was the Caudillo, by the grace of God, whose picture appeared daily on the front page. At military camps, before the parliament, at a factory opening, he spoke with "full pomp and grave ceremony." There was also Franco in the countryside, hunting. And there was his wife, Polo, and the department stores she gathered into her purse. Popularly the people mocked the leader's oratorical frailnesses, his agrammatical sermons delivered in a highly unattractive thin voice. Imitating Franco's speech was a game. Under tyranny, humor saves.

When Antonio had returned to Spain in 1943, world war was raging and Spain was playing its ambivalent role. It sent its crack Blue Division to fight with Hitler against the Russians. Yet despite nice photos of three chummy dictators from Germany, Italy, and Spain, Franco would not let Hitler's troops pass along his highways to take over Gibraltar and choke the narrow neck between the sea and the ocean. As for everyday life in the country, the land was gasping from its wounds. Prisons were full. There was little industry, less trade. The police and army were everywhere, and in Extremadura and parts of Andalusia there was hunger. Yet the nation was recovering.

By 1951 when we arrived, Spain still felt like an occupied country in which the occupiers spoke Spanish. But one got used to guns. Poverty and recovery were more critical than personal freedom and censorship. In the '60s intellectual dissidents signed petitions, risked position and liberty, and there was real change.

By 1975 when Franco died (after coming close several times), Madrid and Barcelona were pleasant cities where Latin American boom novelists came to work in peace. Weary of dictatorship, with the Caudillo and his mystique of fear gone at last, his silly and evil rhetoric buried, Spain came to democracy suddenly and totally. The economy expanded dynamically. Next door, democracy had also come to Portugal after the death of Salazar, who had been in power even longer than Franco.

Back in Spain, Antonio Puig found a job in a tool factory where his wife and daughter were working. They each had an eight-hour shift. He worked a double shift, sixteen hours a day, and between their four salaries he was able to buy his house. The wages were little—yet substantially higher in Catalonia than elsewhere in the country. A worker made twenty-five pesetas a day (a dollar then was thirty-two pesetas). So Antonio Puig worked sixteen hours to take home fifty pesetas—$1.60.

"How could you do it?"

"I did it and I continue doing it. I am stubborn and strong."

"You're a good type," I said, "despite being a Catalan."

"We are what *Dios manda*—what God orders—and though I'm a radical socialist atheist, I admit God did well in ordering us to be Catalan."

"I agree, you are an impossible people," I concurred.

With his wife's and daughter's earnings, and his double salary, Antonio and his family could live *decentemente*. Spain was suffering but the irrepressible Catalans managed.

"By the way, I like my boss and he likes me. He is a good man," Antonio told us. "And an exemplary Catalan. He doesn't set the wages. The government dispenses that charity."

In the 1950s the dollar was gold in Europe, and especially in Spain, so to translate pesetas into dollars is misleading. We were to rent a huge house and garden in Andalusia for fourteen dollars a month. It cost two pesetas to go to a film or to get a haircut. The Andalusian field worker made twelve or thirteen pesetas a day—when there was work. At dawn the field workers congregated in the village, and those selected would be sent to the *campos* to cut *caña* (sugarcane) or, in season, to work in the sugar mill. In the richest agricultural terrain in Spain, the south, where most *campesinos* (peasants) did not own small farms but worked on big estates, and in our own village, there was much hunger. Sometimes there was fish for those who could afford it. Goat meat occasionally. And many poor children sucking sugarcane. Bread, olive oil, and potatoes were a meal for the poor, if they were lucky. Compared to the conditions in Andalusia, life in Gerona for Antonio Puig was good.

The evening was wonderful. Our first night in Spain and we were in a worker's house, talking regional and national politics for hours. Would it happen in New Haven or Bridgeport? At the dinner the family apologized about the quality of the olive oil. "The best we export for foreign currency," said Señora Puig. The pastry was made with that oil. I preferred the macaroni and bread. I am embarrassed to remember how in that good company I couldn't stand the pastry—it reminded me of motor oil laced with sugar—and how hard it was to express my pleasure, which I did as forcefully as I could.

The drama of the evening was when Antonio took us to his workroom, opened the drawers of a big dresser, and there were his prewar world classics in Catalan. "One day I will take these books from their concealment and place them on open shelves."

These were his treasures, his books in a language captive in the dresser.

We were given the bridal room. Of course we were given the best. There may be civil wars and caudillos, but the Spaniard is a noble creature. We couldn't tell whether the room was left empty for guests or whether by some sneaky miracle they had prepared it while we were getting washed or eating. But that evening we had hot water in the bathroom and bridal sheets on a soft bed. I looked at the fluffy pillows, white lace coverlet, and toy house curtains on the windows. Maybe in a few decades the civil war would be over.

Picasso painted and drew in Barcelona. So did Juan Gris and Joan Miró. And Pablo Casals fiddled his cello. Artigas, the ceramist who cast Picasso's ceramics, took us around. He was married to a Swiss who was Albert Schübach's friend. So our first evening in Barcelona we listened to Artigas telling hilarious tales about Pablo the painter and complaining about his Swiss brother-in-law, who with all his fine qualities felt obliged to charge him for local telephone calls when he was staying at his house. Spaniards hate money. Money is a religious sin. Of course it's baloney, and as everywhere money is power and the poorer the country the more rigid the power of money; yet pose or no pose the poorest Spaniard in the Peninsula would not charge his brother-in-law for a phone call, even if for other good reasons he was planning his murder.

In the beautiful city of Barcelona, with its logical grand boulevards, its Rambla for walking, and its *barrio chino* (Chinese district) for whoring and curing venereal diseases, lack of foreign exchange led to colorful solutions. Gasoline was expensive, so most of the taxis burned charcoal and wood in the trunk. Somehow the car trunk was converted into a furnace and hot fumes from burning charcoal drove the internal combustion engine. When a taxi stepped on the gas, the furnace would flame, and since the trunk lid was partially opened, it looked like a car on fire. Often a driver would stop to stoke embers and add more coal. He was filling up. The first days when I saw flame shooting out of a cab, I honked my horn and tried to catch it. Once I caught up and told the man his car was about to explode. The old driver took a look at us and roared.

Carlos Novi was our closest friend in Barcelona and we have never lost touch. Eventually, Carlos left Spain, married an Englishwoman, and worked for the BBC Third Programme. He asked me to do an English version of Pablo Neruda's only verse play, *Radiance and Death of Joaquín Murieta,* which was broadcast in London and later published in America. Carlos took us everywhere and brought sunlight to this port city, to this medieval harbor which Columbus sailed back to after crossing the ocean to find spice in the Indies; by the time of his return the later world decreed that the Renaissance had reached the West. Fourteen ninety-two was the dividing line, except in Italy, which jumped the gun. Our favorite cathedral was the gutted Santa María del Mar, which the Republicans had burned during the war. As in Greek antiquity when Christian iconoclasts and Turkish and Venetian bombs had turned closed temples into freestanding columns catching sun and blue firmament where once there were roofs, so the torching of the church burned the baroque gold altars and the holy intrusive mess at the center of most Spanish churches—in contrast to Greek Orthodoxy and Islam—and in its scarred, barren state the light through high windows came in and mixed with huge open darknesses of the interior, and its mystery was tangible.

In those days Carlos, along with many Spaniards with some literary flare, was studying law. Lorca and Aleixandre took law degrees and never practiced. Carlos complained, "To study modern literature today in Spain somehow means to read classical philology. You end up with interminably tedious courses on Roman coins or place-names. They kill you by forcing you to memorize trivia." Paco Brines, who in later years in Madrid was my closest companion and remains the Spanish poet I most esteem, recounted the siege of boredom in the good old times of literary studies at the university. That too has changed.

In recent years, only very recent years, I have thrown off the last tyrannical cords of the emotion of regret. That wasteful remorse is gone. I look back—whatever the mistake, wrong decision, wrong road—but no regret. Except in Barcelona, and it still bugs me. Because it has continued to do so, despite some philosophical blanketing, it has perhaps positively changed some of my habits. What happened in Barcelona? Nothing happened. It's what I didn't do.

Carlos Novi took us to a bookstore-gallery. The important galleries then in Barcelona were found in that union of letters and brush. In one gallery the owner showed us two drawings by Picasso, drawings Picasso had done as a student at the academy before leaving Barcelona for Paris, while he was in his teens in 1897 and 1899. They were masterfully exquisite, strong pencil drawings. One was three figures at a bar, in berets, smoking pipes, with bohemian defiant laughter on their faces, each drinker with a foot lifted off the ground. The other was a single portrait, just a few right lines of a very lone figure, standing, near a stool with a wineglass on it. There were virtually no foreign buyers, and the art market was minuscule. The prices for the drawings were ninety-five dollars and one hundred seventy-five. I had the money in traveler's checks. Helle suggested we wait until the following year when we would be leaving Spain through Barcelona. It wasn't a bad suggestion to see if, after a year, we had any money left.

When we returned shortly thereafter, the drawings were gone. Of course they were. They were not fakes. They were beautiful drawings, which I wish I were looking at above this computer screen, right now at 12:22 A.M., September 27, 1991, three days after harvest moon rose like Picasso's own face over the Indiana pampas. Above this screen I am looking at a Picasso lithograph, unsigned but genuine, which I bought from a dealer friend in New York for a lot of money. I love the litho and look at it every day—dated 3.12.57—a woman in profile, Greek face, large Picasso eye, framed in colors within the real gold frame—but I also like the two drawings I will never see again. They are the loss, which has driven me at moments to do things *when* I had to. But the notion of loss is also a fixation, or at least I have made it so. It has become the perversion of my philosophy, since in terms of material things, I have lost not so much by not acting but from losing real, valuable objects. What could be more instructive of the perspective of our Buddhist impermanence, of our shadow of transition that Plotinus called our deception and earthly illusion? So, though not intended, I have accepted my actions of loss as an inevitable cult. Thank you, Picasso drawings

not purchased, for endowing me with the permanent glow of
your absence—its memory, though vague, is as real as any object
in time:

Spirit Has a Beginning

Although there's no Director of the Scenes
working especially for me, I bet
what happens is for good. Forgot my jeans
in Hong Kong; on a marble hill in Crete
I left a lens. Yesterday in Nepal
a boy got my glasses. Why do I lose
my things? Alms to the cosmos? When I fall
in love, it lasts a life, but I confuse
my lover, lose her, and walk for years
on fire. It's good. Rain will surprise my heart
one day before I die. Theologies
despise possessions, and I feel no tears
for things—though lost love replays death. Yet these
words come because I lose. Loss is a start.

Barcelona is one of the good cities of the world. We stayed
just a few weeks, and the grace and reason of so many Catalan
hosts amazed me. The Catalans are especially firm about not
being Spaniards. Their country is divided by a political border,
but in French and Spanish Catalonia you have another people,
language, and character. And what they say is true: even apart
from politics and separatism, Catalans are not Spaniards. They
are a people whose land lies between France and Spain. Yet for
all my affection for the region, I was anxious to go to Spain—
even to Spain as the Catalans see their caricature of the Spaniard:
irrational, dark, extreme, severe, emotional. I would be at home
in my second Greece, I knew. And Andalusia was Greece. A big
island. La Mancha up north—Spain's pampas and prairies—are
stark, severe in climate. But who can spend a month in Segovia
and not dream open-eyed like Machado? Through Antonio Ma-

chado's eyes I saw Castilla and those ruinous villages he wandered
through at night like a ghost. They were mine too.

We had been roaming since late spring and now it was fall and
we longed to settle in a rented house and paint and write. We
wanted to be with people not only for a week, a day, or an
evening.

"Put your bike on a train," Carlos suggested, "and go directly
to Sevilla."

It was a splendid idea. We had climbed the Alps on our Lambretta and with it would eventually cover much of Spain. But
the roads were rough, our scooter not a giant vehicle, and to go
directly to Sevilla meant we were close to our white island. From
Sevilla we could roll along the coast until like Odysseus we
washed up on Ithaca.

Spanish trains were a treat. I felt the same sense of abandonment
to nature in Egypt when I took overnight trains into the south,
for the sky as well as its smoke, smells, even clouds entered the
open windows. In Egypt I remember at about four in the morning, at a food stop, a boy jumped in through the window—it
was too jammed to use the doors—was squatting on my lap,
and selling watermelons, which his father tossed him from the
platform. I was already smudged from smoke, whitened from a
bag of flour overhead in the rack that sifted quietly down on me
through the night, and now I was rinsed off with watermelon
juice as the boy used his sharp knife to cut dripping halfs for
his customers. The Spanish trains were not quite so jammed.
Passengers were tired, courteous, and helpful. On every trip, our
eyes hung out the windows to take in the villages and landscapes.
Each time the train took a good turn, the locomotive's hot, black
fumes poured in through the open windows. And we talked to
people.

There are some countries, and Spain is one, where you know
you can speak to anyone, almost anywhere, whoever you or they
are. It is very consoling. I confess an ethnic prejudice. I like
Spaniards enormously. I know there are madmen, murderers of

Lorca, Franco along with Goya and Casals, but I don't care. If I go into a morning neighborhood bar in Madrid for coffee and a piece of bad cake, I'll probably talk to whoever is standing next to me. It's easy and natural. It is perfectly ordinary. I don't have the same desire and pleasure in most places in America, with perhaps the exception of Vermont and Maine villages (where people have the false reputation of being cool and reserved). In America such communication sometimes works but it is not ordinary. I try, but only when I am so pumped up with social energy from some event that I can overcome ordinary barriers with the stranger by way of a joke, the remark, the quick serious exchange. Even then, it is always chancy, always a dangerous walk into silence and disapproval. But in Greece and Spain talk is natural and inevitable. I miss that humanity and mutual curiosity.

On the last evening in Barcelona we were packing for the train. We had bought provisions for the long ride. Carlos Novi was taking us to the station. He was formal as he was intimate. The phone.

"Carlos, *qué tal?*" (How's it going?)

"Are you ready for the train, all set for battle?"

"Armed to the teeth."

"Good. Now get ready for the ship."

"Ship. What ship?"

"Yes, you're leaving tomorrow by ship for Cádiz. I've been trying to reach you all day. I made reservations. You'll arrive intact and fresh after a night's sleep in the cabin."

"What can I say?"

"Don't say anything. Go out and buy some more cheese."

Our ship was sailing for the Andalusian city once called Gadir by the Phoenicians, who, coming directly from Tyre, founded it in 1101 B.C. Gadir was the port city for tin and silver from Tarshish, the biblical word for Spain. The Romans called it Gades, which evolved in a few centuries into Cádiz, the name it had when Columbus left its port in 1493 on his second trip to find

178

the elusive Indies. The city extends out from the mainland on a promontory.

We slowed into port at dawn. The air was blue, bluer than sky or water. Blue daybreak. Upon the land was a gigantic ship with all its sails fluttering. Each house a sail tinted by the sun on the sloping hill. A thousand constellations had fallen to earth and during the night rose as blowing laundry sheets. So was Cádiz that morning at dawn.

Cádiz's poet Rafael Alberti was still in exile in Buenos Aires. But he had given us an exact replica of his city and sea, their inseparable marriage, in his first book, *Marinero en tierra* (Sailor on Land):

> The sea hangs a drapery,
> not a wall, over the street.
> Come out.
> A marine city
> wants to dock at your house.

From Cádiz and Puerto Santa María, we sailed on our little machine over to Jeréz de la Frontera and drank *jerez*—sherry. The winery doors were open, and it was fun to become one-day experts. That afternoon we walked, leaving our *moto* sober at a gas station. The English went to Argentina with railroads and to Jeréz de la Frontera with sherry wineries. They owned the main firms—Sandeman, Gordon, Terry. "Sherry" comes from *jerez*, the fortified wine that takes its name from the city of Jeréz (Xeris) de la Frontera, where it is fermented. *Frontera*, of Jeréz de la Frontera, means "frontier," yet the city was never, as one would suppose, a border town between Spain and Portugal some hundred kilometers away, but between Christian and Moorish Spain, a frontier that moved about for centuries as defeat and conquest alternated with *reconquista* in the battles between *cristiano* and *moro*. Consequently, surrounding Jeréz, and all over Andalusia, are other villages and towns with the same romantic compound *de la frontera*—of the frontier.

The rival Spanish distillery in Jeréz has the resonant name Pedro Domecq, which appears in Lorca's poem about the Civil Guard. Lorca tells us the other side of color and beauty in his ballad of gypsy terror and murder, during festival, in Jeréz de la Frontera. It is said that Lorca's "Romance de la Guardia Civil española" put Lorca on a death list. It was more complex, however. As Ian Gibson's work on Lorca's assassination shows, many factors of chance led to that absurd human horror and violation of art. The first weeks of the rebellion saw the emergence of single grave figures bent on immediate destruction of the enemy. Lorca's brother-in-law, Fernando de los Ríos, the liberal mayor of Granada was executed a few days before Lorca.

This ballad, especially this one, with its depiction of the *tricornio* Civil Guard, whose heads conceal an astronomy of shapeless pistols, added to the rage by the military against the poet. In those years Lorca was decisively Spain's best known poet and playwright, and his *romance* on the *guardias* was known or heard of even by those who read no poetry. "Patent-leather souls" to describe the *guardias* in their three-cornered leather hats was a phrase entering the Spanish language. Now that the actual frying-pan hats are gone, it remains as a linguistic and social memory.

Ballad of the Spanish Civil Guard

Black are the horses.
The horseshoes are black.
On their capes glow
stains of ink and wax.
Their skulls are made of lead
and so they don't weep.
With their patent-leather souls
they come down the street.
Humpbacked and nocturnal,
where they go they command
silences of dark rubber

and dread like fine sand.
They go where they want to,
concealing in their skulls
a vague astronomy
of shapeless pistols.

. . . .

*

They advance in double file
into the holiday city.
The rustle of evergreens
invades their cartridge belts.
Double nocturne in gray cloth.
In their fancy the sky
is a show window of spurs.

*

The city, freed from fear,
was multiplying its gates
when forty Civil Guards
rode grayly in to plunder.
The clocks clicked to a halt,
and brandy in their bottles
wore a mask of November
not to arouse suspicion.
A flight of long screams
rose in the weathercocks.
Their sabers slash the breeze
which their hooves crush.
Along the streets of shadow
old gypsy women run
with their horses asleep
and their jars filled with coins.
Through the steep streets
the sinister capes mount,
leaving behind them a fleeting
whirlwind of scissors.

*

Sunday Morning in Fascist Spain

The gypsies gather together
by the Bethlehem gate.
Saint Joseph, full of wounds,
enshrouds a young virgin.
Stubborn screeching rifles
resound through the night.
The Virgin is healing children
with saliva from the stars.
But the Civil Guard
advances seeding bonfires
where young and naked
imagination burns up.
Rosa of the Camborios
sits moaning by her door,
her two breasts cut off
and lying on a tray.
Other women are racing
chased by their own braids
in a wind where roses
of black powder explode.
When all the tile roofs
are furrows in the earth,
the dawn shrugs her shoulders
in a long profile of stone.

*

O city of the gypsies!
The Civil Guard rides away
through a tunnel of silence
while flames surround you.

*

O city of the Gypsies!
Who could see you and not remember?
Let them find you on my forehead.
The game of moon and sand.

Who could see you and not remember?

As a reader of the Spanish poets, I remember through Lorca in death and Alberti in exile, through Miguel Hernández succumbing at thirty-one in his cell in Alicante, through Aleixandre who remained in Madrid, and Miguel de Unamuno, irascible poet-novelist-scholar-rebel, telling the triumphant generals they may vanquish but never convince.

After Jeréz our destination was Seville. We were sober when we set our Italian wheels on the hill roads of this Spanish Tuscany. We roared quietly down to the olive groves and sunflower fields around Andalusia's capital city.

Sevilla.

Quien no ha visto Sevilla, no ha visto maravilla. (Who has not seen Seville, has not seen a marvel.) The Phoenician city of Roman emperors Trajan and Hadrian, of the painters Velázquez and Murillo, of the poets Góngora, Bécquer, Antonio and Manuel Machado, Aleixandre, of the contorted white streets and sculptured alleys of the Judería and Moorish quarters. When as a young man the playwright Lope de Vega entered Sevilla for the first time, saw the Giralda Tower, the Court of Oranges, and the glittering Guadalquivir River, he felt it was unworthy to be so poor in a city of such richnesses. So he took his one gold doubloon from his pocket and hurled it into the Guadalquivir so as not to be walking the streets of Sevilla with so little money in his pocket.

Sevilla was and is also the city of the *Semana Santa* (Holy Week) parades where the Virgin of the Doves is carried in the streets while doves circle overhead the veiled Virgin beauty with glass, teary eyes, sung to in *saetas*, protected by Civil Guard *tricornios* and the penitents, men in Klu Klux Klan-like hats who walk carrying torches alongside the *pasos* (floats). A week later came the spring *Feria* (the Fair): the dancing of *sevillanas* through the night in the *casetas,* in the afternoon *la corrida* (the bullfight), and meandering through the streets those beautiful women on horseback, dressed like women bullfighters.

One awful sight was to see Cardinal Segura, famous for his draconian morality and medieval politics, leading a religious procession down a grand street. The people on the sidewalks fell to their knees before the glaring priest. But even Segura, friend of Franco, confessor of generals, failed in his efforts to ban dancing in Seville. Tyrants can ban, but not forever. Usually there is a return, as "the banner" himself is overcome. Mao banned the open market in the market city of Kashgar in Turkestan in the center of Asia, and to have succeeded in banning carts with fruit, cloths, and pearls from a Silk Route capital was to drain blood from the vigorous Uighur and Uzbek people. In 1985, when I got lost in the alleys and plazas of mythic Kashgar, a spot in the Gobi just a few miles from Pakistan, Afganistan, and Russia, the market was back in its fullness, occupying most streets of the ancient city that Marco Polo described with colors of wonder. Segura failed to ban the *sevillana* for the same reason that Franco could not wipe out the Catalan language or kill democracy forever.

There are some cultural and political activities that tyranny cannot obliterate—although suppression may endure for decades. When it is over the explosion of emotion is the dance of the world.

We would return to Sevilla in the spring, and, in anticipation, secured a room in the house of an arts-and-crafts teacher for those festive days when lodging would be impossible to find. So with just a week in Seville we got on our bike and headed for Ronda and the coast. We would explore, live, love through these days in Andalusia, and find a place—but only after a decent period. I remember Antonio Machado's discovery of Castilian Soria, where he was sent as a schoolteacher in a rural *instituto*. He wrote, "the fields seem more than young, adolescent." Our autumn fields seemed also to have the youth of adolescence, or perhaps the childhood was in *us* because of our discoveries. In the villages— sometimes only two white streets of sun-mirroring buildings— we'd enter the houses, and sometimes in twenty minutes we knew the whole village and they knew us. Later in England, which we also liked but where good friendship came slow, this instant communion might have required six months. Helle made extraordinary watercolor-and-ink portraits of the children, who fought to pose seriously for her.

From low in Sevilla we went southwest, climbing through wheat and olive fields and land-stray sea gulls, to medieval Ronda, a noble city of impeccable beauty, from the poorest street of regional houses to the richest street of señoreal mansions. It was intact, no blemish of our century's fast-food structures. In Ronda, knights initiated the brutal rite of bullfighting. Much earlier the bull was god or hybrid god in Egypt and Greece. By the maze in Minoan Crete, as the wall paintings tell, in the second millennium acrobatic men somersaulted over the bull and didn't bother to gore or stab the animal.

We spent the night at an inn by the great gorge at the city's edge, where the poet Góngora stayed in the early seventeenth century and Rilke in the first decade of ours. An old English Quaker lady owned the *parador* and had been there most of her life. After supper—there were four guests that evening—she invited us to her library den for *jeréz*. "Read," she said, and kindled the fire. We read from her nineteenth-century travel books. That night we slept under an English quilt; our window overlooked the gorge.

Gospel of Love

We took our cycle to the lovers' cliff
at Ronda where the knights murdered a bull
or fought the Moors. Sore from the road and stiff, we
sat where Rilke (in the fanciful
old Quaker lady's inn) sat by the fire,
hearing the verse of Góngora the Jew.
It seems a century ago: desire
for sun, refinement, and for white and blue
Sevilla, oranges, and the Spring Fair,
five nights of dancing into dawn. Sunday
morning in fascist Spain, the women rode

their flowery stallions. Salt was in the air
as we cycled on the coast. That episode
of wonder was our childhood sun. Our way.

We didn't linger. We headed down to the coast, where we were destined to find a home. Even Alberti's salmon under the sea, floating with open eyes, needs a place in the water to sleep. So we rode along the southern rim of the Iberian peninsula. The coast was so pure it was not yet made for tourists, foreigners, or Spaniards seeking vacations. It was made for Andalusians living there. We found nothing. Only east of Málaga in Torre Molinos were there houses for rent. This spot was the only stain of corruption on a coast that in a decade would disappear and become a ghost whose memory was only in others. The disease spread with alarming speed. The commercial corpuscles seized the land. Yes, hunger disappeared. The government improved. But the world disease, destroying the chronicle of centuries, struck. It is no different from the fires in the Amazon or the razing of Lhasa for the victory of Chinese prefab apartment houses. It was luxuriously done on the Costa del Sol. But the coast is gone. No further apology or comment. Some miles inland, Andalusia still lives. For now.

East of Nerja we passed through dreamlike beautiful villages. It was Mykonos on the continent. But only when we got to Almuñécar did we find a place for us.

The town of Almuñécar was a jumble of styles. Moors and Spaniards threw in balconies and doorways. The Greeks were there and in their important trading post of Mainake nearby. The Carthaginians traced out the streets and stored bones in the caves on the hill, the hill where the paupers slept. The same North Africans (who were earlier Phoenicians) set up fortified fish factories in Málaga and Almuñécar for salting sardines. This was Tartessus. And the Romans left a perfectly intact aqueduct behind the Rancho Chico outside of town. Five hundred meters further east was a promontory connected to land by an orange Roman bridge, unused and perfectly preserved. All along the coast were the *atalayas*, the Arab watchtowers, from which the Moors used fire and smoke to signal information quickly all along their coastal territory.

In the town casino Don Andrés Cuevas said he knew where we could live. He would take us there. It was the Rancho Chico. What an absurd name for a country house in Spain. "Rancho Chico." Spain had *fincas* but a *rancho*, no. That was from Mexico or the United States. The owner, however, don Paco, had been to Mexico, had known about *ranchos grandes* and modestly named his hacienda house and terrain the Rancho Chico. Paco himself was not at all *chico*. A tall, corpulent, and boisterous man, of radically autocratic ideas, he offered us his furnished country house on the water, with its oleander, jasmine, and hyacinths, flowering magnolias, and a few acres of sugarcane within a tall surrounding white stucco-and-stone wall. Behind the house were more fields of cane and then the Sierra Nevada mountains. A small river ran into the sea about twenty meters east of our gate. There on the rocks and in the water women washed laundry. A dirt path in front of us separated us from a patch of bushes and sand dropping down to the Mediterranean. We were about a ten-minute walk from the town itself on a path that usually had some goats on it for us to dodge. The cost for our estate was four hundred fifty pesetas a month, a little less than fourteen dollars— what a farm worker might earn in a month if he worked seven days a week. Cuevas thought it was high, but we accepted.

I don't know who was happier, Helle or I.

If I had the craft and the memory of Vladimir Nabokov, I could tell you about each piece of furniture, the mortise and tenon of each joinery, the beading along the legs and aprons of tables. My memory is more fundamental; that is, it works in blocks of images, and this large apartment, the second floor of the tile-and-stone house, was blocked out large. One climbed a stairway to the grand tile terrace, which was the width of the house and twenty feet deep. We spent much of our daylight on the terrace. On either side of the entrance hall was a large room. To the left was our living room where we read and Helle painted, to the right our bedroom, farther down the hall on the left a bathroom and guest room, and on the right a kitchen with three charcoal-burning cooking pits. A simple, generous plan.

Within hours of unpacking and setting up, came Josefa.

Josefa was there with a white rose in her hair. She always had a white rose in her hair.

Josefa had heard that *franceses*, Frenchmen, the local word for foreigners, had taken Don Paco's house, and she offered us her service. By now we had been in Almuñécar half a day and surely the whole town knew everything about us. The last thing we had in mind was to have a maid. Why? What was there to do in our life, so plain in its needs, that we could not do ourselves? But Josefa was a much stronger person than we. She was fifty, nearly blind from trachoma, a viral disease that scarred and destroyed the cornea, common in North Africa, and still prevalent in Andalusia. Trachoma is a disease of the poor, and treatment, hygiene, good food are its enemies. Many adults and even children had the disease in our town. Across the waters in southern Egypt, trachoma was so widespread it broke your heart to see the children, untreated, in varying stages of blindness. Josefa had had an operation in her youth that saved the little vision she had left. She went to Granada, fifty miles north, for the operation. She walked there and back. Yet her bad, teary eyes, which she rubbed with a kerchief, impeded her little.

Andrés Cuevas, being loyal to his class, tried to protect us, in front of Josefa. "What do you want with a *ciega* (a blind woman)? I'll get you someone good."

Josefa wasn't offended by this blunt defamation. Cuevas was rich and locally powerful; he was the assistant mayor. She was a poor woman scrubbing the clinic's floors. She listened impassively until he was through. She knew her victory.

Yes, we were not a match for her reason and will, and very quickly we had no regrets about our frailty. Josefa was a nation. She was incapable of speech that was not aphoristic. She made Sancho Panza's proverbs and *refranes* (rhyming refrains) seem an amateur's labors. Nothing escaped her humor and burlesquing tongue. Her verbal vision was perfect, despite a few teeth gone here and there. Her voice was loud, coarse as the rocks on which the women scrubbed their laundry, and singsong. She invented words. And she worked, *fregando* (scrubbing floors), going on errands to the town for watered-down goat milk and other provisions, and cooking. Helle was an excellent cook, so even that was not necessary. But she fried good local sardines in olive oil, kept us supplied with *jerez, tinto,* Perico Domecq or the equivalent, and lots of flowers, which she filled the rooms with. She wanted to make herself necessary, and we were glad, because we liked her as much as she did us. We liked speaking to each other. We had Spain living with us. That is, she arrived each morning at her own hour, with a huge "¡*Bueno' día', francese'!*" (Good morning, French people!)

Of course Josefa mocked our speech, the speech of *los franceses de más allá* (the French people from out there). She made fun of our northern Castilian Spanish—we pronounced the final *s* in "*gracias*" (thanks), which the Andalusians (and Cubans and Puerto Ricans) drop. They "eat" the final *s,* as this habit is expressed in Spanish.

"*Gracias,*" I'd say.

"*Graciaz,*" she'd answer, trying to repeat our *s* as the most ridiculous thing in the world, but her *s* would come out as a sibilant *z,* making our exchange hilarious.

"Okay, Josefa," Helle would tell her, "say *estómago*" (stomach).

"*Eztógamo.*"

"No. *Estómago,*" Helle insisted.

"*Eztógamo!*" Josefa yelled.

"Slowly, then, syllable by syllable. *Es.*"

"*Ez,*" the *ciega* repeated.

"*Tó,*" said Helle.

"*Tó.*"

"*Ma,*" said Helle. "We're getting close."

"*Ma,*" said Josefa, obedient.

"*Go.*" Helle.

"*Go,*" Josefa repeated, with eternal patience.

"*Perfecto*. Now, let's have it. *Estómago*."

"*Eztógamo!* Josefa uttered in triumph. And her Andalusia triumphed over *Francia*, triumphed over the barbarians.

Josefa smiled with every tooth, knowing she would never yield. You couldn't tamper with her metathesis.

"*Tú eres astuta y granuja*" (You are cunning and a little scoundrel), Helle said.

"*Y la zeñora ez muy zeñora*." (And the lady is very lady.)

"*Tregua*" (truce), I called.

Although we used the *ceceo* (*c* and *z* pronounced like Greek *theta*), Josefa herself like many Andalusians used the *ceceo* all the time. In her case it wasn't regional as, say, in Baeza. Because of her missing teeth, the lisping toothy joy of her Spanish, fast as a hummingbird's wings, dominated. I was her *francés* from America; Helle her *francesa* from *Grecia,* which often came out as *Suecia* (Sweden). When she said proudly to someone "*La zeñora ez griega*" (The lady is Greek), that too often shifted to "*La zeñora ez noruega*" (The lady is Norwegian). *Grecia, Suecia; griega, noruega*—is there a difference? They all rhyme.

Helle set up her studio. We still found that the butcher, this time Spanish, not Greek, had the best paper in town, and she used oil, gouache, acrylic, watercolor, inks, wash, and all mixed-media combinations, on the strong brown paper she pinned onto her easel. There were favorite models, mainly adolescents, who came to pose: Salamón, María Elena, and Soledad. Salamón was grave and wise as his name (Solomon) suggests. That was his pose, which he would not alter. Off camera he was a scamp. María Elena had a Spanish-Moorish face and in Helle's colors she came from the south of Spain or some Pacific island. Soledad was solitude. Her father had killed someone and disappeared, a fugitive. Her face had the beauty of a sorrow, a depth that never left her smile. She was the blond Andalusian, as most of this particular village was, Visigoth or Vandal (the Vandals gave their name to [V]andalusia), and Helle painted her as if her hair were inch-wide bands of blonde and brunette.

Helle's paintings had not a trace of sentimental Murillo, the peril of those who observe children on canvas. Who gave her strength was another Spaniard: Diego Velázquez. Her figures were Velázquez's dwarfs (except hers were not short, deformed adults but *were* children) and with iron emotion and veracity. They also had in spirit, if not form, the outlines and whimsical pathos of Modigliani. Helle Tzalopoulou was and remains a European colorist. During her three years at Yale studying with Joseph Albers, the master of color, her Greekness, her own colors, her emotion, were never diluted by whatever external movement she was close to. Living the warmer months of the year on the Greek island of Serifos, on Perseus Street (where Perseus ate yogurt when he was not conspiring against the Medusa up on the slope overlooking the Orthodox church), she has taken much from the movement of the windy sea-surface and its mists of color and energy.

In Spain Helle painted every day. It had already become her life habit. One she began in Greece. I think back to that persistence.

Recalling a Life with a Greek

September melancholy. You are there,
sketching the island of the moonhigh wheat
and enigmatic tides. The iron chair
out on the terrace with your form. You eat
the Euboian yogurt cured in sacks and drink
sage tea with honey which the hotel stored
for us. And sketch the chapel. As I think
about our hills, the cave and brook, its sword
of water glittering the pepper tree,
I sigh for us. A thousand years have not
erased your drawing. Hold the sun. The fall
of Thera and our ghosts are a white dot
before your charcoal eyes. Near that spring wall
we pause. You sketch the tombs of porphyry.

In Greece I read the morning newspaper and the poets in Greek. Now in Spain, the newspapers were so offensive it was painful to glance at them, but both Helle and I read books mainly in Spanish. Our Spanish intellectuals, the poets and essayists, were in books. We found an edition of Greek classical drama in fluent, modern Spanish, and I was fascinated to find that Euripides, the most dramatic and swiftest of the tragedians sounded, in resonant Spanish, like Lorca's *Bernarda Alba*. Lorca's plot is static, but the dark tension, the anger, the violent resolution, the primitive forces joined in psychological combat echo in Spain's murdered author of the rural trilogy.

In Paris, Greece, Barcelona, our friends were writers, painters, students. Here there were visitors from London and Paris who wandered by and dug us out, but our days were spent with the people, of all classes, the people of Almuñécar. So the children were our first friends. Others came quickly, and Josefa named them. She was Adam the namer, and once in our house the guest accepted the new title. There was Antonio of the clothing shop who became Antonio de la Tienda. (*Tienda* means "tent" and "store," a union unlikely in the colder north.) There was also Antonio the artist-painter who worked at a gasoline station. He had two names: Antonio el Pintor and Antonio el de la Bomba de Gasolina: "Anthony the Painter" and "Anthony he of the Gasoline Pump." There was Andrés del Casino—which is where Cuevas spent his day, playing cards with cronies, and Justo el Gitano del Pico —Justo the Gypsy of the Pickax. Justo used his pickax working on the highway, a dubious occupation for a legitimate gypsy.

Justo the "Just." Josefa liked Justo and didn't mind that he was a gypsy. He was poor and she was poor, and he even worked at a nongypsy profession—pounding the roads with his pickax and sledgehammer. When he arrived—we had no phone so everyone arrived by surprise—Josefa would call out his name, with particular glee, "*Aquí tenéis este joven, el Gitano del Pico, que quiere deciros algo*" (Here you have this young man, the Gypsy of the Pickax, who's got something to tell you).

"What's the news, Justo?"

"A troupe's coming to town."

"A good one?"

"Good? I'm going to dance with them."

"Not so good then," I said.

"*Muy bueno ez ezte gitanito*" (Very good is this little gypsy), Josefa protested. "Even with *my* eyes, I can see he's good. I see him with my ears."

"So it's a good troupe," I relented. "What's it called?"

"*La compañía del niño con la voz de oro.* (The troupe with the boy with the voice of gold.) Now *he's* good. He's like the virgin, a miracle."

Justo had gravity and dignity, not much talk, and an occasional big smile with valuable gold fillings among very white teeth. His regular dark features, tall athletic build, the grace of his manners and walk, made him a striking figure in the village. He seemed to have come directly from Rajasthan, in northern India, the gypsy homeland and origin of their dances and songs that unfolded in Spain. Before these wanderers entered Europe they passed through Egypt to pick up the name "gypsy," an Egyptian. I suppose the belief that the gypsies' actual passing through Egypt is the source of their name is about as accurate as the word *turco* (Turk) in Latin America for anyone from the Near East, including all Arabs. So in Argentina my friend Amanda, whose parents were from Lebanon and Syria, was *la turca*. The best feeling for the gypsies in Spain you find in George Henry Borrow's nineteenth-century classic travel book, *The Bible in Spain,* where the author, who learned *calé,* gypsy speech, describes among other stories, his adventures with gypsy gentlemen and ladies along our Andalusian coast.

Sometimes Justo was willing to dance for us. In the course of the winter he broke a few tiles doing so. He was not very good, not a superb flamenco dancer, but a serious one. He would dance if the radio were on and playing flamenco. Then Josefa, who was a one-woman orchestra, would grab a spoon and start beating the chair seat rhythmically to his steps. Once when we went to the film in the village, Josefa insisted on staying to guard the house until our return. We left while there was still light. When we came home and opened the gate that stood one hundred meters from our house, we could already make out *zapateado* (stamping) and loud singing of a fiesta, as if the radio were on full force. As we walked through the garden, among the redolent jasmine, we deciphered the source. No radio. It was blind Josefa, in her fifty years with the rose in her ear, amusing herself, singing away, shouting her songs against the night that lay outside on the terrace and in the living room lighted by a single bulb hanging from the ceiling, where the singer-dancer was carrying on.

The movie house, where the troupe would perform, was next to the church. "Do you like *las películas* (the movies)," I asked Josefa.

"I like them, but it costs."

"How much?"

"For me one peseta. Downstairs it's two, but since I don't see anyway, I sit upstairs for one, with the *probeticos* who work in the *frábica*." *Probeticos* was her version of *pobrecitos* (the little poor) and *frábica* was her revision of *fábrica* (factory).

"Do you go to church?"

"Every Sunday morning at eight."

"So devout. I thought you hated the priest."

"I hate the priest. *Con ezta bolita de plata que ez el mundo, el único que juega ez el cura.*" (With this silver ball that is the world, the only one who plays the game is the priest.)

"So why so early at church."

"*Pa' fregar.*" (To scrub.)

In the endless warm days of December, when the almond trees on the ridges were blossoming, we went for a long "work" walk in the hills, Helle with her paints, I with a notebook. These landscapes were later to be replaced by her islands and Indiana barns. She talked about them with concise philosophical language. She had the words always to explain. In her case it helped her motivation, gave her strength and ideas. I'm reminded of the

194

opposite of her self-aware art, the words of an old black jazz musician interviewed on public radio about his improvisations. "Do your read music?" "Sure, but I never let it get in my way when I'm playing." By contrast, Helle liked to know what she was doing. I was putting together a book of poems to be published in Málaga. While Helle painted, I sat on the ground, writing lines, fiddling with words. Nothing makes me happier than the freedom of scrawling lines. It was a good afternoon. When we reached the *finca*, a little tired and hungry, we heard Josefa making a racket. She was rushing about among the citrus trees, in circles, weeping and shouting, "What will they say, I didn't steal the money?"

"What is it?"

"It's the five hundred pesetas you gave me to buy food. Why did you give me so big a bill to change? A month's rent. It's gone."

"Gone?"

"I walked into the *tienda* and no money. I had it right here in my pocket. I've been walking back and forth to town all afternoon looking for it. I went to talk to the Virgin herself—not the piece of dead wood behind the *cura*'s altar, but to the good one in the small church for the poor. That Virgin María works. But not today. The money's gone."

"Forget it," I was saying, when Helle cut me off as she spotted the five-hundred-peseta note lying on top of a bush, a few feet from where Josefa was standing.

"You never got out of the *finca* with it," Helle said. "You dropped it after you came down the stairs. It's right here, next to your feet!" And she scooped it up and handed it to her.

"*Zeñora!* I knew that little Virgin didn't have her ears stuffed up with wax."

"*El zeñor Cuevá,*" Josefa announced. "*Ezte amigo vueztro*" (This friends of yours). Even Cuevas, for all his toughness, had to yield, with a sheepish smile, before her loud, formal sarcasm.

For all his faults, Cuevas was one of our intimates. It was an experience that we could be friends with a fascist, and he was an unrepentant admirer of Mussolini, not to mention Franco. We knew each other's views, but that didn't stop him from coming to see us, from standing handsomely middle-aged on our blue-and-white *azulejo* tile floors, smoking, gossiping, spitting on the floor—but always stooping a bit before each shot so as not to make an untidy splatter—and thoroughly engaging us. The war was not over until Francisco Franco died. But one could not live by civil war and hatred. Moreover, it was important to know everyone. Otherwise the *other* is a caricature.

His friend the mayor, Juan Morelo, I cared for much less. He was from Granada and a cousin of Federico García Lorca. His ideas about Lorca were government slander and guilt, but in his case he added his own scorn based on family information. However, I became responsible for a piece of art that was in the hands of Juan Morelo.

The mayor Juan Morelo had lent me his own first edition from the thirties of Lorca's early verse play *Mariana Pineda*, a drama that takes place in the city of Granada. We were living on the coast in the *provincia* of Granada. I read the piece. Inserted in the edition was an original ink drawing, signed in Lorca's hand. It was a portrait—wistful, poignant. A few lines for the face and body. And a flowerpot on a table.

"Are they worth much?" Morelo asked me. "I hear his nonsense is worth a lot."

"*Mucho*," I said, "and for many reasons. There are few drawings around by Lorca."

Since those days more pencil, crayon, and ink drawings have turned up, mainly illustrations of scenes from his plays, and they have been gathered in interesting, excellent art books published in Spain. Now that Lorca has been rehabilitated, his face is on an oversize memorial postage stamp—for thirty-five years only Franco was on the stamps—streets are named after him throughout Spain, and his plays, which were banned during the *dictatura* (dictatorship)—are everywhere on stage. Like the Chinese—to my knowledge uniquely like the Chinese—Lorca wrote words on his drawings and paintings, phrases of poetry, as classical Chinese poets brushed a line of characters vertically alongside the image on a scroll painting. Goya's savage titles for the *Caprichos* and the *Disasters of War* etchings are also aphoristic poems, but not inscribed on the pictures themselves. Among those drawings with words—the words are like concrete poems—are the drawings Lorca did in Buenos Aires for Pablo Neruda for a special edition of Neruda's *Twenty Poems of Love and a Desperate Song.*

"Did you know Federico?"

I said Federico. It's how readers and critics speak of Lorca the person. In his life he was adored as no Spanish literary figure in modern times, and to everyone he was Federico. (Similarly, Borges had no other name in Buenos Aires but Borges.)

"No. Not really. I saw him with the family, but even then they told me he was a crazy *mariquita* (a faggot) who stayed up all night playing the piano. He was a famous writer but a bad man."

"You're an idiot, Juan Morelo."

"Maybe you're a *rojo* (a red)," the mayor answered.

"*Tan rojo como tu culo.*" (As red as your ass.)

Cuevas was there to help me. "Juan, he's calling you an idiot in your capacity as *alcalde* (mayor). Everyone knows that. He's not talking about your personal intelligence, which some of us also know, but that fact is not public. It's only your friends who recognize what a genius you really are."

"Cuevas, sometimes I think you too are a *rojo!*"

I felt indebted to Cuevas. Thanks for the out. I always teased but was rarely aggressive, even if young, political self-righteousness was overtaking me. Aggression and insult make good reading, but my nature rejected those emotions; when I surrendered to them, I disliked myself. Living so often in countries under autocratic regimes—which was and remains most of the world—I could bite my tongue. That spat between Morelo and me couldn't have been more poorly timed, for what it foreshadowed.

Cuevas and Morelo stayed for coffee and Greek preserves that Helle made. She charmed them, and they thoroughly enjoyed the food and the charmer. Even Juan Morelo could bring himself to speak to a *rojo*, which in those times meant not "red" but anyone who was not *azul* (blue). Spain was littered with monuments and inscriptions reading that in March 1939 Generalissimo Francisco Franco defeated the *rojos*. Officially, you were for Franco or were a *rojo*, thereby making that division of loyalist or traitor that all extremist regimes make: Communist or Fascist, virgin or whore, nun or witch. "Politically correct" or "evil reactionary" were the terms I heard in China in May and June, 1972, during the Cultural Revolution. But since in Spain we were outsiders, we were expected to have wrong, uninformed opinions. The most ardent Falangist (I never really met one) knew that Europe, the United Nations, and Latin America from Mexico to Chile spurned the Spanish government. After the war, it was not a politically courageous act for a nation to condemn Francoism.

A few days after the tiff over Lorca, Jean Vigneras, an American professor of modern Spanish history at the University of Maine, was passing through the village. He heard about us at the *parador* where he was staying, and he dropped by. We spent a leisurely afternoon talking. Vigneras gave us information about Spain drawn from his own career. As for foreigners, only Laurie Lee, the English poet, whom we were soon to meet, was personally more informative.

Vigneras recounted how he had been sent by the U.S. government to Spain during the last months of the world war. He went all over the country, obtaining general intelligence. "I was not a spy. I was not after secrets. I looked at the country, spoke to the people, and reported my impressions. No more." As a historian, in the military, he was a member of a presidential advisory board. What should be the Allied role after Hitler's defeat? Should the Allies send divisions to the Spanish border? Even Franco could not have resisted. The Allies were no French Napoleon against whom Spanish *guerrilleros* could or would rally. If the war victors had said go, the regime would have collapsed. The decision was a close call. In the end the Allies did and said nothing. In 1946 the United Nations condemned the Franco regime, refusing to recognize its legitimacy. But the cold war had already begun. When Eisenhower made an official visit to Franco in 1953 to negotiate air bases and two years later Spain was admitted to the United Nations, Spain's diplomatic isolation was formally over, and Franco was assured there would be no diplomatic or military move to restore democracy to Spain.

"What are you reading?" Vigneras asked me, noticing *Mariana Pineda* on the table.

"An early play by Lorca."

"I'm bored in the *parador*. Can you lend it to me? I'll bring it back in two days, on Sunday, the day before I leave."

I have seldom been able to turn down requests for borrowing a book. But I said I couldn't lend it to him, since it wasn't my book to lend. It belonged to the *alcalde*.

"That fool? I met him my first night in town. What's he doing reading Lorca? Don't worry, I'll get it back to you."

"I'm sorry."

Vigneras insisted. I gave in.

"Be sure to bring it back yourself."

"I will."

Then, in one of those flashes of bad judgment, I failed to remove the drawing. After my reluctance to lend the book, to remove the drawing would have been an act of pettiness. I have often got into trouble out of politeness, which is a cover for cowardice. So Vigneras went off with the first edition and the drawing.

On Sunday we waited for Vigneras's return. It was an unusually windy day. Maybe the Greek *melteme* got lost and blew over to Andalusia. Despite the wind, I decided to read and write in the garden in order not to miss the historian's knock at the big wooden gate. Our landlord, don Paco, insisted the gate be kept closed and locked to keep out stray animals and poachers. As it got dark, we said he would surely come by supper. There was no knock. I went down the road as far as the village, looked around, and came back. The next morning before breakfast I was at the *parador*.

"The American, he left two days ago, on Saturday."

"Did he leave anything for me?"

"Nothing."

"Ask the maid."

"The maid is my wife."

The owner came back with some American magazines taken from the trash. He was pleased to give me the magazines.

"Nothing else?"

"Nothing. Hold on. I remember. My little son tore up some old worthless books the American left behind. We threw them in the fire, since when he got through playing with them, they were a pile of loose pages."

I went to the fireplace. It was clean.

"You're getting on my nerves," the *dueño* said, impatiently. "If that cheap little book was so important, why didn't you pick it up yourself before he left? I throw trash away every day. Is this a library? *Me cago en Dios.* (I shit on God.)"

Morelo didn't believe a word of my story.

Six months later I ran into Jean Vigneras in Tangiers. He told me that he had come to the *finca*, knocked, and we probably couldn't hear his knock because of the wind. He had to leave a day or so earlier and left the book with the *dueño* so we could pick it up.

The Picasso drawings disappeared but were not lost—except to me. In the instance of Lorca, I was the destroyer.

The Boy with the Golden Voice. The theater was packed. The village was there. Josefa was with us. No guard was necessary, and she had to see her Justo perform.

The crowd was very silent. I expected noise, but within a few minutes of the theater's filling up, talk disappeared and the farm workers sat back like a lump, waiting. I could not imagine they had any life in them and was disappointed.

The first number, however, woke the *labradores* (field workers). An old man, a regular with the troupe, danced a flamenco *alegrías*. He was not very good and he missed his steps. This audience knew its art and started to jeer. Then it booed, clapped, and the old man, who was looking up fearfully from his dancing duties, finally stopped struggling, looked back at the *público,* and walked off the stage. The old man was followed by a female dancer, about forty, who had eaten a lot of bread and sweets in her life. She was a good professional gypsy dancer and she glared fiercely into the audience as she stamped fire out on stage. If the *público* had been unkind to her, she would have bitten its head off.

When the fire lady finished, Justo came out in glaring white trousers, shirt and vest, and black Andalusian *sombrero*. He had his supporters, we among them, and we shouted "Justo!" Justo was too professional to smile. He began to dance, intense, slow, and clumsy compared to the professional who preceded him. But all his force went into his own way. He was neither flaring nor fully traditional, but himself. I think in a freer, even more corrupt period in which tradition altered, his way could be accepted as cool and superior. I liked to see Justo dance. I was corrupt. The gypsy received a decent applause and was not unhappy with his village reception. After all, only Justo had been asked to join the roving company for that evening.

The Spanish word *olé,* from Arabic "Allah," I thought was reserved for the *corrida*—the bullfight. It is not. Allah is everywhere.

We were waiting for the *niño con la voz de oro.*

In this case the *niño* (boy) was really *niño,* about thirteen years old. His mesmerizing voice was changing, so he was part man and still part angel. When he came out on stage, the crowd came totally awake in a new silence. He was known to them. He began. The boy was singing the grief of centuries. Lorca caught it in his best of books, *The Poem of the Cante Jondo,* in which he has a poem about Juan Breva, who sang deep with the voice of a girl, blind behind a smile:

Juan Breva had
the body of a giant
and voice of a girl.
Nothing like his trill.
It was pain
singing
behind a smile.
He evokes lemon groves
of Málaga asleep.
In his lament are
flakes of sea and salt.
Like Homer he sang
blind. His voice had
a speck of lightless sea
and crushed orange.

When the Almuñécar boy sang his first notes, the silence turned
into a hush. John of the Cross in the "Spiritual Canticle" says *la
música callada* (the music of a silence). It is precisely that music
we hear in Fray Luis de León's country retreat and in the Tang
dynasty Buddhist poet Wang Wei when Wang goes to Deep
South Mountain by himself and shares his aloneness with a few
friends:

Seeing all this I hope to leave the peopled world.
Across the water in my small cottage
at year's end I take your hand.
You and I, we are the only ones alive.

So art in its aloneness gives us that union of sound. When the
niño hit the high note, there was a tremendous oneness, a harsh
thundering *olé*, as the somnolent crowd woke into their scream
of alert communion.

Yet there was no bombast, no rhetoric, no Beethoven's Ninth

making crowds collectively joyous. This was the boy, the single artist, and for twenty minutes the earth of Andalusia turned on his song.

Who has heard must still hear.

The crowd with its poverty and humility (that is lost too, except in memory) and its centuries of art tradition was rich that evening. They were cruel to the old man, good to the boy. It was a satisfied *público* when it left its artist.

As we left we met for the first time an American couple, about our age, who were living about half a kilometer to the east, in a small house directly under a cliff and by the water. He had a motorcycle, a real one, and she had her weaving and books. They were Americans from the West Coast. We said we would see each other. That was the beginning of something I would never see end. It was initiated then, though neither they, nor I, knew what it was, and we were only the beginning actors, whose role was small, but critical, for at that moment the seeds of an ordinary passion and obsession began.

As we walked back, the night of Andalusia lay on our necks. I held Helle's hand tight. We were there. And our shared life in Spain was eternal because it was transient. Its timelessness was not the repeating endless afternoons of Machado's poems but the *now* of a year in Spain—a now limited by approaching forces, a now enduring only in memory. Greece would be personally repeated. Andalusia would be once. But Andalusia on its own, for purely commercial and political reasons, had a shorter life as we knew it, independent of us and our return to it. Not we but *it* disappeared. The coast of so many invasions was near the end of its millennia. It was not invaders and settlers from Carthage, nor Athens, Rome, Vandals, Visigoths, Moors, or the reconquering Catholic Kings of Castile and Aragón. It was a prosperity of invading Spaniards and foreigners, an architectural blitzkrieg of highway and condo, which in a decade would transform, beyond return, that long historical coast into another Miami strip of the world (the *Costa Brava* up north fell about the same time). In Greece at least the obscure island I still inhabit hangs on.

Came the friends. For the first months our visitors were from the village. That was best. There was someone every day—children, workers, small store-owners, the pharmacist's two daughters, and Justo, Cuevas, Morelo. After Vigneras there was Bruce Mill Holland, an American yogi playwright and film scriptwriter, who stayed with us a while; and a French painter and his wife with whom we went on painting trips.

Laurie Lee and his wife showed up one morning on our sunny terrace. We were already linked through Robert Payne. In Paris, Payne told me the most romantic story I had heard. Laurie Lee, forty years old, an English writer known for his poetry and travel memoirs, whose book of poems *The Sun is My Monument* was featured in *Life* (as was Gary Snyder's poetry and ecology), went to a performance of the Sadler's Wells Ballet. During the performance he was smitten by a young dancer exactly half his age, waited at the stage-door entrance, and when she came out, saying nothing, he swooped her up in his arms, placed her in his waiting car and drove off. They were married a few weeks later. Laurie and his dancer wife, Dottie, were having coffee with us.

Laurie had a long history in Spain. As a young man Laurie Lee had gone around pre–Civil War Spain, playing a violin in the streets to make his way. Then he fought with the Republic. When he returned to Spain in 1952, he also passed through Almuñécar and found us out in the Rancho Chico. Now he was not here as a fiddler, a soldier, but a poet with his wife, looking. He and Dottie brought sunlight to an already very sunny region. Stories, humor, warmth. I was immediately very fond of them. I told them so.

"You just came, and you're leaving. You're killing us."

"Spain has a violent soul. We're conforming."

"Not conforming. To me you're just dreamy, dreary idiots," I said. "Like honeymooners. How is it you look so happy? Did you bump off a few *guardias*?"

"We got our hands on only one today," Dottie apologized. "They were shy when we came near and they ran away."

"Maybe tomorrow?"

"Tomorrow will be better," Laurie assured us.

Laurie and Dottie did look like honeymooners. Or recent lovers.

"By the way," I asked Laurie, "is Robert's story true about your sweeping this lady up gallantly from the stage door and marrying her into submission?"

"We all have our failures," Laurie said. "You can see what a mistake it was."

"Yes, I see clearly. I agree. Dottie made an irremediable error."

"Thank you for seeing what a monster I have to run around Spain with," Dottie protested.

"My pleasure," I said.

Laurie Lee's writing has an unusual vision. He sees fine detail and an elemental sun feeding that detail with energy. Behind the scene rules a delicate sensibility. He is a lucid miniaturist, both in form and observation, as Nabokov is in fiction. Like Louis MacNeice and Stephen Spender in Greece, Lee belonged to a clan whose membership he earned by his writings. Laurie mentioned that MacNeice and Payne had told him to look me up if he was in southern Spain. That gesture was the friendly clan keeping us together.

As a young American I felt comfortable with diverse circles of writers—though most at ease with Greeks and Spaniards. I didn't care whether or not I shared the same language with a writer. The feeling and recognition were there—or were not. Yet it was also crucial to be with people struggling to learn the writer's speech. I fight with English, trying to learn it each day. Is this line right?, I ask. Each sentence is a possibility, a chance. Shaping the awkward ones into something better redeems. Of course words don't work, are finite, are never the object or idea they speak, but I'm never jaded in the struggle. How can I be jaded since I can't win? My confidence with lines is growing. But I have never escaped, nor wish to, from the notion of the learner.

Being an enthusiast and controlling it poorly, I suppose my passion for literature and my cottage of insecurities have served me well. I can very easily be the hermit, lock myself up for weeks, see no one—or be months apart from any connection with club or literary friends—and work solely on the page. That hermitage of writing is a joy. At least mine. Of course there is the unconscious notion that the words will reach a secret reader, and that hope makes the isolation deeper and good.

Now, after six months of disconnection, to talk to a poet working in English was a treat. It was buoying.

"What are you working on?" Laurie asked.

"A sequel to the book that came out in Athens. I write from my life in Spain. Only here, however, am I finding an idiom for recording Greece. I've also been writing songs, plucking out the melodic line on a guitar. Have you written songs?"

"I played the fiddle. Most of my poems are songs, I think. It's true of me more than other poets."

"Yes, I hear the lyrics."

"Some critics think I'm too lyrical, too beautiful. I'm not. It's my way. What else are you working on?"

"Antonio Machado. Since we're in Spain, and I already did some poems from Antonio Machado in my first book, I'm trying to do a full book of Machado translations. New Directions sent a letter asking to see the finished manuscript." (New Directions said no, but later took my Saint John of the Cross book. It was appropriate, since when Machado lived in Segovia, on the Street of Abandoned Children, just below his window and down the slope were buried most of John's limbs.)

As we were talking it also came out that Helle and I were polishing a draft of *The Other Alexander*, the novel we translated from Greek, and that we had done a batch of poems from Angelos Sikelianós.

"Give me a copy of the Sikelianós. I'll send it to a friend at the BBC."

"Sure, I'll type one out for you."

Before the year was up, while we were still in Spain, the Angelos Sikelianós poems were broadcast in London.

I look back with strange nostalgia to that easy process of writing and publication. Now I take my work, which a Toshiba laptop writes for me, and drop it in the mail. No gentle friend to hand-carry things. Of course networks exist today, and will always. But the gentleness is largely gone. Everyone is an eager professional. And personally, I am never free of the anxiety of time. As I face a messy mountain of pages, though I'm quick and lucky to be doing literary work I care for, I have forgotten calm. And there is never time. In Spain there was. Time to learn by writing, time to read books unrelated to what I was working on. Could I today read *Anna Karenina* as I did in Almuñécar? There was time to make copies, slowly, and make blurry carbons. I shouldn't beef. But it was just as intensely exciting then, and there were no watchdogs of the brain, taking nips out for hours, days, and weeks ill-spent.

After Laurie and Dottie departed, I remembered Gerald Brenan's memoir, *South of Granada,* where he describes his life in villages of the Alpujarra and talkative madames in Almería's bordellos. The same Brenan was to write a major volume on the life and poems of Saint John of the Cross. In his memoir, the author, who was then a young man living south of Granada, recalls a 1923 visit by Leonard and Virginia Woolf. About Virginia Woolf, he speaks with disturbing appreciation: "I want to emphasize Virginia's real friendliness on this occasion and the trouble she took to advise and encourage me, because her recklessness in conversation—when she was overexcited she talked too much from the surface of her mind—made some people think that she lacked ordinary sympathies." In the end, after some self-deprecating remarks about his own self-centered isolation, he speaks with resentment about scant treatment as "their intellectual equal." Brenan began living in the white island of unknown southern Spain three decades before our stay and remained there much of his life. I admired him as much as I regretted his disappointment in the friendship of writers. Friendship in the arts is the deep family. It is hope as it is reason. For him then, as for so many today, that communion is fencing for position. The trade neurosis of writers over station is Brenan's when he concludes, with undisguised disappointment and bitterness: "Virginia had a strong sense of the continuity of literary tradition and felt it a duty to hand on what she had received. She was also intensely and uneasily aware of the existence of a younger generation who would one day rise and sit in judgment on her. It may be, therefore, that she thought that my strange way of life and my passion for literature showed that I might have something to give. If so, however, both she and Leonard decided a few years later that they had been mistaken."

In the pharmacy I ran into Misty, the woman living with the other American somewhere up the coast.

"Hello, how are you?"

"Lonely."

"How's that?"

"Matt's taken his moto and is off in France?"

"Is he coming back?"

"I suppose so. I think he has a woman there."

"You're alone in the house then."

"The authorities are so concerned they have stationed a Civil Guard about two hundred yards from my house, I guess to protect me. This tall guard, with all his weapons, comes at night and stands on the cliff over the beach."

"Is it scary?"

"No. Just lonely. Why don't you drop by?"

"I'd like to."

We walked out of town together, saying goodbye at our gate, and she kept going. Misty was wearing sandals, a light blue skirt; she moved away like a dancer. It began then. I wanted to go to her house. I wanted to very much. I didn't and regretted that I had not. Even today it is easy to invent the next hours of the sensual visit I was rehearsing then, again and again. It didn't matter that I never went, but Helle was away for a week in Granada and during the week I made no visit to that unknown house under the cliff.

From foreigners we found out that in Tangiers, a free-market city not yet incorporated into Morocco, the banks gave you the commercial value of the dollar at seventy pesetas, rather than thirty-two, the in-country tourist rate. It was legal to bring 5,000 pesetas into Spain, a sum we couldn't spend in six months. So I went to Tangiers to change dollars and double our stay in Spain. I took a bus to Algeciras, where Molly Bloom said yes, yes, and then the ferry to Tangiers.

On the ferry I met colorful Sean, an Irish Jew who was running away from his wife in Dublin. Within minutes he pulled out a wallet photo of a whore in Seville.

"She cared for me."

"That's what you think."

"My wife made scrambled eggs the day after our wedding for supper. And it went on that way. I put up with it. But when my father-in-law socked me, I left. The two of them swore at me. That I could take, but when he socked me, I left."

Tangiers was a city of the Europeans and the Casbah. The French and other Europeans lived in the European section. Berbers, Moors, and many Spaniards were in the Casbah. The Zócalo Chico reminded me of Mexico, except that the smell of kef, a hemp narcotic stronger than marijuana, was in the air. Kef was legal and available at all kiosks. In the Casbah, usually next to the whorehouses, there were tiled stores with open doors where men, usually older ones, sat on elevated tile platform benches smoking their kef pipes.

I had to wire New York for money that should have come through in four or five days. In the Casbah I found a hotel room. At night there was a strange singing, which I suspected was rats. The landlady said it was swallows singing in the attic, but one morning when I woke up to find a rat jumping out of my shoe by the bed, I thought it best to find another room. I wandered that city from street to street. The Beat Generation was in and out of Tangiers in those years, though I ran into no one. Jack Kerouac I had seen in Paris, and in 1959 I invited him and Gregory Corso to Wesleyan for a weekend of readings; Allen Ginsberg I saw often, especially in China when I found a place for him for a week in the dormitory at the university in Beijing where I was teaching that year. But in Tangiers, on several stays, I met no one of that movement. I met their opposite. Other outsiders to responsible citizens of the middle class.

There was a cabal of wealthy titled Europeans who lived in tax-free Tangiers and formed a community, much like the group described in Thornton Wilder's book *Cabala*, where the wealthy are described in their elaborate decadence. I had two friends in this Tangiers society: a French baroness and a French count. The baroness I spent many days with. She took me for an afternoon at a walled-in mansion in the Casbah where our Arab host entertained us with talk and platter after silver platter of cakes, piled in high geometric shapes. His wife had rooms on the floor below. Because she was a woman, the wife of the family head could not be seen, even in a veil, by anyone other than one of the core family. The baroness also took me to the count's house, really a museum of small and massive sculptures he had collected in Burma and Cambodia in the twenties, when his comrade André Malraux was up to similar uncertain ventures (Malraux faced arrest for his art hunting). The count was a boxer, aviator, and archeologist. But most clearly, despite the photographs and other evidence of those other professions, what came through was his wonderful battered face, bald head, and iron build of the boxer with the cultivated gentle voice.

The baroness, in her late fifties, was svelte and elegant. I liked her speech, which was as shocking as she could make it. Her religiosity bothered me, however. I didn't take her on. One day, she asked me, "*Vous croyez en Dieu, n'est-ce pas?*" (You believe in God, no?)

"Non."

"What religion are you?"

"*Je suis juif.*" (I'm a Jew.)

"You killed our Lord." I recall that I said to her that she believed in a Jewish Lord. We saw each other another time. Why not? The baroness was not expressing an original idea.

I was obliged to stay some twenty days in Tangiers because there was a mixup, and I couldn't leave till the bank transfer came through. A pathetic cook, I bought an alcohol stove and ate boiled eggs, boiled potatoes, and hot cereal. I stayed healthy and was even proud of my stinking cooking. The odor was the raw alcohol. As I moved away from the cabal, I found increasing delight in climbing towers where one could order tea and look at the Atlantic Ocean into the sun mirror that extended into an infinity of beauty. There I sat for many hours, writing, thinking.

A Tower in Tangiers

Some place among onions of pain I lose
my nerve. Gone is the table in that tower
on the west coast of Africa I used
to climb to in the afternoons, where hour
on hour I'd smoke, sip tea, and look at ships
fall off the glass of fire into a throat
of stars. Back in my room a bone rat slips
along the walls, singing the infant note
of swallows as I boil the milky smell
of oatmeal on the green alcohol flame.
The green casbah moon floats over the square
like a knife patient in the dusk. I came
to climb jail steps to you. The Moors in prayer
yell from the towers. I climb, crazed, infidel.

As I was walking downtown, happy in this French-Spanish language city, where I regretted my ignorance of Arabic, I ran into Sean the Irishman. It was early after supper. Sean insisted I go with him to a Spanish whorehouse. So I went. He had been

the night before. I went in, as if I had entered the scene of
Cervantes' "Rinconete and Cortadillo" in which the whores and
thieves and constables all sit together and eat, at the end of the
evening, after those friends have gone through their nominal
daytime occupations. Sean got fixed up right away. There was
a blond woman, very pregnant, sitting at the far edge of the
bench. I nodded to her and she took me up to her room. She
was from Málaga.

"*De dónde eres?*" (Where are you from?)

"Almuñécar."

"Very good," she said, with her wistful smile. "But you are
American, no?"

"Yes."

"This one," tapping her stomach, "is also an American. A little
sailor." Then she showed me the dresser with baby clothes in
preparation. "Are you *soltero* (a bachelor)?"

"No. I'm married."

"What did you do? Fuck her?"

"Yes."

"Be easy with me," she said. "Do it on the side."

A Blonde in Tangiers

Sean is an Irish Jew crossing on the ship
from Algeciras. He's just dumped his wife.
He has a snapshot of a Seville whore he whips
out in a flash, "She loved me." His bum life
with his old bag is over when her father socks
him. "No more fried egg suppers." Sean pops by
one hungry evening, saying, "Buddy, shall we wet
    our cocks?"
We go. A new moon stabs the virgin sky
over the Zócalo. Veils and kef are in the air
as we stroll eager through the Casbah streets.
The *azulejo* parlor jammed with Berber men on benches

smoking dope. The whores next door
  on chairs.
"You first," says Sean. I choose a blonde. She treats
me fine. She's knocked up. Sideways I plop in.

When I left my head was different. In my uncertain life I went
with other prostitutes, but only with the woman from Málaga
do I have a strong feeling. Perhaps it was sexual when I thought
of it afterward, as I did. Of course it was sexual. It was also
another life. That is not to be read or told. Like the colors yellow
or blue it is only known when one sees the colors yellow or blue.
I like all kinds of people. I should not be embarrassed to say I
liked her realities and her. Her name I recall. Anita Hernández.

In recent years I have written about *clochards,* the homeless,
the executed. That is easy. To write about a whore might be
easy if it is not a personal confession. It is not very easy for me,
although it is also natural. How could I dare to write a selective
memoir? I suppose one can do anything one wants. As a writer
I can't ignore what began as a sensual force and exploration that
eventually split a marriage. With my stupid mouth, my wife was
to find her own way, only she never had the slightest sentiment
of guilt, which I envied her, and of course why should she have?
Her own eternities and purities did not admit those negative
emotions. A bit more than a decade after our divorce—which
friends say was our success—we are close as in those good years.
There is no division.

As spring came Helle and I finished our revision of *The Other
Alexander.* It was my only apprenticeship in fiction. (It was good
to do a work in collaboration, and it prefigured my chance, after
our children found their own voices, to do books with Aliki and
Tony.) I say apprenticeship, since literary translation is not only
its own activity but a school for the author's fantasy and craft.
And while in Andalusia I made the Seville-born poet Antonio
Machado (1875–1939) my closest poet friend for life.

I worked through translations from the poetry, which recorded childhood Seville memories, Madrid adolescence, Paris with Henri Bergson, and Soria in Old Castile as a rural school teacher where in 1909 the young poet married his love, Leonor, who was only fifteen. Two years later, his wife took sick during a stay in Paris, and the couple returned to Spain. When later I went to Soria, I met an old gentleman, present at Machado's wedding, who told me how he would see don Antonio pushing young Leonor in a wheelchair, high in the hills overlooking the Duero River, in the spring of 1912 when his bride was dying of tuberculosis:

Antonio Machado in Soria
(Jotting in a Copybook)

Walking in Old Castile the widower
(a young schoolmaster in his dirty clothes)
is gravely recreating Leonor
who left him in the spring. He almost loathes
the adolescent fields, merino sheep,
blue peaks, the first whitening brambles, plums,
her child voice in his ear—yet walking numbs
intolerable whispers of the bed. "To keep
your face, it's best to learn to wait. I will
know victory (or so the proverbs go),
and see an elm the thunder could ignite
and burn. Dry elm, a century on the hill,
still graced with leaves, my heart would also know
another miracle of spring and light."

After Soria, the widower went south to Baeza, in Andalusian isolation, and recalled a lost Leonor and the austere beauty of the old ruinous city and late highland spring; and then went north again to New Castile, to Segovia where he lived on the Street of Abandoned Children, overlooking the tomb of the dismembered corpse of the Spanish mystic Saint John of the Cross. In Segovia, his crippled landlady told me, he wrote through the nights, filling the wastepaper basket with drafts of poems which she dutifully threw away in the morning. After the Republic was declared in 1931, Machado went to Madrid and followed the Republic's fate through the civil war, going first to a Valencian farmhouse where he wrote most of his last poems, and then to his own death in Collioure, France, a month after flight into exile:

Antonio Machado in Segovia, Daydreaming as Usual of Soria, Baeza, and Sevilla

Our secret. One day we meet next to John
of the Cross's bones down in the cypress grove.
You're living up the hill in a small room on
the Street of Abandoned Children. You keep a stove
under the round table, a blanket on your knees,
and each night scrawl till dawn, throwing away
the papers with their dream of orange trees.
The maimed lady scrubs your ashes off the gray
floor. The toilet is a red clay bowl. Your cell,
Antonio, big dreamy, Chaplin-walking man,
has (like small Saint John's) a cot, chair, and field
around for solitude. The Andalusian
fountains laugh blue. Your eyes, a far moonbell,
are grave and funny like an orphan child.

A poet of memory, during that terrible war, Machado became a reporter of the moment, of the droning warplanes over the city. His sonnet "The Death of the Wounded Child" ends with a repetition of coldness (like Lear's "never, never, never, never"), a cold whose meaning escapes no one:

Again the hammer through the night is heard:
the fever in the bandaged temples of
the child. "Mother, look, the yellow bird!

215

and black and purple butterflies above!"
"Sleep now, my son." The mother near the bed
squeezes the little hand. "O flower of fire!
Who can freeze you, tell me, O flower of blood?"
In the bleak room a smell of lavender.
Outside, the round full moon is whitening dome
and tower across the city in its gloom,
Somewhere a droning plane one cannot see.
Are you asleep? O flower of blood and gold.
The windows clamor on the balcony.
O cold, cold, cold, cold, cold!

As Almuñécar March and April came, Helle's work defined
itself, I wrote the poems that were to be in a second collection,
and we were both itchy to leave our hermitage. Spring and full
moons make the blood crazy. We were glad to have an excuse
to go out for a few weeks on the road. Our Lambretta was right
for travel. It was our convertible. With its limited speed, we saw
everything as if we were walking.

Spring in Andalusia is a carnation and a butterfly. All the songs
say so. In the back hills away from the coast, outside Baeza and
Úbeda in the north of the province, spring shares with La Mancha
the true equinox of nature. There, on Spain's mountainous under-
belly, herbs come in adolescent shyness out of winter-moist earth
and emerge before the retreating snows. South of Granada, in
the Alpujarra's lofty villages where the Moors held out longest,
those African-white buildings—the fantasy of native sculptors—
are suddenly overgrown with flowers of fire and groves of citrus
and fruit trees in blossom. As in the Himalayas of Nepal, the
Alpujarra is high enough to have more snow than any region in
Spain, yet far enough south to grow citrus trees when the sun
is warm.

One popular song says

How beautiful my child is
when he is sleeping,

216

a butterfly in green wheat.
And the almond trees sob,
and the almond trees sob
with infinite joy.

When the almond trees sob with spring, it is also the season
all over Spain for those macabre processions bringing dread and
hope for salvation into the sighs of the faithful. That celebration
is the *Semana Santa,* the Holy Week. While the penitents march,
the soul is threatened with torches yet hears drops of heaven in
the mournful saeta songs. *Semana Santa* is followed by the sane
madness of the *Feria.* The *Feria* is Seville, especially Seville, and
there is none like it. We set out in the sweet rhetoric of Andalusian
spring for dread Holy Week in Málaga and the happy fair in
Seville.

But before we got to Málaga, we stopped in the small city of
Nerja. It was having its own *Semana Santa.* Before the hell and
rapture of the big city processions, why not a Holy Week in a
modest setting? There was to be a very brief parade. The floats
would come by under the balcony window of our hotel. The
floats carried a statue of the Virgin, who had many fanciful alluring names. The singers "threw *piropos* (flirtations)" at her through
their song, which was the *saeta,* meaning both "arrow" and the
African-wailing lament of the song to the Virgin.

As the elegiac bugles and drums sounded under our window,
and the priests, Civil Guards, and penitents in their tall hats were
passing by, there was a knock at the door. Two young gypsy
girls were there.

"*La niña quiere cantar su saeta a la Virgen.*" (The girl wants to
sing her *saeta* to the Virgin.)

"*Anda.*" (Go ahead.)

"*De su balcón.*" (From your balcony.)

"Come inside."

They came in, and the gypsy girl in her long polka-dot dress
went out on the balcony, and stood there, petrified with the

spirit of God. When they spotted her from below, the procession stopped and awaited her song. Everyone looked up at us. The gypsy girl opened her eyes, looked down, then dramatically cast her eyes up toward the dark night, opened her mouth, and out came resounding silence. The procession waited. She closed her mouth again, looked down at them all, took a breath, and this time leaned over the balcony. We were sure she would blast the Virgin of the Crystal Doves off its float with her passion. Nothing came out.

One penitent lifted his hood, saying, "*Pepe, la niña perdió la lengua.*" (Pepe, the girl's lost her tongue.) The comment resounded clearly in the otherwise silent street. It was a signal. The bugles and drums started up, and in their humble cacophony the parade moved on.

The two gypsy girls sat down on our bed, inconsolable, each crying louder than the other. The singer had tremendous lungs for weeping. We tried to comfort them. Helle put her arm around the singer of silence. They thanked us profusely, stood up together as sisters and, with their garments ruffling, slipped out the door.

We went to sleep with all the confusing music in our ears. We had strange dreams. There was a movement in the bed but no sign of bedbugs. The next morning we discovered our mutual crabs and made a quick stop at the pharmacy for powder before getting on the road to Málaga.

José Luis Cano, the critic, poet, and biographer of Lorca once told me how he spent the entire evening walking the beaches of Málaga with Federico García Lorca. Cano was about fifteen, the poet a young adult already the author of *El libro del Cante jondo* and other books of poetry. They had the moon, the walk, the conversation. Cano said to me he was walking with a prince of poetry. Cano's parents were so alarmed about his disappearance that night that they called the police to look for them. But the police had no idea where the two poets were, and so they were able to walk till dawn along the strand. Cano was to know Lorca well, but this first friendship was paramount. Knowing Cano for so many years, in many cities, each time I come near Málaga, on its western and eastern sides skirted by beaches, I cannot see the city without thinking of Lorca's and Cano's walk and guessing their words.

With regard to Málaga I also think of Vicente Aleixandre, who spent his childhood there, and recorded it in his *Shadow of Paradise,* and remember my last conversation with Jorge Guillén, who after three decades of exile in America had retired to Málaga. Guillén and I were talking on the phone. Our last conversation was about teeth. He was on the way to the dentist that afternoon. Guillén was the author of two great books: *Canticle* and *Clamor,* which he characterized by personal song and public reality. There was always both canticle and clamor, yes and no, light and pain, in his poems, whatever the division of books. The teeth was surely at the *Clamor* end, but as we talked, because of the indomitable enthusiasm of that poet of "being, and more being," he might have been going to the *Feria.*

> Ser, nada más. Y basta.
> Es la absoluta dicha.
>
> To be, nothing else. It's enough.
> It is the absolute happiness.

The religious spectacle in Málaga was enormous. It took over the city. At no moment did it stray from neo-medieval Christian pageantry, except for the Guardia Civil who walked alongside the priests and *penitentes.* Smoke of Inquisition hung low clouds of intimidating memory amid the masses of towering white hats. It persisted each night for five hours and for five days. Thousands of men, looking like slaves or executioners in hoods, marched, some carrying the enormous wooden floats that were glittering platforms of sentimental kitschy religious decorations and glorious Zurbarán austerities. Alongside the horizontal galley slaves were the men in white robes, the Klansmen in huge duncecaps.

Many carried torches. Doves floated above the floats. The Virgins were sculptures of young Spanish women. They lacked all Near Eastern reference. They were the statuary from the richest churches in Málaga. Each Virgin was an idealized daughter of the great landowners or breeders of prize bulls. Her glassy, often teary, eyes were at the same time rich in Murillo tenderness. The Virgins were truly virgins, robed in sumptuous modesty, with Eros protruding with cool fever from every fold of the dresses, in the hair, in the arms that were embracing the crowd.

To satisfy these Virgins with song, the *saeta* singers, the *cantaores*, were all along the route. They were masters of this gravelly and yet soprano range of Near Eastern melodies whose coarse, rapturous melismata carried the crowds into stilled wonder. The *saeta* startled by its ability to halt the huge procession. Here was an angel, usually a poor gypsy, with a traditional voice, singing his or her heart out for the holy parade. Or a worker, in his small beret, who climbed two meters up to the window of a building, and while hanging with one arm onto its *rejas* (wrought-iron bars), his eyes closed blind, directed his spirit and voice to the incarnation in wood and plaster of an ancient Jewish woman from Bethlehem, whose son was a rabbi and she a virgin. Or a woman in resplendent garments of the rich or poor, from a high balcony dispersing her fierce nightingale over the crowd.

Dawn

But like love,
the archers of saeta
are blind.

Over the green night,
the arrows
leave tracks of hot
lily.

The keel of the moon
breaks purple clouds
and the quivers
fill with dew.

Ah, but like love,
the archers of saeta
are blind.

Lorca

Each rendition came as a surprise in the torch-lit night, enhanced by the sudden stopping of a thousand marchers as the voice shot out of nowhere. I waited for other glories of the flamenco, but the *saeta* did not yield to likenesses. Lorca described all the *pasos* and songs in his *Poema del cante jondo*. The Lolas and Carmens of Lorca were as real as the avenue of marchers and singers, for in twenty lines he resumed their history. In his instance a word was a hundred images. Occasionally, some ordinary humanity would intrude into the theater and mystery when one of the galley slave float-carriers saw a pal and momentarily lifted his hood to shout "*Hola Pepe!*" Spaniards, for all their gravity and actors' pomp, always have a safeguard of plain realities when everyday speech and comportment take over and save us.

Procession

Through the tight streets
come strange unicorns.
From what fields,
from what mythological forest?
Nearer,
they look like astronomers.
Fantastic Merlins
and the Ecce Homo.

Sunday Morning in Fascist Spain

> Enchanted Durandarte.
> Orlando Furioso.
>
> Lorca

We watched for hours. The re-creation of heaven on the floats was never tedious. It was fearful, exhilarating. Finally, even the *saetas,* each one more impassioned and innovative than the preceding, moved into satiety. I loved them until I couldn't suffer them anymore. Helle and I breathed the medieval air, watched and bowed to austere yet colorful opera, felt the shadows of the three-cornered-hat *guardias* with their old rifles and clubs, were angered by the blueshirt Falange leaders and acolytes, went tense before the godliness of the priests in red, black, and blue velvets. We witnessed the night-lighted ideology and solemn beauty of regional religion, politics, and military.

At one moment I thought of the athletic, naked gods of Greece, whose bodies were their candid beauty. When my mind began to fantasize about how the Virgins would perform on a nudist beach on the Yugoslav coast, I realized that my profane spirit, which liked philosophy, was relishing yet crying out during the procession of decorated god idols. I had my own heroes—John of the Cross and John of Patmos—the sensual mystic who re-created the lovers of the Song of Songs and the dissident Jew of Ephesos who soared into filmic apocalypse in accord with other intertestamental apocalypses and noncanonical apocryhpha of that period of rebel faiths. With such a wandering mind, I knew it was time to edge away from those great voices singing to the beautiful and fearful floats.

We went to our room. The next day we would motor up and down alongside wheat fields and move to the candy-white city of Seville and its spring *Feria.* Having wandered in the Gobi, through market after market of the Silk Route in central Asia, I now hold some measure of comparison for the controlled beauty and passions that awaited in Seville's *Feria.* Seville, so European, so Moorish, Jewish, and Roman, would do very well along the Silk Route in central Asia.

That evening as we slept, there were neither bedbugs nor crabs. Clean fresh sheets. Above them, however, three feet over the dreaming blanket, were torches lighting the darkness and then the *saetas*, those songs of the poor becoming rich as they mesmerized, flattered, and battered the soul and guts of the crowd.

Morning on the road. Helle and I were birds. Rolling of course. It was a companion joy of the pícaros. We were open to any venture. Our immediate destination was Antequera, where the roads crossed for Seville. Then for the first time our Italian wheels gave out.

We pushed the scooter to a small village that luckily had a garage and a family of mechanics. It was impossible to know how many fathers and sons there were among the seven who tinkered with our vehicle, the first of its kind they had seen. They marveled. They were determined to understand its every labyrinth, and starting from the front wheel they took everything apart in search of the elusive noise. Nothing would escape their hands. All day they broke down the scooter until it looked like a pocket watch a child had picked apart and spread on the floor. They found the cause in the rear wheel, which was the last piece they disassembled. We ate with them, and by twilight we were ready to fly off. We did so, got a hundred meters from the shop when the culprit back wheel flew off. Helle fell off, unhurt, as the wheel rolled like an Italian ragazzo, impudent and independent, into the field where it finally lay down under a fig tree. The bike tipped on me, but I was also unhurt. Our friends came running after us. They had scarcely stopped waving goodbye when they came to rescue us. They put the wheel back on, tightened the bolts this time, and again we zoomed away.

As the year went by we saw Spain opening up, slightly. It was not dramatic yet, not the pace of China from 1984 to 1985 when in everything from personal dress to the kinds of publishable novels and showable paintings there was radical change. In another decade, Latin Americans would live in Spain's cities to write their novels in a peaceful, stimulating setting. But in 1952 Spain was not a visited country.

Sevilla during the *Feria,* however, was the exception. Its fame made it a place where not only Spain came to enjoy the spring fun, but continental Europeans, Americans, and English. There was electricity and a touch of madness in the air as in Hemingway's Pamplona of the twenties during the running of the bulls. But Seville was not the Basque country. Seville had its bulls but they didn't run them through the streets. Andalusians danced in the streets. They also had dances, *las sevillanas,* and their song. The *Feria* was a party, and when the people drank it was not a wild journey.

We were smart to have reserved a place with our schoolteacher. We spent scant time there, however, for during the week in Seville we slept little. At night we danced, some evenings till dawn. During the day there was the sun, the streets—one should walk in Seville as many streets as one can—and I loved merely to hear Spanish spoken by a *sevillano.* And still do. It has salt and *gracia.* Many good restaurants occupied side streets, closed to traffic, and the tables were scattered in the *callejuelas* so that to walk down those narrow streets you were walking through those outdoor restaurants and somehow participating in the feast.

While you walked in Seville, the women rode their horses. These were the beauties. For the most part, in miserably and hypocritically puritanical Spain, the women riders, with many flowers in their hair, were not wearing dresses (the permitted Spanish bathing suits then were more dresses than swimsuits). They wore men's riding outfits—black trousers with large silver buckles, and boots. Some of the best women flamenco dancers, the solo performers, danced in the same male outfit.

In the years I went to Spain I saw only two corridas. I will not see another. The last one was in 1962, in Baeza. El Cordobés fought. He was a nimble dancer, and I suppose brave, but had little chance to prove his courage since the bulls didn't care to fight, even when they were gored and stuck with banderilla arrows. So the crowd booed him. In Seville we went in the afternoon to see

Conchita Citrón, the Portuguese woman bullfighter who did all the rites of the matador on her white horse. It required extraordinary acrobatic coordination to race toward the oncoming bull, swerve her mount, and, at a four o'clock lean, jab the banderillas into the neck and shoulders of the bull. She didn't dismount even for the kill.

At night we went to the little houses, the *casetas*, where the city dance, the sevillanas, kept going till dawn and into the morning. The *casetas* are set up just for this week, to accommodate natives and invaders with tables for food and drink and wooden floors for noisy abuse. There is nothing like the dance at the Seville fair. The sevillanas do not require a life of preparation and professional training—unlike classical ballet or *alegría, bulería, seguidilla, farruca*. The latter formal flamenco dances, solo or as couples, are nominally regional folk dances, but, like their counterparts in Asia, require years of rigorous exercises and practice to achieve a modest mastery of basic steps. The *zapateado*, poorly translated as "stamping," with its infinite improvision and complexity, defines the dancer. A solo flamenco dance may last ten minutes, in which the feet are a percussion instrument, changing tempos and rhythms in the most subtle variations of volume, speed, and mood. It ends, often, in a smashing, erotic climax. The sevillanas (plural because it is danced in four "sets") had a court origin and were once a dance of the aristocracy. Today they are also danced by professional artists of the flamenco. But in a professional troupe, the sevillanas are an interlude of amusement, a mirror of its real life, which, like the *jota* up north, lies in its being danced widely by large numbers of people in Andalusia and Spain. They have the same national and popular function as the Greek *kalamatianós*. More than the *malagueño* or the *fandango*, sevillanas are the dance of Andalusia. And in Seville everyone, including cripples and the blind, dances sevillanas.

The sevillanas are performed by a man and woman, facing each other, in four sets, with a specific series of steps for each set. It includes the *zapateado* (stamping), as the partners come apart and turn sideways for a burst of footwork. The soul of sevillana is not in the feet, however, but in the movement of body and hands, in *las palmas* (the palms). Usually, both dancers have castanets. It is the hands that distinguish, and the best hands carry no castanets. The sevillanas are especially linked to their Asian past in the critical arm and hand movements.

Helle had great hands. The Spaniards loved to see the Greek dancing sevillanas. We had been instructed before going to Seville. (Not until a decade later in Madrid, however, did we study flamenco for a winter in a freezing basement studio down in the old *rastro*, with a one-legged instructor, Diego Marin, who was belligerently severe. I studied *alegrías*, and after a year I was at the beginning. Helle perfected her sevillanas.) In Seville we followed our partners. Knowing Greek dances helped us. We could perform the steps with some dignity and joy. I emphasize the joy, because the sevillanas are not religious, mystical, austere. You don't frown. You shout and laugh. And you swish about for hours, drink, and dance more, changing partners. In our case, improving a bit. The truth is that Helle, a natural dancer, danced superbly and there were not enough partners for her in the *casetas*. They all wanted to dance with the *griega*.

The sevillanas—with their brio, exhibitionism, controlled choreography of sweeping steps, *zapateado, palmas,* happy craze, and shouting—are not Norwegian, not French, Greek, or Italian. They are not Spanish or Andalusian. They are of Sevilla. And it is good to dance them there. And best to do so night after night for a week, at the *Feria,* at least once in your life.

We had been in Spain much of a year and had not been to Madrid. We had been *campesinos* before going to the capital. Yes, I wished to go the *rastro* and loaf around the old section where Lope de Vega, Cervantes, and Francisco de Quevedo had their apartments within a block of each other. Of the poets of Spain, Quevedo was the most tormented, the most offensive, and for me the most profound. In the Greek and Latin manner he was luridly obscene in his insult poems, dark in his meditations, and in those sonnets where nation and person were interchangeable, he saw sixteenth-century Spain and its empire as weary:

He Shows How All Things Warn of Death

I gazed upon my Country's tottering walls,
one day grandiose, now rubble on the ground,
worn out by vicious time; only renowned
for weakness in a land where courage fails.
I went into the Fields. I saw the Sun
drinking the springs just melted from the ice,
and cattle moaning as the Forests climb
against the thinning day, now overrun
with shade. I went into my House. I saw
my old room yellowed with the sickening breath
of age, my cane flimsier than before.
I felt my sword coffined in rust, and walked
about, and everything I looked at bore
a warning of the wasted gaze of death.

Quevedo I could read, but Vicente Aleixandre we could see. And so Madrid, at least on this brief trip, was only Aleixandre.

For a few years before and during the civil war, Aleixandre was sick. He was confined to a couch much of the day. His doctor kept him on a strict regimen of food and medicine. In his house on Calle Velintonia he said to me, "Because I was the sick one, I thought of the three poet friends closest to me, Federico, Miguel, and Manolo, I was the least likely to survive. And here I am and they're dead." García Lorca was executed, Miguel Hernández died of consumption in prison, and Manuel Altolaguirre returned to Spain after exile to be killed in a car accident on the murderous road through the mountains where Castile meets Andalusia. After seven early years of sickness, Vicente discovered that the doctor's diagnosis was wrong. As soon as he quit taking the medicines he got up from the couch and lived in good health till 1986, when he died at age eighty-eight.

Because of his earlier precarious health, Aleixandre was alone among the major poets in Spain who didn't leave for temporary or permanent exile. So he remained and was for the younger generation their model, hope, and constant support. The threats, punishments, and struggles with the ministries were recounted by José Luis Cano in *Cuadernos de Velintonia: Conversaciones con Vicente Aleixandre* (Velingtonia Notebooks: Conversations with Vicente Aleixandre). The book engraves a steel-gray picture of early Franco years and the efforts of Aleixandre, Dámaso Alonso, Cano, and others to outwit censorship and return some measure of quality and freedom to Spanish intellectual life and the arts. When Aleixandre was awarded the Nobel Prize for Literature in 1977 (which might have gone to equally worthy Jorge Guillén, who was still in exile), the committee selected Aleixandre in part because he had remained in Spain throughout, despite the government, and was there for its generations. We hear Aleixandre in "My Voice" from his early surreal book *Swords like Lips,* which now reads like a prophecy:

> I was born one summer night
> between two pauses. Speak to me: I hear you.
> I was born. If only you could see what agony
> is in the easy moon.
> I was born. Your name was joy;
> under a radiance a hope, a bird.
> Arriving, arriving. The sea was a throb,
> the hollow of a hand, a lukewarm medal.
> And now lights are finally possible: caresses, flesh,
>   horizon,
> meaningless talk
> turning like ears, snails,
> like an open lobe that wakens
> (listen, listen!) in the trampled light.

When we got to Madrid, I rang Aleixandre. We met in a restaurant. Tall, bald, handsome, Vicente had a natural kindness not blemished by shrewd intelligence and the lessons of survival and resistance in a duplicitous time that was to endure for thirty-six years of dictatorship (1939–75). He was a poet of consistent, varied, and extraordinary dimensions. Despite his natural discretion, his opinion on each issue, writer, and book was candid as it was original. Freshness and insight were his person and poems. No poet I have known or read has that combination of cosmos and pebble, of idea and dirt. He wrote a love poem and asked, "O fish friends, tell me the secret of your open eyes, / of my gazing that will flow into the sea, / holding up the keel of distant ships." With the moon he was an intimate as he was with breakfast or a lover's lips. Sometimes I thought of Aleixandre as the poet of "or," the word by which he linked worlds, as others might use "like" in a simile or no word at all when slipping into metaphor.

When you read Aleixandre the warm fantasy persists in energy of the word, the image, and the thought. You don't get off easy.

We began as a continuation. It was that way thereafter. When he signed his recent volume, *Shadow of Paradise,* the inscription was "On the first day of friendship. Affectionately, Vicente Aleixandre. 26 June 1952." It was—and impossible to guess then—a prophecy for three decades.

I suppose Vicente Aleixandre was the most loved literary figure in Spain in the postwar period, as was Lorca, the *enfant terrible* and fire of Spanish letters, before the war. The poet from Velingtonia Street developed a special affection for my daughter Aliki, and when an edition of her book *The Real Tin Flower* was being prepared in Spanish he wrote a piece for her, remembering her as a five-year-old child who used to climb all over him:

. . . .

Aliki was the big little one.
Gracefully she ascended on one flank,
first reaching a knee, then climbing to my chest
where she rested a moment;
   then with new Alpine drive
she shimmied up to a shoulder and there,

as if what she described from that height
   were the universe,
she extended her gaze all about
and, bending her arm of over the peak,
rested her small hand in her hand
where she remained ultimate, supreme on the mountain
   summit.

. . . .

Today I do not see her but I feel her.

. . . .

Aliki, lift your hand, open it. Where do you
come from?

And there, great, immense, against the horizon,
I see her raise her arm and trap impossible birds,
surprise blinking stars, catch summers, steppes,
furies, sounds, tiny colored butterflies
or simply the intact aroma of the world.

An example of the comraderie of that generation is the bor-rowing of lines from each other, as in the Aleixandre poem "Life," which begins with "*Un pájaro de papel en el pecho*" (A bird of paper in my chest). Jorge Guillén puts the "bird of paper" in a poem; Lorca uses the first two lines of "Life" as the epigram for his poem "Streets and Dreams" in *The Poet in New York*. Whatever and all the two first lines have in them will change, for this poem is alive as any that was composed:

> A bird of paper in my chest
> says the time of kisses hasn't come.
> To live, to live, the sun crackles invisibly,
> kisses or birds, late or soon or never.
> To die a tiny noise will do. . . .

When I saw Aleixandre last, in 1985, the name of his street, Velintonia (after Wellington), had been changed to Calle de Vicente Aleixandre. A herpetic infection in the cornea had left him blinded in one eye. He published in his late seventies a volume that I liked as an entity, as a sequence, perhaps more than any single volume (which I say diffidently, caring so much for earlier books). That book is *Poemas de la consumación* (Poems of Consummation)—*consumación* meaning "consummation" and "consumption." The title and notion came from many sources but mainly from Saint John of the Cross's *"todo me voy consumiendo"* (and I burn myself away).

"Guillén keeps writing poems," I said. "He said he has insomnia."

Vicente, discreet yet truthful about his old friend Guillén, said, contrasting his attitude toward his writing, "My work is completed. I have peace of spirit, but not of mind, because of this facial herpes. I need peace to work."

"Since *Poemas de la consumación* is so good, I find it hard to think you are unwilling to write any more."

"Well, I do compose poems, but I don't record or remember them."

"How's that?"

"I compose them when I am dreaming. You see I am at peace then, but I don't remember them when I wake. I've tried, but I don't remember. But I do know and remember clearly the process of writing them."

"Are they any good?"

"Of course."

"But since you don't remember them, how do you know they are good. You're just being arrogant."

"You are cruel."

"*Mira Vicente,* since you know the process is going on, why don't you imitate it while you're awake and compose poems called *poemas no recordados* (unremembered poems)?"

Vicente, magnificent as always, was hesitant. "I'm not sure I can do it."

"Of course, you're not sure. You're not that arrogant. Just write some unremembered poems."

"Maybe I'll try," he said without conviction.

These were our last words, before the goodbyes. Vicente died in the course of the year. His voice is always here.

After we returned to Almuñécar, we made plans. In student days in Paris, Arun Mitra, a Bengali poet, friend, and classmate at the Sorbonne, had convinced me that I should go to India and get lost. He was right of course. And while we had a little money, it would have been the best idea for us to go there immediately. To India. In France and Spain I knew the languages, and in Greece I learned. But to go to India without being able to speak to the common people or read the poetry was wrong. So we would not go to India. I would first try to learn Bengali, and so I wrote to and was accepted at the School of Oriental and African Studies of the University of London. Perhaps later I could get a fellowship for India, with the credential of the language. Since the independence of the colonies, Oxford and Cambridge didn't teach modern Indian languages—there were no English colonels and colonists to train. SOAS was the place.

I would also like to have gone to China, but in 1952 that was out of the question. I should have studied Chinese then, in their wonderful program, which included Arthur Waley, but I thought I probably couldn't get into China for twenty years. Exactly twenty years later, in 1972, during the enthusiastic worst of the Cultural Revolution, I did go to China—invited there as a "guest of China" for having translated a book of Mao's poems. Even in 1952, however, I had misgivings about not throwing myself into Chinese. Yet with its thousands of characters, Chinese is a life's devotion. Though I did later put a few years into its formal study I'm glad Chinese didn't become my life. There are too many temptations in the world. How, for example, could I have spent years reading and writing about intertestamental pseudepigrapha and Gnostic scriptures (in preparation for *The Other Bible*) if I'd become a real sinologist? I am a dispersed man, and am glad. One friend, Scott Sanders, said to me that there was a pattern to all the apparent scattering. There is. I just have a different bag, with personal labels. Why not lump the Gnostics and Sappho and Wang Wei and John of the Cross and Billy Budd together? They are fine company. How lucky to have all those real friends. There are more. Can one have lived in our century without being comrades with Cavafy, Stevens, and Borges?

So, as a wanderer I spent a year at SOAS, as a full-time student in Bengali and Indian studies, and learned the tongue pretty well. Helle studied Byzantine literature at Kings College and was full-time in the School of Arts & Crafts, which, despite its hokey name, was London's very good art school with excellent painter instructors. The next year I failed in getting a Fulbright for India (in those days, having studied abroad disqualified me, for awards were for those who had not had the chance to study abroad). Instead I got drafted. The U.S. Army classified me, of all things, as an "oriental expert," and put me in a secret ARA program where I was to overhear radio messages in Bengali. But I was soon kicked out of ARA, since my Greek wife was not an American citizen and I couldn't pass the security clearance. These were McCarthy times. I forgot Bengali very quickly.

Many plans. It seemed that this Andalusian country of endless afternoons was to become English evening, the early winter darkness of the north. Soon we would leave Eden. Time—for poetry, painting, reading, voyage—would never be so kind to us again. Outside of Eden time began again. As I write this in my concrete office at 1:00 A.M., I am taking the time to relive these memoirs. And it is an intoxication to do so. I hope some of you are there with me. But I think back with anxiety. On my other desk is a pile of mail and manuscripts—they're good friends too—which make me feel guilty for my hours. I am weary of time squeezing me. I hope it will let up. My daughter, Aliki, who is the poet love of my life, called an hour ago to make my complaint. Why? Why is Eden today so stingy? Age should have given me wisdom. And time.

Before the autumn in London we each had duties. Mine took me to Marseilles. Coming back I would stop at Prades in the

Pyrenees for the Casals Festival. Then Helle and I would go for a while to Morocco, where we would be with William Bird, Ezra Pound's printer in Paris who had printed the first collection of the *Cantos, A Draft of XVI. Cantos,* 1925. Bird had retired to Tangiers, where he had a little commerical printing shop. He showed us all his vellum-bound books and gossiped about the American authors of the Paris twenties. An old friend of Pound, he was in the States when Pound was being arraigned for his trial for treason. "What can I do for you, Ezra?" he kept asking him. Pound insisted on talking about nineteenth-century economic policies in America that had ruined the country. His lawyers couldn't keep him on track either. Obsession, if not "insanity," which ultimately kept him out of prison, was not incorrect, Bird said. While in Tangiers, we spent a day in Fez among the three ghettos of Arabs, Jews, and French. In the market were barbarically beautiful pieces of jewelry, made of amber, silver, buttons, animal teeth, strung on heavy, soiled cords.

When we got back to the continent there was a strange adventure. In Paris, in a small hotel on the Left Bank, we were sound asleep, when there was a firm, rapid knock at the door. I opened. Two policemen asked me to identify myself. When I had done so and they were satisfied that I was the true husband of Helle, one of them soberly announced, "*Monsieur, votre motocyclette a été volée*" (Sir, your motorcycle has been robbed). It was necessary to identify my identity in order to be certain that the driver was not Helle's drunken husband, racing off in a huff.

"*N'ayez pas peur.* (Don't be afraid.) The thief will soon be apprehended."

The matter came to the attention of the police after a wild drunk, who had been refused a room at the hotel, walked out, spotted my motorbike, wrenched the handlebars until the thin, protecting chain broke, and then flashed away (Lambrettas had no built-in key lock) on my bike.

A few blocks into his adventure the thief fell, cut his forehead slightly. Then he ripped off his shirt, which was getting bloody, and continued his mission, whatever it was. When he was racing down the Champs Elysées, down the wrong side of the street, bare-chested and dripping blood all over his stomach from his very small wound, he smashed into a cyclist, toppled over, smacked the cyclist in the jaw for being in his way, again raced off, and finally skidded to a halt in the arms of about five policemen. When I got the call to come identify my vehicle, they took me to a basement jail where a drunken Irishman—drunk he explained to me in order to give him courage to ask a French woman to marry him—was standing behind bars, shoeless and shirtless. He immediately told me he was raging hungry and could I get him a sandwich, and being silly and surprised by his silver tongue, I ended up chasing down a sandwich for him.

An hour later, a bit more sober and slightly repentant, the Irishman settled, for small sums, with three civilians whom he had run into during his tour of Paris. The pedestrians were more amazed than angry. At one moment in the informal brief he won the sympathy of the presiding officer when he drew from his wallet a battered newspaper obituary about his father. Its impact was lessened, however, when an official noticed that the devoted son's clipping was dated seven years earlier.

After Marseilles, Paris, and other "errands," Helle was in Spain, and I paused a week in Prades in French Catalonia. Then a few days after the festival, I took a train back to our Andalusian village, where Helle and I packed our things. We wrapped her paintings in a roll, which we carried with us, safely tied on the baggage carrier rack along with a few clothes, and sent the rest of our books, papers and belongings—no Picasso drawings—to London, where they were waiting at South Station when we arrived.

Before setting out from Spain to London, though, there had been a week in Prades and music.

A journalist friend from Rome, John Forest, had asked me to come to help him out in Prades. John told me that Casals, just a few months before, for the first time since the civil war, actually went to Barcelona for an afternoon to attend the funeral of an old friend. His presence in Spain was hushed up so that neither side, the Spanish government or Casals, its opponent, would be perceived as having taken a public position. This was far different from the immediate postwar period when a Spanish general threatened that he would cut the hands off the famous cellist if he were to set foot again in Spain.

In 1951 the Casals Festival had been held in Perpignan, a lovely city in French Catalonia. Now it was in Prades, a village some thirty kilometers to the north, at the foot of Mount Canigo. The concerts themselves were not in the village festival headquarters but in a medieval chapel halfway up the mountain. I took a room in a schoolteacher's house and the first evening walked up to the chapel where a rehearsal would take place. These were the most interesting days of the festival. All the performers were there, and most of the recordings were made during the days of rehearsal. I had a job—it didn't pay but it gave me free entry—which was to keep people quiet during rehearsals. The "people" usually meant other performers.

It took an hour to reach the chapel. It was much better than taking one of the free vans. The region was beautiful. Wild, tame, green, rocky, meadowed, forested. Canigo leaned over into Spanish Catalonia. France was a free country, and this feeling of freedom was palpable, even by the fact that we were on the French side of the range. Only four or five of us were there to hear the rehearsals. Our lone presence among the empty seats increased our rapt involvement in the music. That nineteenth-century German music was rising from this mountain on that night, from an old chapel high on French Canigo, was sweetly implausible. No more implausible, I suppose, than that an American Jew and a Greek Byzantine were living together on the southern coast of Iberia. Our century of natural conjunctions of opposites is reassuring. Of course I always thought that putting old Homer and the Bible together was impudently smart and accounted for most of Western culture and its footnotes. Helle and I were its complicated annotation.

The following afternoon I was at my post. Joseph Szigeti, the

Hungarian violinist, was recording in the chapel. Earlier he had been very nervous, disturbed by a noisy bird that liked the sound of his violin and was flying in circles inside the chapel. There was no one to hush until two black sedans drove up and the stars spilled out, loud, energetically talking stars. Eugene Istomin, Dame Myra Hess, Mieczyslaw Horszowski, Alexander Schneider, Jennie Tourel, and Rudolf Serkin descended. What could I do? I recognized most of them. At the center was a short, older man who looked like the Prades baker, and he was certainly a Catalan. He was making the most noise, and with his kindly and amused face he seemed the least forbidding. My strategy was that if I could quiet one, the others would understand and submit to silence. So I went up to the old fellow and shushed him. He smiled at me, and I will not forget those fully opened laughing eyes. And again I shushed. I felt curiously uneasy, reached into my pocket to look at the program, and there, on the cover, in honor of his seventy-fifth birthday, was Pablo Casals, the local baker. I faded back and thereafter voluntarily surrendered my post as music cop. In retrospect we had an intersemiotic discourse. And it was the only conversation I had with the maestro Casals. I shushed and he laughed.

That evening a bunch of us ate together in the schoolhouse where beds were set up for the less wealthy among us. In our group was Josette Belzon, whose mother had offered the summer-empty schoolhouse for the festival. We talked. Josette was a classical southern French beauty. She would have denied the certainty of the "southern," because as she soon explained to me, she had never known who her father was. Her mother would say nothing.

"*Pourquoi?*" (Why?)

"I don't know why. So I don't know whether he is alive, dead, in France, in Australia. That's why it drives me crazy."

"Crazy?"

"Well, yes. When I was eighteen I was placed in a hospital. Some of the inmates had tuberculosis. And one man, he was an engineer, had sex with me."

"How are you *now?*"

"Yes, I'm better, but I'm talking to you about it."

Josette's mother came in for a few minutes to see if we needed anything. Josette stayed on her missing father a while.

"Your mother's here."

"That's all right. She won't let herself understand. That silence is the way she is when I speak of him."

"Shall we go up? *Tu es prête?* (Are you ready?)"

Josette looked at me. We had fallen immediately into the *tutoyer* form, the familiar "you" address. In those more stuffy years that "familiarity" was unusual and a sign of intimacy. Today it would not be so.

We piled into a van and went up to the chapel. Again there were few of us at the rehearsal. Schubert's "Trout" swam for fifteen minutes. In the small talk between pieces, Casals was clowning. Then the musical athletes switched again to the serious mask. It was brilliant. I've moved away from most German music in recent years, preferring French, Italian, Spanish, and Greek, and avoiding big, bombastic orchestras. Bach had the good sense to like single instruments. In those times I was less fussy and could be carried away by the *Eroica.* But at Prades it was chamber music. I've never been a bigot about chamber music. We walked out of the chapel as high as the mountain.

And with a tremendous intimacy. We had hardly spoken. Yet, there were assumptions and so we began in the middle of the story.

There was enough moon for us to find our way. To be walking down the mountain through that night was a peak of serene intensity. The darkness was our shelter. In the Song of Songs the lovers climb the mountain to the lion caves. But in San Juan de la Cruz's "Spiritual Canticles," the bride speaks (Saint John takes the voice of the woman in his three major poems, including "The Dark Night of the Soul") and stunned by love goes indoors, into the the *interior bodega* (the interior cellers) of her love and comes out dazed in the light:

Deep in the wine vault of
my love I drank, and when I came
out on this open meadow
I knew no thing at all.
I lost the flock I used to drive.

He held me to his chest
and taught me a sweet science.
Instantly I yielded all
I had—keeping nothing—
and promised then to be his bride.

We walked and talked. I don't remember what we said. Yet I recall every word. The deeper the music of silence, the clearer it was.

"Where are you?" she asked.

"Here and happy."

"*Moi aussi,*" she said. She had my hand.

"I'm where I've never been."

"You are descending Canigo, and, yes, you have not been here before. Nor have we."

Josette spoke ordinary truth. It was easy. It was also true that wherever I was, in time, it was once, and has not been repeated. Life was there and cannot be removed either.

It was. And so it is.

San Juan had words. He didn't invent the Spanish language or even the words he used to describe his night, since his words came from his re-creation of the Song of Songs:

My love, the mountains and
the solitary wooded valleys,
the unexpected islands,
the loud sonorous rivers,
the whistling of the loving winds.

Sunday Morning in Fascist Spain

> The night of total calm
> before the rising winds of dawn,
> the music of a silence,
> the sounding solitude,
> the supper that renews our love.

When we reached a lower part of the mountain we went off the road into the fields. We took our clothes off. Even my watch. I entered her warmth. We stayed while the stars got brighter and brighter. We did not come down till a cow came near us. It was waking up for breakfast. We got dressed. I didn't find my watch. Time stayed there. And we walked down into Prades. Pablo Casals's favorite piece was the Catalan folksong "Song of the Birds," which he played in his own version, and which, like American spirituals, was the voice of his people:

Song of the Birds

> After Pablo Casals had taped the Song
> of the Birds, high on Canigo, we went
> by foot, from the old French convent, along
> the mountain rug of stars, down to the scent
> of wheat. We couldn't see. You held my hand
> because the trail was steep. Then in the grove
> we saw ourselves. Naked. By the command
> of natural soul, we lay down young and drove
> our blood. Our tongues were water, our eyes huge,
> earth an unknowing fire until the dawn
> of cows and village children screaming led
> us back. I loved you in our pure refuge
> against the law. The night was sun. Now gone,
> our virgin mountain is a lucent thread.

We woke in the afternoon and didn't leave our bedroom during the afternoon.

"*Pourquoi tu pars?*" (Why are you leaving?) I had no answer.

Why does one leave happiness, fulfillment? Futile to say what if. Time does not allow such distortions and, well, absurdities, since what *was* cannot be translated into *later* without indulging in deceptive romance. It was and so it is, it remains, then.

"*Je ne sais pas*"—I don't know." We were happy then, even the last day. Is the unexpected island not a lifetime?

There is no way to handle time. It's all we have, and all we have not. At that age I couldn't conceive of not leaving. I was leaving the mountain. It is impossible to sort out the confusions of love. It has happened to me a few times. This was not the love of absence, but of presence.

8

HIDING FROM

LANDLADIES

IN LONDON

OF THE

GREAT FOG

On the ferry to free England, the inspectors treated us with firm, official suspicion. In Spain the guards didn't think we would be a burden on the economy.

"Do you have your tickets to leave England?"

"Not yet. We're students. We're not leaving for a while."

"How much money do you have?"

I took out my travelers checks.

Then I thought briefly, maybe we should have gone to India. Since we never reached the subcontinent, it was, given that fact, a mistake. But we couldn't know that fact then, and it was not a mistake to have the experience of London. I'm sorry I've not returned. The vagabond I am took me elsewhere. Apart from Greece and Spain, the regulars, I discovered the atlas, and spent years in Latin America and Asia, and on certain peripheries— North Cape in Lapland, Cappadocia in central Turkey, Manaus in the Amazon, black Nubia in southern Egypt. I thought I had arrived when I went from place to place in the Gobi—especially in Silk Route Kashgar in Chinese Turkestan—the white island in the desert. In Tibet we arrived someplace else, at the end, with the Han Chinese leaning terribly upon the nation. Tibet gave me a dream. It was there my father came back, more clearly than he ever had since his death. The reality of place was so overwhelming, despite the fury we felt about the massacre of people and culture, Tibet, especially away from city and monastery, in the mountains, held a peace detached from normal referents. And then, there was no place to go after those mountains—we could hardly breathe—but to walk down and out of Tibet, as we were allowed to do (just in that brief period when the border was open to individual crossings) and cross through into Nepal:

Gospel of Peace

The mustard fields and mountains in Tibet
    waken with dawn and frogs
crooning on snowlakes. We go out, forget
the Hans, and hack the fields. I toss some logs
    on a burnpile.
    My daughter wakes
happy, unburned (except by passion) while
    her birthday breaks
out over violet plateaus. Nomads pass. We claw
    the dirt of peace. I guess
    I lose my scream.
Without a book, with you, and with a thaw
    in loneliness
and no Han soldiers near, we loaf and dream.

I was surprised that these stern officials on the ferry were speaking English. When we landed it was even stranger. After four years on the continent, it was a shock to hear people in the street and in the stores speaking English. And it was not a foreign language to them. The rain we remembered from Paris.

In London we found a flat in the Chelsea district. Our landlady was a Tory who loved Ike, who was about to beat Adlai Stevenson into the ground. I liked our room. It was not a great mansion as in Spain with its own gardens and a Roman aqueduct for our back wall. Justice and better economies don't offer those anomalies of privilege for ordinary citizens or foreigners. Apart from murkily unpleasant notes from our chatty landlady, Mrs. Brightbottom, it was a fine place to live.

The surprise was Mr. Brightbottom. We had some nice talks. Very tied up with politenesses and inhibitions, he was a mild, distinguished-looking gentleman and French horn player in the Sadler's Wells Ballet orchestra. Four nights a week he came home from the theater a little after midnight, full of love for his profession and horn, and blew melodies and scales into the wall where, on the other side, the pillows were on which our sleeping heads lay. There were at least four inches of building material separating his horn from our ears. Curiously, if Helle and I exchanged whispers, in virtually any corner of our room after midnight, the next morning on the mail table in the hallway there was sure to be a note for us, requesting silence and consideration for the other tenants.

SOAS, the School of Oriental and African Studies, was a natural place for me. It was my first move toward the East. We had a large common room, a natural meeting place, and there I made friends. It was a treat. All my curiosity for Asia and Africa had a field day. Richard Robinson was then a student too, a Buddhist, knew Tibetan and Chinese, and though he was to die young, apparently tragically, he published important books on Buddhism and a translation of Buddhist poetry texts. I read his manuscript of the Buddhist poems. I envied his knowing Chinese, and again the forces for me to turn to East Asia were building up.

Arthur Waley, the sinologist of the century, was there each day. I'd see him come into the main school entrance and turn right, where the faculty hung out in a common room like ours on the left. He had a fine face, that scholar and poet who claimed that he had never visited China because his dream of it was perfectly intact and it was best to keep it that way. Along with tense propriety a good Englishman or Englishwoman should be loyal to an eccentricity.

Arthur Waley's most public one derived from his bicycle. He cycled to school each day, always elegantly dressed in his gentleman's uniform. To save his trousers from grease and dirt, he wore bicycle clips. These he never removed during the day. Wherever he was in the school, his clips went with him, in place, protecting his trousers from untold other dangers.

While I read and owned a library of Waley's books—I don't think he was yet knighted up to Sir Arthur—I was too shy or zombielike to speak to him. What a failed opportunity! To have been at SOAS and not to have studied and worked with Waley now seems to me painfully stupid. I don't wish to inflate my error, but since I had always read whatever poetry I could find translated from Chinese, since I eagerly went through bookstores in London for books from the Chinese, and since I not very secretly saw myself as a Chinese poet who happened to be born in a cover of Western skin, now not to seek out Waley was equivalent to being a young novelist living next door in a rooming house to Nathaniel Hawthorne and being too foolish to knock and say hello. In Greece or Spain the human shyness would never have happened, but in England inhibitions grew like the grass around Roman monuments and even Stonehenge. There should not have been grass around those antiquities; they should not have been so tamed into formal correctness. Can you imagine proper golf course grass around the Parthenon? But the catchy nervous inhibitions were in the English air (the English themselves claim to feel freer outside their island where the air had some good smells in it and the grass was disobedient), and so I never knocked on Arthur Waley's door. In tribute to the man and his work, however, when I did the Wang Wei book, I gave it the title *Laughing Lost in the Mountains: The Poems of Wang Wei.* The title I stole from combined lines of Wang Wei and Arthur Waley.

Among the young professors I did get to know was George Weys. He taught Chinese and Japanese language. George was born in Austria and was, like Waley, of a central European Jewish family, though his parents, like many Austrians Jews, had converted to Catholicism. When Hitler came rumbling into Vienna in March 1938, with Anschluss, his parents, fearful, sent George to a Catholic orphanage in London. Their own Christian faith did not save them from later arrest and the gas chamber. Refuge in London saved George. But the orphanage was horrendous, mainly because, for whatever reason, it didn't give the children enough to eat. George was so desperate, he dreamed up the crazy scheme of writing anonymous letters to the Home Office, denouncing himself as an Austrian spy, hoping the authorities would investigate, put him in a well-fed jail, do something to get him out of the orphanage. It had no effect. But by 1940, since he was a seventeen-year-old Austrian, he was sent, as an alien from an enemy country, to a prisoner of war camp in Canada, where he worked in a factory for two years, and ate well. He did manage to talk his way out and before the war's end got back to London and entered college, where he majored in Chinese.

George played the recorder beautifully (though several of his fingers were deformed or missing from birth); he knew everything I wished I knew then about Eastern religions and literature and was in every way my closest friend throughout the year. I have not known a more gentle person. I had no idea when we met that our lives would become so entangled. That was for a few months later.

My courses were all in Indian studies. I took a course in the history of Indian Buddhism with Professor Friedmann, a kind and thoroughly boring Dutch scholar. I went to each class, did the assigned reading, memorized categories and categories, names and more names, and desirous though I was to learn, learned little. The course in Indian history with A. L. Basham, though, was fascinating. Basham, an excellent scholar, was also a fine lecturer of his storybook knowledge. My daily class was with Major Reginald Clarke, retired officer of the British Indian Army. I learned the Bengali script (which has a separate letter for each phoneme, so several hundred letters to its writing system) in a separate class, but the daily, two-hour morning instruction was with Mr. Clarke. The formality was absolute, although I was his only student, and the only student in Bengali in Great Britain. The former officer from India never wavered from the tasks. He did bring me into an ability to read Tagore's letters in poems in Bengali, and we got through a novel. It was only the last day of classes, after a year, that we had no regular exercises and we talked. On that day, perhaps because I had earned some chips, for two hours he told me his life and we said goodbye.

One day George told me that "a Thai girl, studying Sanskrit, was looking for someone to tutor her in French." Could I and would I like to do it? I said yes. And so I met Oussa Shenakoul. Oussa, meaning daybreak in Sanskrit, was from Bangkok, daughter of a professor of engineering and granddaughter of an Irish engineer who had come to Thailand to install electricity in the palace of the king. While there he married a Thai and stayed on. His name was O'Shea. The "O" was dropped and the Thai ending added, creating "Shenakoul." On her mother's side she was part Chinese. Because of her Irish blood, and perceptions unknown to us, her friends, she told me, thought of her as a Westerner with a Thai culture.

"What's a Westerner?" I said.

"I can smell one."

"Meaning."

"My girlfriends and I can stand on a corner in Bangkok, looking at the street and we all can smell who is walking by."

"How do you smell them?"

"With my nose."

"That's not what I'm asking."

"I smell them by what they eat. Indians smell of curry, Chinese of rice."

"What do Westerners smell of?"

"Steak and milk. Especially Americans."

"What do I smell of?"

"Not much, but nice."

"I'm not even a vegetarian."

Oussa had an Asian frame, meaning she was thin-boned and delicate. Her English was perfect—in direct line from Grandfather O'Shea—and in all ways her thought was original and sophisticated. She was scarcely familiar with Western classical music, and was curious; her comments were refreshing, telling. She didn't reject out of hand, but neither did she accept all discoveries without running them through her insight, and that was a very good test. Instinctively her intelligence and candor were there, inviolate and attractively so. In speaking to people she was sensitive, not Asian-woman shy, and laughingly enjoyed things. Oussa, however, didn't laugh about the London fog and rain, which depressed her.

We were just friends, but I fell in love with her voice. It was its own country.

Her voice was water-music. Birds in the marshes. Tweeting and stillness between tweeting. Clanging wind in the reeds of bird-pond. Her laughter was a whistle and low thumping of light on the milk drum of an arum lily. Then were the knife blades and metal cries in the no-time of rice fields.

To be in England and hear the voice of Asia.

But from the voice of ivory, heard from another continent, I went back to an English poet's voice, made of a leaden echo and a golden echo that went unheard during his lifetime.

To be in England. Yes, where its people gave a language to a Victorian poet, who converted to the Society of Jesus, and who lived in Ireland as a monk and teacher.

I am soft sift
In an hourglass—at the wall
Fast, but mined with a motion, a drift,
And it crowds and it combs to the fall. . .

Gerard Manley Hopkins, who wrote "Some candle clear burns somewhere I come by," gave us a tongue in poems neither he, nor his century, saw published. Not until 1918, nearly thirty years after his death, did his friend Robert Bridges, the poet laureate, who disapproved of his poems in his life, agree that the world might be ready to accept the Jesuit monk's work. It is heartbreaking to read Hopkins's letters to Bridges, defending his "Wreck of the Deutschland" (from which those four lines of stanza 4 above). Hopkins was led to write to his "affectionate friend" in 1878, acknowledging his failure to convince him of his experiments. "[My 'Deutschland'] unsettled you, thickening and clouding your mind with vulgar mud-bottom and common sewage." Hopkins ends the paragraph to Bridges asking him to read his work more than once.

Yet how can one feel sorry for Hopkins who, despite all the lashing self-pity in the incredible "terrible sonnets," could rock the English language, blast it with joy, noise, and apocalyptic distortions when he left us the brightness of?

A heart's clarion! Away grief's gasping, joyless
days,
dejection.
                              Across my foundering deck shone
A beacon, an eternal beam. Flesh fade, and mortal trash
Fall to the residuary worm; world's wildfire, leave but
ash:
                              In a flash, at a trumpet crash,
I am all at once what Christ is, since he was what I
am, and

This Jack, joke, poor potherd, patch, matchwood, im-
mortal diamond,

                     Is immortal diamond.

It was a strange thrill to be living now in the country where
Hopkins wrestled with his God and his own tongue. In America
I never felt strange about the notion that I, grandson of East
Europeans, spoke and wrote West Insular Germanic (modern
English). What else was I to speak or write? I spoke English
kraut, the good plain dim stuff Hopkins and Borges loved, which
was mixed up with some elevating polysyllabic Latin. But in
England, for the first time, I saw myself participating in, enjoying
the drumbeat of, our Saxon dialect. From birth on, we are all
foreigners to the tongue we inherit through our ears. When I come
to death, perhaps my head will have forgotten or be incapable of
using it any more, a true foreigner again, ready for the last tongue
of silence.

One of the friends I liked to chat with in the common room
was Charles Went, a Londoner, who was studying Hindi and
Sanskrit. Charles's father was killed in an air raid. The lanky,
red-cheeked East Ender was always broke. I wondered how he
was making it through the term.

"Where do you get the money for college?"

"I 'ave a London borough fellowship."

Charles spoke good cockney, with some self-conscious efforts
to raise his diction, at which moment his speech slowed. As
soon as the English opened their mouths, they made a class and
education statement. Perhaps it's less true today, but only less.
So Britain was a green bowl in which were stacked many nations.
The nations were its classes, sometimes changing levels, but those
who tried to pass upward into a higher nation were usually easy
to spot. You could lose your money and your job, but it was
almost impossible to lose your speech, so if you were "born
well," your tongue was by birthright safe. Good English was
language Eden. It knew no fall, since there were no lurking
phonetic sins to hide. Charles often talked about class; he was

concerned. I'd say disturbed. Finally, I said to him, "Charles, what class would you say you come from?"

He paused. There was hurt. Then he blurted, with as much dignity as was appropriate, "I come from what you might call the *upper* lower class."

In the mornings we usually left our place at seven-thirty so I could drop Helle off for her Byzantine readings and I could be at SOAS to read with Major Clarke. It was still dark when we left Chelsea and dark by the time we returned. At four in the afternoon the light was falling. England for us—until after the spring equinox—was a dark northern edge of the globe, opposite in latitude to Labrador. Its warmish, rainy winter, heated a bit by shillings in gas heaters, lacked snow but the light, or its absence, revealed how far up we were on top of the purple earth.

When we ate out, we sought a Cypriot or Indian restaurant. English food was the limit. In Burma, which was my favorite refuge in the mid-eighties, the great, dilapidated Strand Hotel in Rangoon served English food, beautifully served by Burmese waiters, and it was, as in London of those days, overcooked, bland, and pleasant to consume only because of the heavy tableware. In Spain it was hard to eat before nine. In London the eating was all over by nine and so were most other things. Lights stayed on in friends' houses, though, especially as our clan of painters and poets grew modestly.

When we went out one morning the London fog had turned to ash. Day was brief enough, but on that day it never came. It was too dangerous to go to school on my cycle so I took the tube. The yellow journal tabloids were de rigeur. The day's sensation was that Christie was captured. He was the multiple murderer of London prostitutes. A necrophiliac, he buried his women in his back yard or inserted them, in chunks, between walls of the boarding house where he had a room. London had a lot to read about. Five years earlier, Christie was the state witness in a successful murder trial against a retarded tenant, Timothy Evans, living in the same boarding house. Evans was accused of killing his wife and was in due course convicted and executed. In prison Christie confessed to that crime as well. The Home Secretary, Sir David Maxwell Fyfe, rejected Christie's confession as "the more the merrier" and rammed through an inquiry in a single week, completely exonerating the official conduct of the court, but the outrage and uproar over the earlier execution led Parliament, soon after Christie in all his banal evil was hanged, to banish execution from Great Britain.

That evening of fog the theatres were closed. The conductor could not see the orchestra in Covent Garden, and the performance was halted. Thieves walked nimbly up to people and fingered their pockets with impunity. It was very difficult to find our flat, since from the sidewalk the houses, fifteen feet back, were a blur. Once inside I blew my nose. The handkerchief was black.

Next morning we woke early. It was a little lighter than the day before, but not much. We heard a slow crashing and crunching of glass. I rushed outside and the good citizens, most in their bathrobes and pajamas, were already cleaning up the street, kicking the broken milk bottles to the curb with their shoes and slippers. I joined them. A taxi had rammed a horse-drawn milk cart. Slowly, but effectively. The black-and-white scene reminded me of the first moments of De Sica's *Miracle at Milano*, which begins with the camera following a stream of milk from an overflowing boiling pot, through the street, up to its destination, a cat's tongue.

There was a calm London miracle to our fog. When it lifted, the papers reported many deaths of those with pulmonary conditions. All twelve prize exhibition bulls died at Hampton Court. Thereafter the very softest coal was banned from London, and the British Museum was air conditioned. They would never again have to sandblast stolen Greek marble statues because of the romantic London fog.

Word came from Greece that Vassili was dying. He had gone to Paris to see specialists, but the creeping paralysis was unrelenting. A few days before he died, he received an official appointment for a chair in medicine at the University of Athens. He had published books, articles, and waited long for that honor, tied up with myriad academic politics. By then he couldn't speak.

Helle had to go immediately to Athens. She was always very close to her father. She loved him. And he loved her above all. I had to get her a ticket in a hurry. An Indian law student, Radjine Singh, who sometimes came to SOAS to soak up our Asian atmosphere, lent me money, on the spot, for Helle's plane fare. It was Radjine's book allowance for the next semester. We were little more than acquaintances. I felt no hesitation, however, about asking her, and was able to return the English pounds to her in a few weeks. I was moved by her spontaneous help. Helle reached Athens two weeks before her father died.

There were legal matters, murky ones. Since Helle was married to "an American millionaire," why care about property in Greece. But Vassili left Maroussi to her, where we had lived two years, stating in the will his wish that his grandchildren (not yet conceived) live there some day. After the initial move by relatives to disinherit the doctor's daughter, there was to be no settlement for two decades. Ultimately, Helle made it possible for Vassili's grandchildren to live in Maroussi and in the islands.

After her father died, she felt empty. In a call that came one night from Athens, Helle told me that she had met a sculptor who was, for the moment, filling the emotional void.

It was November. If I could borrow some money for myself, I would come to Greece at the end of December and stay some weeks until the second term at SOAS began again.

I saw George, and saw Oussa, who had moved across the street into another building owned by Mrs. Brightbottom. Dear Mrs. Brightbottom.

Sometimes Oussa came across the street to my flat and cooked me something. Or I went to her place. We were very close. It was not Josette, black fire and joy of a week, and then time. With Oussa it was another kind of immediate recognition. For me it was endlessly interesting when we spoke. I looked forward to each encounter. And there was full confidence. She was and remained, with George, the people in England.

In addition to her studies, Oussa was broadcasting in Thai for the BBC news service and, on her own, translating a long medieval narrative love poem into English from Thai. Eventually, she published her translation, with commentary, in book form. She did everything with grace and strength—an unusual and good combination.

In mid-December SOAS had an end-of-term dance. Oussa was acting strange. Clearly something was wrong. Since she was the most naturally candid person I knew, and since she said nothing, I said nothing. As for the dance, she asked me to go with her. She had a white dress for the occasion, though it was winter. Her plan was the following. She would go alone and call me from school. I didn't know why, but that was fine. She left at nine o'clock. At eleven the phone rang.

"Willis, you must come immediately."

"I'm on my way?" I could hear her tears.

"What happened?"

"Just come now."

When I reached SOAS—and it was December cold, even in England—I was shivering. I looked for Oussa.

"Let's go," she said.

"One dance."

"One dance," she agreed.

I decided to leave my motorbike in the parking lot and come back for it the next day. We found a taxi and went back to her place. In the black English cab, in that miniature velvet backseat living room, she leaned her face on my shoulder and said nothing. Her face was buried in my shoulder.

We went inside, and as soon as the door was shut, she clung to me.

"What is it?" She removed her arms from me and sat down on the bed.

"I'm pregnant."

"Are you sure?"

"I am regular, and my period didn't come this month."

I went to the bed and sat by her.

"He's an Indian, a horrible man in my class. He asked me to his place and forced me. He's so ugly and horrible."

"Are you sure you're pregnant?"

"I'm sure. Apart from the period, I feel different inside. And also I've been upset. For weeks, before I knew about a baby, I couldn't stand thinking of him."

I put my hand on her waist.

"You mustn't leave me tonight."

"I can stay."

"Since I am already pregnant, your sleeping with me won't add a second child."

"I would be surprised if it did."

Oussa put her hand on my face, kissed me. We took our clothes off. It was a tender night.

At seven in the morning, as Oussa warned me, impossible Mrs. Brightbottom would be around to empty the trash basket. There was no way. When we heard the knock, I went into the wardrobe closet and tucked myself behind the clothes. Mercifully, the gorgon was cheerily efficient and left us after a few minutes.

Hiding in a Wardrobe Closet from a Landlady in London of the Great Fog

Winter mornings. London is dark. The fog
comes in the common toilet window (which
we're not allowed to shut). I read and hog
the quarters on my freezing buttocks. Bitch
and scrooge, I call Mrs Brightbottom who
leaves me her nasty notes. My lovely Thai
friend will redeem the day. I'd like to screw

her royally (I confess, ashamed, since I
am also dreamily in love with her
thin smile, her wistful arum lily throat).
The fog has killed the bulls at Hampton Fair
and I can't get to SOAS. Through the blur
I walk to Oussa's sheets. The night we share.
Morning. I'm in hiding in her closet coat.

Later that morning Oussa and I went to my place. We spent the next day together, and then another night. Thereafter we were not in the same bed again. Two weeks went by, with no less affection. Oussa decided on abortion. I began to gather information. I cared for Oussa immensely. She was in love.

As was the earlier plan, at December's end I got ready to leave for three weeks in Greece. How life was getting complex. Good, but even more confusing. Helle told me she was still with the sculptor.

Oussa took me to the airport. She said she had something very important to tell me. I could tell by her voice that she was going to tease me terribly. And I was glad to see her so happy.

"Well, what are you going to tell me that's so important?"

"I'll tell you. Be patient."

"Are you pregnant again?" The abortion had not yet taken place. It was to be in three days.

"It doesn't seem so."

"You are making me sweat for nothing, and it's December."

"Willis, you could have made me pregnant?"

"You mean, from two people in a week?"

"No just from one. You see, last night my period came. It skipped a month. So I was never pregnant at all from the horrible Indian."

Greece felt cold and sunny. In the evening it was almost winter. People walked briskly in the streets. But during the day, it warmed up to a sweet, temperate pause. There was no glint of darkness in the air. Helle spent some days with me, some with the sculptor.

Then we decided to leave Athens. It would be good to go to the islands in the winter. Only die-hard residents would be there. We thought of Hydra, that rocky island only three hours from Athens. The Polytechnion (School of Fine Arts) had studios for foreign painters available, for a negligible payment, and Helle, as a Greek residing abroad, qualified. We spoke to the friendly director, the painter Bizantinós, who suggested Hydra over Mytilene or Mykonos where there were also studios for painters. Mytilene, Sappho's island, was far. Mykonos we knew in the winter.

With canvas, paints, and books, we left on the ship for Hydra. At noon we saw the amphitheater, which was the stone port itself, rising in arched rows of houses to high hills. The houses had for the most part cypress doors and were colored with subtle washes. Not the gleaming white of the Cyclades. Here the palate was stone-hued. Many of the houses were imposing eighteenth-century mansions designed by Venetian and Genoese architects. Our first walk was steps on stage under the extraordinary theater behind us.

In the early nineteenth century, the Hydriots threw their merchant fleet and wealth into the War of Independence against Turkish rule and many naval leaders were Hydriots, including Commander Tombazis. The House of Tombazis was the international hostel for artists, where our room and studio was. The mansion lay at the right-hand edge of the amphitheater, by itself, commanding the port and the sea. In January we had Tombazis to ourselves.

One large drawing I remember well. Helle did a life-size drawing of me in charcoal. It survived many years until a fire in Bloomington burned all our possessions. We have talked about it and it survives in both our heads. An interesting metaphysical question. For me it has reality, as much as the certainty that if I look up I will still see that Picasso lithograph of the Greek woman with the big black eyeball, the melon breast, and fingers like

scissored cut-outs. While I am not focusing my eyes on the lithograph it still exists, if I call it into memory. So too does that
drawing, when I call it into memory.

When we are dead, the drawing dies definitively. Such disappearance of knowledge occurs eternally, and so the earth and its
being—its being is in our minds—is transient. We lose, and best,
we are obliged to start again and invent. Imagine what a bore if
everything were intact and still. Then being would be a massive
tombstone.

The evenings were cold, and there was no heat, which made
our studio somehow more humanly intimate. We had to be close
and aware of our physical presences. Our late evening wanderings
found us alone. Nothing open, except the sea, the salt wind, the
sky, and the hills whose houses blinked with candlelight every
now and then.

Next day the sun was unusually warm. It was a perfect time
to hike up to the center of the island. Our destination was the
monastery of Zourvas. First we followed a coastal path to the
village of Mandhraki. I left Helle in the village, where she wanted
to sketch, and went about twenty minutes into the island to a
meadow outside the house of Greece's best known painter, Hadji
Kiriakos-Ghikas, who was much of the time in Paris. After London, the island was wonderfully warm, and we had been eating
good Greek food in ordinary *tavernas*. Now I sat on a rock and
it was pure sunlight just to sit there.

Then that feeling came which has turned out to be my life. I
looked for a piece of paper but had none. When the feeling is
not there, paper won't help. But if the feeling is half there, it is
good to sit down and move toward it. I sat and bathed in the
meditation. I was wearing espadrilles and a pair of shorts. Nothing
else. I had a ballpoint in my pocket. Starting from my left shoulder, I wrote stanzas of a poem about the village carefully on my
arm. Then at a moderate pace so as not to sweat too much, I
walked back to the village *taverna* by the sea. After twenty minutes
I could still read the arm, sat down at a table, and with the

ballpoint copied the verses onto the permanence of a paper napkin.
Then I plunged into the sea, letting the tattooed arm wash out.

> Windmill, bread oven on the hill,
> white walls and tile, blue windowsills
> the color of the sea below.
>
> Under the godless sun the town
> is a glare of cubes. The air blows
> with smells of salt, dung, jasmine, heat.
>
> Out of the rock heart of this island
> seven round fig trees face the sky
> and an acacia tree cools the well.
>
> The tiers of homes nap in the noon
> like a deserted amphitheater
> around the bay. Village of light!
>
> Light and tedium. A pomegranate slowly bursts in the
> heat, its bloody
> seeds are eyes firing at the wind.
>
> The village, a sculpture of time
> in dead cubes, is Greek and here to
> say the silence waits everywhere.

By our studio that night a crowd gathered. To celebrate St.
John's Day, the cross, the Roman torture instrument revered in
miniature and worn on the breasts of Christians, was about to
be thrown into the sea. First the *papa* blessed it. It was cold again,
but a young *palikari* hero dived into the waters, went deep, and
retrieved it.

After many good days in Hydra we went back to Athens,
finished a few finishable legal matters, and flew to London. We
felt restored.

There was news. During these three weeks George had fallen in love with Oussa. He was not out of his mind, since that was not his way, yet he was. Oussa was affected by it all, but not convinced. George persisted.

Oussa told me it was very hard for her.

"I love you," she said.

"I know."

George won over her. They asked me to be the witness. We went to the legal office where marriages were performed. Oussa wept. And they were married.

It turned out to be a lasting and good marriage. When I saw George last it was in Vermont. He had become very dignified-looking with age. I have not seen Oussa. Not yet. Ivory and song do not worry about years.

When the weather broke, we got on our cycle and went to the Lake District and up to Stonehenge. It was lovely of course. We had seen little of England, in contrast to Greece, where we were so often on the road. But the memory I have of England's beauty is a long weekend we spent in the country with George and Oussa, in a farmhouse they rented for a week, some seventy miles south of London. Spring is nature's birth and everywhere good. That genesis of life is very gentle in England, at least I recall it so. England was Roman warm. That messy, detailed quality of this less formal countryside, scraggly woods, and uneven meadows infused with spring was delicious.

The farmhouse had a piano, and we discovered a Spanish songbook, with old regional songs I didn't know. One of them could have been set by Falla.

We were four friends. And we were all in England's pastoral paradiso.

At SOAS the students elected me president for the coming year. It was a surprise, since I didn't know there was a student president or that I was a candidate. It was not a political post—but rather one that suggested that I liked to talk to Asian and

With poets W. S. Merwin (seated) and David Wade (in beret), 1964

In Asia Minor, at the ruins of Troy, continuing my life as a
vagabond, despite and because of the academic life, 1970

With novelist Ye Chunchan when I was a Fulbright professor at
Beijing University of Foreign Studies, China, 1972

In central China during the Cultural Revolution, May 1972; I am
standing in the center

In an Argentine café, 1975

With Jorge Luis Borges in a
bookstore, Buenos Aires,
1975

With Borges in Buenos Aires, when I was Fulbright professor at the
Profesorado, Argentina, 1975

Giving a poetry reading in the 1970s

Our children (*bottom to top*) Robert, Aliki, and Tony on a camel in Turkey

Under a portrait of Jorge Luis Borges, noted Argentine author and poet, whose writings and personality were a major influence upon me

Inscription card for the National Autonomous University of Mexico, in the Faculty of Philosophy and Letters, 1947

Inscription card for the University of Paris, Faculty of Letters, 1948–1949

Aliki, Robert, and Tony in Kashgar, Chinese Turkestan, near the
Afghanistan border, 1985

In Kashgar, 1985

African friends. I was flattered, but had to decline. We had no funds to stay another year. Had we, it would have been India.

In the last months, we spent many evenings with Helle's painter teachers. And I was frequently with Jon Silkin, the English poet, or Lucien Stryk, the American poet, who was already interested in the Persian mystics and Japanese Zen poetry and publishing his Marine Iwo Jima invasion poems in *Poetry*. "My name is 'one, two, three, Stryk, you're out,'" he'd say. Lucien and I had been classmates at the Sorbonne. In Paris he lived in the smallest apartment I ever saw. There were six inches of throwaway space lapping the rectangle of his bed over which hung a few shelves. Now, married to an Englishwoman who had had tuberculosis— Helen had been Sir Jacob Epstein's model for many sculptures— he had to wait out her five-year "after-cure period" for an American visa before they could go back to America together.

I was closest to Jon Silkin, not a student at SOAS, but because of a Persian woman connection he was frequently there. We'd meet in the common room and go off together. Jon always had a book of Hernández or Lorca or a Czech poet crammed in his pocket. Years later in America he said to me, "I must have been obnoxious in those days." Not at all. Maybe he was embarrassed because, like poets everywhere, he believed in what he was writing and said so. His son, by his Iranian wife (if I remember right), had Down's syndrome and died when he was about a year and a half. The poem he showed me in manuscript was immensely moving. It ended when the child closed his big eyes, turned over, and died. Already he was accumulating poems for his first very successful volume, *The Peaceable Kingdom*. Yes, I liked my obnoxious friend, who was gutsy, feisty, and had a dark anger that he was certain to turn into good ambitions. With Lucien and Jon and a few English poets I hung out with, we were a circle. England, atmospheric England, had lost its strangeness. Now America would be a curious place to see after five years.

The vagabond I was, the poet and loafer in the service of the poem, was on his way home. There were other titles I could dig up, but vagabond and poet are the most complimentary and, whether I was good or bad at those professions, they accurately described intentions. Five years earlier I had left Maine with a few poems in my bag but after a recent wakening that had given me conviction. Helle had gone to Europe with an intention to write a book of stories about Epirus. She painted. Paintings and poems, the same. Home for the next year would be New York, but home would be inconstant until I reached Indiana where I live in a cement-block office, my tower, and remember.

However, even in a work tower, with its boulder stability of a regular salary, the vagabond was neither dead nor reformed. What led me down to Mexico and through Europe and North Africa had shifted to parts of Asia. I suffered the same reckless hope that in the next part of the desert or beyond the next lake in blue Tibet, there would be a truckstop, a place to sleep, catch fleas, and wake up from dreams that still spoke almost discernible secrets:

Vagabond

Who cares what people say? I need to go
into the Fayuum desert or share tea
with Uzbeks in the Gobi. A rainbow
shone over Yangshuo as we were biking free
from rainy villages to the airport
where we were locked in. Not one open door
until the plane got there. Yes, my passport
wasn't dust. I forgot my desk. The poor
were friends. Only the weak and poor and lost,
the chubby janitors and peasants came
to share our food up in the icy hills.
When two Tibetan nomads fought in the frost
over a prayer wheel, when another's shame
dazed him in song, I ate a sack of daffodils.

I put in the years. Maybe I was safe. One is formed from childhood, perhaps. If that is so, I had a double one.

Europe turned me around. It might have happened in Kansas City or the Ozarks. We have our exotic pampas and Alps. But Paris of the red room, the sea-clean islands, Sikelianós, the buffoon moon at four in the morning, which had the habit of coming over the Sierra Nevada and the Roman aqueduct just before the Andalusian cocks yelled at it, damp London and my Thai and Austrian angels, all those parts of the world out there helped whatever could happen inside. The precarious inside is changing with every forkful of bad food, good food, bad news, deep kiss, rebuff, yet it does have a mass and persists despite the protean waves. Now that I am, as always, precarious, I look back at what persuaded me to be in the years 1948 to 1953.

By the time we were leaving Europe, I knew little about love and its confusions. Is love, as Machado wrote, in the absence? Is it longing, multiple, one? And then all the cousins of love— affection, lust, dream, madness. Fool of love, yes, that was the young whim of Ramon Llull, the fourteenth-century Catalan mystic and philosopher. Our love was to be best when it was not known, not seen. When it was. Then came the three children who were born in love. When after our decades together we formally split, love came back naturally. It had no legalities any more. Just tenderness, interest, endless friendship. I wonder what is most permanent. Don't ask me to understand. I suppose I'd be dead if I understood anything fully. In my lack of wisdom I guard youth and adolescence.

As a writer, before I became a happy writing-machine, it was only poetry. It still is. But then women came on stage. Then fiction and memoir. It made me happy. And I add those scholarly ventures, which I never thought less of, since to write about Wang Wei or the ancient rebel religions and their literatures has been another joy. There is no writing I tried that I did without passion. Borges said close the book if it doesn't bring you pleasure. So too with writing. If you don't like to do it, stop. Of course there is agony. As in love. And the confusion of the several women, the several genres, gives us richness, instability, weakness, all the good and true things.

I still have time. Maybe a good decade or two. Will I find peace? Little I suppose. For a while I thought I was on my way. Now, I believe more in work, life, women, thought, and passion than ever, so there may not be much peace and that may save me. Yet I could very well dump anguish. Once it seemed like a source of intellect. In the last year, when it showed up for external reasons, it carried a knife. It would be fine if it were to go away and not come back.

Yet without some *angoisse,* what will I do? Without barbarians, Cavafy's Romans in their North African colony were lost. So I will keep it, some of it, along with assorted ignorances. And write a letter to you, the world, asking for things. Not fame. That's a silly secret, which loses its secrecy if it comes, and does so, as is its habit, with mountainous corruption and the loss of solitude. It's here already anyway, since in the poems I have the arrogance of belief.

But I write a letter, a plea, for that elusive love. Don't ask me more. It's there. It's still the one thing I could die for. Emily Dickinson could and did die for it. She called it eternity, death, a certain slant of light, wild nights, poetry, and left most of it tied up in letters and fascicles for us. Here's a letter I wrote a while ago. The years of Europe were of the wanderer. I am just as nowhere as then. And that wasn't a bad place to be.

Happiness of the Patient Traveler

I wrote a letter to the sun
to shine on us again for one
more life. Then begged him for the time
to let our tongues agree to rhyme
for one more year. And then I asked
for just a day, but he unmasked
me with the alphabet of night,
and when I pleaded for more light

he spat on me with hours of rain
which finally washed away the pain
of time. I wrote a letter to
the sun and said I would let go
of love. He led me to a tree
inside, where I could be to be.

When I look back to being nowhere it was very good there. Paris, Greece, Andalusia, London. Inside each proper name were those winds where we hung out. And better even than being outside or inside, than being the cosmos with a few blind eyes to explore it or through it, is to have the sun shine on us for one more life, and let our tongues agree to rhyme for one more year. There is so much pain, so many walls erected invisibly by builders, imperceptibly closing us off from the outside world; there is so much endlessly deep aloneness, that it is good to remember and hope today to be with sun and rhyme.

And since memoirs are mainly for you, I spit on you gently with hours of rain to wash away the pain of time.

SUBJECT INDEX

INDEX OF POEMS

SUBJECT INDEX

Subject Index

INDEX OF POEMS

Index of Poems

Willis Barnstone is Distinguished Professor of Comparative Literature and Spanish and Portuguese at Indiana University, and Professor of West European Studies. His books include *The Poetics of Translation* (1993), *The Poetics of Ecstasy from Sappho to Borges* (1983), *The Other Bible* (1984), and a memoir-biography of Jorge Luis Borges, *With Borges on an Ordinary Evening in Buenos Aires* (1993). Other recent books include his Spanish poetry anthology, *Six Masters of the Spanish Sonnet* (1993), and his collected new poems, *Funny Ways of Staying Alive* (1993). A Guggenheim fellow twice nominated for the Pulitzer Prize in poetry, he has received the Emily Dickinson, Lucille Medwick, and Gustav Davidson awards from the Poetry Society of America and the W. H. Auden Award of the New York State Arts Council.